THE
AFRICAN-AMERICAN
BABY NAME
BOOK

THE
AFRICAN-AMERICAN
BABY NAME
BOOK

Teresa Norman

BERKLEY BOOKS, NEW YORK

This book is an original publication of The Berkley Publishing Group.

THE AFRICAN-AMERICAN BABY NAME BOOK

A Berkley Book / published by arrangement with
the author

Berkley trade paperback edition / February 1998

The Penguin Putnam Inc. World Wide Web site address is
http://www.penguinputnam.com

ISBN: 978-0-425-15939-2

BERKLEY®
Berkley Books are published by
The Berkley Publishing Group, a division of Penguin Putnam Inc.,
375 Hudson Street, New York, New York 10014.
BERKLEY and the "B" design are trademarks
belonging to Penguin Putnam Inc.

21   20   19   18   17   16

For Christine

INTRODUCTION

UNIQUE, CLASSICAL, ELEGANT, ARIS-tocratic and unusual names have been a hallmark of the African-American naming process, a trait that endures to this day. Even names taken from the standard European pool are often altered to be somewhat different in character than the originals. In recent times, invented names and those of Spanish, French, and Irish origin and influences are becoming quite popular choices for baby names. Among members of the African-American community, cultural pride and revivalism and a sense of spiritual rebirth have spurred the use of African names and those that reflect the religion of Islam.

Yet while there are many "name your baby" books on the market, few specifically target the African-American audience. Of those that do, the majority deal exclusively with African names. Most baby name books are a general listing of names that are typically of European and Hebrew origin. Some books offer a more diverse selection and include a small number of Japanese, Chinese, Indian, and Arabic names, along with a token few in popular use by Blacks, such as Deion and Sharlayne. Few names of truly American origin are acknowledged, and the vast pool of modern coinages in use by African-Americans is barely touched.

In writing *The African-American Baby Name Book*, I have given well-rounded recog-nition to the names used by this major cultur-al group. This book offers names that reflect modern African-American naming practices, giving you a new and exciting source in which to find a special name for your child.

NAMING YOUR CHILD

A NAME IS ONE LABEL THAT A PERSON CARRIES for life. In fact, among many African ethnic groups, it is a person's most important posses-sion, for it is the only thing that survives after death. Therefore, great care should be taken when considering a name for your child.

A name has the power to shape a person's personality and can influence future success and popularity as well as the perceptions of others. Give your child a name like Harry Butts or Robyn Banks, and you've sentenced him or her to years of teasing and ridicule. Even the repetition of sounds, as in Mavis Davis and Harley Marley, can provide fodder for teasing and will make your child long for another name.

When choosing your child's name, say your selection aloud, including first, middle, and last names. Listen carefully to the sound and rhythm of the name. A general rule of thumb is to combine first and last names that have an unequal number of syllables. For a one-syllable surname, consider a first name of two or more syllables. For a surname with two syllables, think of names with one or three syllables. Most people would find the name Shameeka Harris to be better in sound and rhythm than Shameeka Washington. Remember, however, that this is a *general* rule. It is more important to listen to the name with a critical ear and to consider it with a loving heart.

The initials of your child's name are another consideration. It's a good idea to make sure they don't form a word that could prove to be embarrassing. No child will enjoy having the initials P.I.G., D.U.D., or I. B. Greene.

Pronunciation is another concern. No one likes to have his or her name mispronounced, least of all a child—an important thing to remember if you are considering an alternative spelling for your child's name. Antwan is a popular variation of Antoine, as Andray is of André, but even though the spelling is different, the pronunciation is obvious. If you see the name Alys, however, you might wonder whether it is pronounced as Alice or Aleece. If you are seeking an African name, be aware that many of these names sound and look foreign to Americans and are apt to be mispronounced. A shortened form for everyday use is something to consider.

Religion can play a role in the selection of a name. Christians often choose biblical or saints' names for their children. In the United States, Islam is the fastest-growing religion among African-Americans. New converts adopt Muslim names and also give their offspring Muslim names. According to the Prophet Muhammad, the best names are those derived from the root *hamida* (to praise) or derived from the ninety-nine attributes of Allah in conjunction with the prefixes Abd (servant) and Abd-al (servant of)—for example Abd-al-Karim (servant of the Generous One). Other popular choices are those taken from the Prophet's family and those that reflect the Islamic themes of benevolence, charity, and morality.

Modern coinages, or made-up names, are a fast-growing trend. Many names today are formed by adding elements from parents' or other relatives' names or by expanding on popular name elements, such as *shon* or *eesha*. In many instances, it is apparent which names or elements contribute to the new names. In other cases, new names are formed from vocabulary words, while some are simply the products of the parents' contemplation. These new names are listed in this book as *contemporary* names and are often without established definitions.

As you begin your search, remember that naming your child is one of your first and most important parental responsibilities. Your child will bear the name you choose for a lifetime. Take care to select one that he or she will bear with pride.

HOW TO USE THIS BOOK

THE ENTRIES IN *THE AFRICAN-AMERICAN Baby Name Book* are easy to read and will give you an accurate history of the names, their origins, and their meanings. They also provide examples of noted African-Americans bearing the names. Some names are common to more than one language or country, and this is noted as well. Other names originated in one country, yet have their etymological roots in another language. In this instance, the country or language of origin is listed first, with the root language preceding the definition. Most African names are referenced first by country or geographical area, with the root language second. The following examples explain how each entry works:

Main entry   Root language   Definition

BARBARA Latin: "foreign woman."
Barbra. Babs, Barb, Barbie. Barbara Jordan, former congresswoman. Barbara Reynolds, columnist.

Variant spelling/Short forms

African-Americans of note

Country of origin

Main entry   Root language   Definition

AFRYEA Ghana. Ewe: "born during happy times."

Etymological root

Country of origin

Main entry   Root language

SHON American. Irish. Hebrew: "God is gracious." Shon is a phonetic spelling of Sean, an Irish form of John. **Shahn, Shonn.**

Variant spelling

Definition

Main entry   Root language   Definition

BAILEY French: "administrator." English: "worker at the outer court of a castle." **Baily, Baylee.**

Root language   Variant spellings

THE
AFRICAN-AMERICAN
BABY NAME
BOOK

FEMALE NAMES

AALIYAH Hebrew: "to ascend." **Aliah, Aliya, Aliyah.** Aaliyah, singer.

ABA Ghana. Fante: "born on Thursday."

ABAM Ghana. Twi: "second child after twins."

ABANA Hebrew: "stony." **Abanah.**

ABAYOMI Nigeria. Yoruba: "she brings me joy; she brings happiness."

ABBEY English: "monastery or convent." Also a short form of Abigail (father of exaltation). Abbey Lincoln, singer.

ABEBI Nigeria. Yoruba: "we asked for her."

ABEJE Nigeria. Yoruba: "we asked to have this child."

ABEKE Nigeria. Yoruba: "we asked for her to pet her."

ABENA Ghana. Fante: "born on Thursday." **Abenaa.**

ABENI Nigeria. Yoruba: "we asked for her, and look, we got her!"

ABIA Nigeria. Hausa: "friend." Efik: "small as a bird." **Abiah.**

ABIDEMI Nigeria. Yoruba: "born during her father's absence."

ABIJAH Hebrew: "the Lord is father."

ABIKANILE Malawi. Yao: "listen."

ABIMBOLA Nigeria. Yoruba: "born to be wealthy."

ABIONA Nigeria. Yoruba: "born on a journey."

ABLA Arabic: "having a fine, full figure."

ACACIA Greek: "thorny."

ACADIA American: Contemporary name borrowed from that of a Louisiana parish originally settled by Acadian exiles from Canada.

ACCALIA Latin: Meaning unknown.

ACENITH Africa: The name of an African love goddess.

ADA Arabic: "fulfillment of a duty." Nigerian. Hausa: "custom, manner."

ADAMA Hebrew: "woman of the red earth."

ADAMMA Nigeria. Ibo: "child of beauty."

ADANNA African: "she is her father's daughter."

ADANNE African: "she is her mother's daughter."

ADARA Hebrew: "noble, exalted." Adar is the sixth month of the Jewish calendar.

ADEBOLA Nigeria. Yoruba: "the crown is hers." **Ade.**

ADEDEWE Nigeria. Yoruba: "the crown is shattered." **Ade.**

ADEDOJA Nigeria. Yoruba: "the crown becomes a thing of worth." **Ade.**

ADELE French: "noble."

ADELEKE Nigeria. Yoruba: "crown brings happiness."

ADELINE French: "little noble one." **Adelina, Adelinah. Addie, Addy.**

ADEOLA Nigeria. Yoruba: "crown brings honor."

ADERINOLA Nigeria. Yoruba: "the crown went toward wealth."

ADERO African: "she gives life."

ADESIMBO Nigeria. Yoruba: "noble birth."

ADESINA Nigeria. Yoruba: "this child opens the way (for more children)."

ADETOKUNBO Nigeria. Yoruba: "crown has returned from overseas." Bestowed upon a child if the father recently returned from a trip. **Ade.**

ADEYEMI Nigeria. Yoruba: "crown benefits me." **Ade.**

ADIA Swahili: "a gift from God."

ADINA Hebrew: "slender." Sanskrit: "one who is not poor." Nigerian. Hausa: "religion." **Adeen, Adeena, Adine.**

ADIVA Arabic: "gracious."

ADRIA Latin: "from the city of Adria." **Adreea, Adreeah, Adriah.**

ADRIANNA Latin: "from Adria." **Adrana, Adreana, Adriann, Adrienn, Adrienne.**

ADUKE Nigeria. Yoruba: "she whom one competes to cherish."

AFAFA Ghana. Ewe: "first child of second husband."

AFFIAH Nigeria. Efik: "cloudless, clear."

AFIYA Swahili: "health."

AFRICA English: A borrowing of the name of the continent. Irish: "pleasant."

AFRYEA Ghana. Ewe: "born during happy times."

AGALA Nigeria. Hausa: "rope."

AGNELIA American. Greek: "chaste, pure." Variant of Agnes.

AHMA Nigeria. Efik: "beloved." Bini: "omen."

AIDA Italian: Coined by Verdi for the central character in his opera *Aïda* (1871).

AILETHA American. Greek: "to heal." A variant form of Althea. **Aleitha, Alethia.**

AIMEE French: "beloved." **Aimée, Aimie, Aimy, Amee, Amie, Amy.**

AIN Arabic: "precious; eye."

AINA Nigeria. Yoruba: "the birth was difficult."

AIRENE American: Contemporary, based on the name Irene.

AIRLIA American: Contemporary.

AISHA Arabic: "life; alive and well." Aisha was the name of the prophet Muhammad's third and favorite wife. **Aiesha, Aishah, Ayesha, Ayeshah, Ayisha, Ayishah.**

AISSA American: Contemporary. **Aissah.**

AIYETORO Nigeria. Yoruba: "peace on earth."

AJALON Hebrew: "place of gazelles." In the Bible, Ajalon was the name of a valley where the Israelites defeated the Amorites while the sun and moon stood still. **Aijalon.**

AJEYA India. Sanskrit: "unconquerable."

AKEIBA Hebrew: "supplanted."

AKEISHA American: Modern coinage based on the name Keisha. **Akeesha, Akeeshah, Akeishah, Akisha, Akishah.**

AKEYLAH American. Arabic: "one who reasons; intelligent." **Akela, Akeyla, Akyla, Akylah.**

AKILAH Arabic: "one who reasons; intelligent." **Akila.**

AKINA Swahili: "relations."

AKOSUA Ghana. Ewe: "born on Sunday."

AKUA Ghana. Ewe: "born on Wednesday."

AKYLIE American: Elaboration of Kylie (from the narrow channel).

ALABA Nigeria. Yoruba: "second child after twins."

ALAIN American. Greek: "light."

ALAINA American. Greek: "light, torch, bright." **Alayna, Alena, Allaina, Allayna.**

ALAKE Nigeria. Yoruba: "she is to be fussed over." **Alaka.**

ALAYNÉ American: Contemporary name, probably based on Alaina (light, torch, bright). **Alainae, Alainay, Alaynay.**

ALBERTINE American: Contemporary name, influenced by Albert (noble and bright).

ALBERTA German: "noble and bright." **Elberta. Bertie.**

ALBERTINA American. German: "noble and bright." **Elbertina, Elbertine. Bertie, Bertina, Tina.**

ALBRETTA American: Most likely a variant of Alberta (noble and bright).

ALCÉE American: Contemporary, influenced by the French language.

ALCINDIA American: Contemporary.

ALDERCY American. English: "from Aldersey (Aldred's island or the riparian island)."

ALDIS German: "old and wise."

ALDONZA Spanish. German: "noble battle."

ALEECE American. French: "noble one." **Aleace, Alease, Aleese, Allece, Alleece, Alleese, Allese, Alyse, Aylese.**

ALEESHA American: Contemporary name based on Alicia (noble one). **Aleeshah, Alisha, Alishah. Alli, Allie.**

ALEHA American. Arabic: "sublime, exalted, elevated."

ALEITHA American. Greek: "truth."

ALETHEIA Greek: "truth." **Alethea, Alethia, Alithea.**

ALETTE French. German: "noble one." **Aletta. Letti, Lettie, Letty.**

ALEXA Greek: "defender." **Elexa. Lexi.** Alexa Canady, first Black woman neurosurgeon in the United States.

ALEXANDRA Greek: "defender of mankind." **Aleksandra, Alekzanndra, Alexandrea, Alexandria. Aleksa, Alexa, Lexee, Lexi, Lexie, Sandee, Sandi, Sandie, Sandra, Sandy, Xandee, Xandi, Xandie, Xandra, Xandy, Zandee, Zandi, Zandie, Zandra, Zandy.**

ALEXIS Greek: "defender, helper." **Alexys.** Alexis Herman, assistant to President Clinton and director of the White House Office of Public Liaison.

ALEXZINE American. Greek: "defender." Variant of Alex.

ALFRE American: Possibly a shortened form of Alfreda (elf counselor). Alfre Woodard, actress.

ALHINA Arabic: "a ring."

ALICE French: "noble one." **Ales, Allice, Alyce, Alys.** Alice Walker, Pulitzer prize—winning novelist for *The Color Purple* (1983). Alice Childress, playwright, novelist, and actress.

ALICIA English. French: "noble one." **Alecia, Alisia, Alissa, Alycia, Alysa, Alysia, Alyssa, Alyssia. Alli, Allie.**

ALICIANA Spanish: Blending of Alicia (noble one) and Ana (grace, mercy).

ALICYS American: Contemporary, probably based on Alice (noble one) or Alissa (noble one).

ALILE Malawian. Yao: "she weeps." **Alili.**

ALIOUS American: Contemporary.

ALIPHA Nigeria. Hausa: "thousand."

ALIRA American: Contemporary.

ALISHA Sanskrit: "protected by god."

ALISKA American: Contemporary.

ALISON English: "son of Alice." **Allison, Alli, Allie.**

ALISSA English. French: "noble one." **Alyssa.**

ALIYA Arabic: "sublime, exalted, elevated." Hebrew: "a going up, ascent." **Alia, Aliah, Aliyah, Aliyyah.**

ALIZABETH American. English. Hebrew: "God is my oath." **Alyzabeth. Allie, Ally, Beth.**

ALIZAH Hebrew: "joy." **Aleeza, Alitza, Aliza.**

ALKANA Nigeria. Hausa: "wheat."

ALKEYRA American: Contemporary.

ALLEAH American. Arabic: "sublime, exalted, elevated." Hebrew: "to ascend."

ALLEGRA Latin: "merry, cheerful." **Alegra, Allegria, Elegra, Elegria, Ellegra.** Allegra Bennett, columnist.

ALLENDA American: Contemporary, based on the male Allen (handsome, fair).

ALLURA American: "allure, attraction."

ALMA Spanish: "soul."

ALMEATHA American: Possibly a variant of Almeta (shapely).

ALMETA Welsh: "shapely."

ALMIRA Arabic: "princess." Spanish. German: "noble one." **Almirah, Elmira, Elmirah. Mira.**

ALODIE American: Contemporary, perhaps influenced by the Spanish Alodio (marsh, shore; plain).

ALONA Hebrew: "oak tree."

ALONZIA Spanish. German: "noble and ready."

ALTAIR Arabic: "a bird." Altair is the name of the brightest star in the constellation Aquila.

ALTHEA English. Latin and Greek: "to heal." In classical mythology, Althea is the name of the mother of Meleager. Althea Gibson, tennis pro, first Black to win the U.S. Tennis championship (1957).

ALUNA Kenya. Mwera: "come here." **Aluma.**

ALUSINE American: Contemporary.

ALVALEE American: Blending of the names Alva (friend of the elves) and Lee (a wood, clearing, meadow).

ALVERA Spanish. English: "elf army." **Alvira, Alviria, Alvra.**

ALVINA American. English: "friend of the elves." **Alveena.**

ALYSSON American. English: "son of Alice." **Alisson, Alissyn, Allisin, Allisson, Allisyn, Alysin, Alyssin, Alyssyn. Alli, Allie.**

ALZENA Nigeria. Hausa: "spirits." **Alzina.**

AMA Ghana. Ewe: "born on Saturday." Nigerian. Efik: "beloved."

AMADA Spanish. Latin: "to love." **Amadia, Amadida.**

AMADI Nigeria. Ibo: "rejoicing, celebrating."

AMALIA German: "industrious." **Amalya.** Amalya Kearse, U.S. Appellate Court judge.

AMANA Hebrew: "established."

AMANDA Spanish: "lovable, worthy to be loved." The name Amanda originated as a coinage of English playwright Colley Cibber (1671–1757). **Amandah, Ammanda. Mandi, Mandie, Mandy.**

AMANI Arabic: "wishes, desires." **Amany.**

AMARYLLIS Latin: Of uncertain meaning. In the classical pastoral poetry of Virgil and Theocritus, Amaryllis is the name of a shepherdess. In recent times, it is most commonly associated with the flower of the same name.

AMASA Nigeria. Hausa: "important; abundant."

AMAZIAH Nigeria. Hausa: "a place to rest."

AMBER English: a translucent fossil resin used in the making of jewelry. Sanskrit: "the sky; fabric."

AMBIKA India: "The Progenitor." Another name of the goddess Parvati.

AMERYLUS American: Modern variant of Amaryllis. **Amerilus.**

AMIEE American. French: "beloved."

AMINA   Arabic: "faithful, honest." **Aminah, Amineh.**

AMINU   Nigeria. Yoruba. Arabic: "faithful, honest."

AMIRA   Arabic: "queen."

AMIRAH   Hebrew: "speech." **Amira.**

AMISA   Hebrew: "friend." **Amissa, Amissah.**

AMISHA   Sanskrit: "honest."

AMITY   English: "friendship."

AMORETTE   American: Contemporary, possibly based on the Latin-word *amor* or the Italian *amore* (love).

AMORITA   Spanish: "little loved one."

AMRITA   American. Spanish: "little loved one."

ANACA   Nigeria. Hausa: "small rabbit." **Anaka, Aneca, Aneka.**

ANADA   Nigeria. Hausa: "entangled."

ANAN   African: "fourth child."

ANATALIA   Spanish. Greek: "sunrise, daybreak, dawn."

ANAVIA   American: Contemporary.

ANDAIYE   Swahili: "a daughter comes home."

ANDELEE   American: Contemporary.

ANDRAYAH   American: Contemporary, based on the name Andrea.

ANDREA   Greek: "mankind." **Andreah, Andreea, Andria. Andie.**

ANDRÉE   American: Contemporary, based on the name Andrea (mankind). **Andree.**

ANGEL   Greek: "messenger, messenger of God." **Angele, Angell, Anngell. Angie.**

ANGELA   Greek: "messenger, messenger of God." **Angelah, Angella. Angie.** Angela Davis, author and educator. Angela Bassett, actress.

ANGELICA   Greek: "angelic." **Angie.**

ANGELIE   American: Contemporary, based on Angel and its variant forms. **Angelia. Angie.**

ANGELINA   Greek: "little angel." **Angeleena. Angie.**

ANGELINE   French. Greek: "little angel."

ANGELYNNE   American: A compound of the names Angel and Lynn.

ANGIELINE   American: Contemporary spelling of Angeline (little angel).

ANISA   Arabic: "friendly, a good companion."

ANISHA   Sanskrit: "lord; supreme."

ANITA   Spanish. Hebrew: "grace, mercy." **Aneeta, Annita, Nita.** Anita Baker, singer. Anita Hill, University of Oklahoma law professor. Anita Pointer, singer.

ANITHRA   American: Contemporary, probably based on the name Anita.

ANNA   European. Hebrew: "grace, mercy." Anna Deavere Smith, performer.

ANNEENE   American: Contemporary.

ANNIKA   Swedish. Hebrew: "grace, mercy." **Anika, Anike, Annike.**

ANNISA Spanish. Hebrew: "grace, mercy." **Annisa, Annissia. Ann**.

ANNISE American: Contemporary, possibly influenced by the name Denise (of Dionysus) or the Spanish Annisia (to carry out an obligation).

ANONA English: Contemporary, of uncertain derivation, possibly influenced by the Latin *annona* (a seasonal planting). **Annona**.

ANQUIA American: Contemporary.

ANTOINETTE French. Latin: "priceless, of inestimable worth." **Antoinetta. Netti, Nettie, Toni, Tonie**.

ANTOLIANA Spanish. Latin: "priceless, of inestimable worth." **Antoliona. Toni, Tonia, Tonie**.

ANTONIA Spanish. Latin: "priceless, of inestimable worth." **Andonia, Antionia. Toni, Tonia, Tonie**.

ANTWANETTE American: Contemporary, a phonetic spelling of Antoinette (priceless, of inestimable worth). **Anntwanet, Anntwanette, Twanette. Netti, Nettie**.

ANTWENE American: Contemporary.

ANUHEA American: Contemporary.

ANULI Nigeria. Ibo: "joyous, delightful."

ANURA India: "knowledge."

ANZELLA American: Contemporary.

APHRA Hebrew: "young deer." **Afra, Afrah, Aphrah**.

APOLLONIA Greek: "belonging to Apollo."

APRIL English. Latin: "second, latter." The first month of the ancient Roman calendar was March, with April being the second month. **Apryl**.

AQUANETTA American: Contemporary, containing the element *aqua* (water) and perhaps inspired by the hair spray *Aqua Net*.

ARA African: Borrowed from the name of the Ekoi sky maiden.

ARACELA Spanish: "altar of heaven." **Arasela, Arizela**.

ARCHERINE American. German: "genuinely brave."

ARDA Hebrew: "bronze." **Ardah**.

ARDELLA Latin: "enthusiastic." **Ardell, Ardelle**.

ARDICE American: Contemporary. **Ardiss, Ardyce**.

ARDINE American: Contemporary.

ARDITH English: Originated as a variant of Edith (prosperous in war) or a blending of Arthur and Edith.

ARDONA Hebrew: "bronze." **Ardonah, Ardonia**.

ARETHA Greek: "best, choice." **Areetha. Reetha, Retha**. Aretha Franklin, singer.

ARETTA Nigeria. Bini: "a charm used to make one reveal a secret." **Areta**.

ARIA Latin: "air, a melody for a single voice." In classical mythology, Aria was a nymph and the mother of Miletus, by Apollo.

ARIANNE   French. Greek: "the very holy one." **Ariane, Arrianne.**

ARIELA   Hebrew: "lioness of God." **Ariella.**

ARIESA   American: Contemporary name, possibly based on Aries (ram), the name of the first sign of the zodiac.

ARIZA   Hebrew: "cedar panels."

ARLENE   American: Contemporary. **Arlana, Arlean, Arleen, Arleyne, Arline. Arlie.**

ARLETTE   French: "eagle." **Arleta, Arlett. Arlie.**

ARLINDA   American: Contemporary. **Arlie, Linda.**

ARLYNN   American: Contemporary.

ARMEIA   American: Contemporary.

ARMELIA   American: Contemporary, possibly influenced by Amelia (work). English. Latin: "bracelet." Armelia McQueen, actress.

ARMIDA   Latin: "little fighter."

ARMINDA   American. Latin: "soldier, warrior."

ARMONA   Hebrew: "palace; oak tree."

ARMONDA   Spanish. German: "soldier, warrior."

ARNEDA   American: Contemporary.

ARNETHA   American: Contemporary, possibly a variant of Arnett (little eagle).

ARNETT   English: "little eagle." **Arnet, Arnetta, Arnette. Netti, Nettie.**

ARNONA   Hebrew: "stream."

ARRIE   Nigeria. Bini: "reincarnation."

ARTELMA   American: Possible blending of the names Art (bear) and Elma (amiable).

ARTHA   Hindi: "wealth, treasure."

ARTHELEA   American: Contemporary.

ARUBA   Arabic: "she loves her husband." Alternatively, the name may be borrowed from the name of an island of the Netherlands Antilles, off the coast of Venezuela.

ARUNIKA   Sanskrit: "the glow of the sunrise."

ARUSI   Swahili: "born at the time of a wedding."

ARVADA   Danish: "eagle."

ARVELLA   Italian: "from the coast." **Arvelle.**

ARYIOLA   Spanish. Latin: "fortune-teller."

ARZATA   Nigeria. Hausa: "prosperous."

ASAASE AFUA   Ghana. Akan: In mythology, Asaase Afua is the daughter of Onyame and goddess of fertility and procreation.

ASAASE YAA   Ghana. Akan: In mythology, Asaase Yaa is goddess of the earth's barren places.

ASABI   Nigeria. Yoruba: "she is of superior birth; she who is chosen to be born."

ASALE   Malawi. Yao: "speak."

ASELA   Spanish. Latin: "little burro." **Acela, Asalia.**

ASHA   Sanskrit: "wish, desire."

ASHAN   Hebrew: "smoke."

ASHERAH Middle East: The name of a Canaanite goddess frequently associated with Baal.

ASHIA Swahili. Arabic: "life." **Asha.**

ASHIKA American: Contemporary.

ASHIRA Hebrew: "wealthy." Nigerian. Hausa: "born during Ashur."

ASHLEY English: "dweller near the ash tree forest." **Ashlee, Ashleigh, Ashlie, Ashly.**

ASHNI Hindi: "a flash of lightning."

ASHURA Swahili: "born during the Islamic month of Ashur."

ASIA American: A borrowing of the name of the continent.

ASISA Hebrew: "young."

ASISYA Hebrew: "the juice of Jehovah." **Asisia, Asisiah, Asisyah.**

ASKIA American: Contemporary. **Askea.**

ASPASIA Greek: "welcome."

ASYA Swahili: "born during a time of grief."

ATARA Hebrew: "a crown."

ATHALIA Hebrew: "the Lord is exalted." **Athaliah.**

ATHENA Greek: Meaning uncertain. In classical Greek mythology, Athena is the goddess of skill, wisdom, and warfare. **Athene, Athina.**

ATIFA Arabic: "compassionate." **Atifah.**

ATIRA Hebrew: "prayer."

ATIYA Arabic: "gift."

ATLANTA Greek: Meaning uncertain. In classical Greek mythology, Atlanta is the name of a beautiful, fleet-footed maiden. **Atalanta, Atalante, Atlante.**

ATSUFI African: "one of twins."

AUBREY French. German: "elf ruler." From the name Alberich. **Aubree, Aubri, Aubry.**

AUBURN English: "reddish brown."

AUDARSHIA American: Contemporary.

AUDEAN American: Contemporary, probably a blending of Audrey (noble strength) and Dean (a dean).

AUDREINA American: Contemporary, based on Audrey (noble strength). **Audreena, Audreenah, Audreinah.**

AUDREY English: "noble strength." **Audree, Audrie, Audry.**

AUGUSTA Latin: "august, venerable, great."

AUNJUANE American: Contemporary.

AURELIA Latin: "golden." **Auraelia, Auraella, Aura Lee, Auralia, Auralie, Aurelie.**

AUVILLA American: Contemporary.

AVERY English: "elf ruler."

AVIVAH Hebrew: "springtime; fresh." **Aviva.**

AYAH Swahili: "bright."

AYALAH Hebrew: "a deer, a gazelle." **Ayala.**

AYAN African: "bright, beautiful."

AYANNA African: "beautiful flower; she is beautiful."

AYLA Hebrew: "an oak tree."

AYO Nigeria. Yoruba: "joy."

AYOBAMI Nigeria. Yoruba: "I am blessed with joy."

AYOBUNMI Nigeria. Yoruba: "joy is given to me."

AYODELE Nigeria. Yoruba: "she brings joy to our home."

AYOFEMI Nigeria. Yoruba: "joy likes me."

AYOKA Nigeria. Yoruba: "she brings joy to all."

AYOLUWA Nigeria. Yoruba: "she is the joy of our people."

AYOOLA Nigeria. Yoruba: "joy in wealth."

AZA Arabic: "short shadows when the sun is high in the sky."

AZARIA Hebrew: "helped by God."

AZIZA Arabic: "esteemed, beloved, precious." Hebrew: "strong." **Azizah**.

AZUBA Nigeria. Hausa: "born on Monday."

AZUBAH Hebrew: "forsaken, deserted."

AZUKA African: "support is paramount."

BAAKO Ghana. Akan: "firstborn."

BADERINWA Nigeria. Yoruba: "worthy of respect."

BAHATI Swahili: "fortunate, lucky."

BAINA Nigeria. Hausa: "dear."

BARBARA Latin: "foreign woman." **Barbra. Babs, Barb, Barbie**. Barbara Jordan (1936–1996), congresswoman, voted one of the ten most influential women of the twentieth century. Barbara Reynolds, columnist. Barbara Reynolds, restaurateur.

BARIKA Arabic: "successful, excelling."

BARNESA American: Perhaps influenced by Barnaby (son of exhortation).

BASHIRA Arabic: "joy, joyful."

BAYO Nigeria. Yoruba: "joy is found."

BEBE American: Possibly a variant of the Arabic Bibi (lady).

BEJIDE Nigeria. Yoruba: "born during the rainy season."

BELIKA Sanskrit: "a small creeper."

BELINDA German: Of uncertain meaning, possibly "snake."

BELVA Latin: "beautiful view." **Belvah**.

BENECIA Italia. Latin: "blessed." **Benicia**.

BENELLA American: Probable blending of Ben and Ella (light). **Benni**.

BENINA Latin: "kind."

BENISHA American. Latin: "blessed." **Benishe**.

BENITA Spanish. Latin: "blessed."

BERDINE German: "bold as a bear." **Berdina**.

BERLEAN American: Possibly influenced by Merline (blackbird) or based on the male name Berlyne (from Berlin). **Berli**.

BERLIN   German: "from Berlin."

BERLYN   American. German: "from Berlin." **Berlyn, Berlynn, Berlynne.**

BERNADETH   German: "bold as a bear." **Berni.**

BERNADETTE   French. German: "bold as a bear." **Bernette. Berni.**

BERNADYNE   American. German: "bold as a bear." **Bernadine, Byrnadine. Berni.**

BERNARDINE   French. German: "bold as a bear." **Bernardina. Berni.**

BERNITA   American. German: "bold as a bear." From the name Bernard. **Berni.**

BERTALINA   Italian. German: "little Berta" (bright). **Berti.**

BERTICE   American: Contemporary. **Bertie.** Bertice Berry, author.

BERYL   English: "beryl, a green gemstone such as emerald and aquamarine."

BETHANNE   English: Combination of Beth (God is my oath; house of figs) and Anne (gracious, full of grace). **Bethann.** Bethann Hardison, model and mentor.

BETHANY   Hebrew: "house of figs."

BETHENA   American. Hebrew: "house of figs."

BETHENNY   American. Hebrew: "house of figs." **Bethanee, Bethani, Bethanie, Bethanni, Bethannie, Bethanny, Bethenee, Betheni, Bethenie, Bethenni, Bethennie, Betheny.**

BETT   Hebrew: "daughter." Also, Bett is a short form of Elizabeth (God is my oath).

BETTY   English. Hebrew: Pet form of Elizabeth (God is my oath). **Bettee, Bettie, Bettye, Betye.** Betye Saar, assemblage artist.

BEVERLEY   English: "dweller near the beaver stream." **Beverlee, Bever-Leigh, Beverlie, Beverly. Bev.** Beverley Anderson-Manley, former Jamaican first lady and international consultant on gender issues.

BIBI   Arabic and Persian: "lady."

BINA   Sanskrit: "intelligence."

BIRDIE   English: "little bird."

BIRDINE   American: Variant form of Berdine (bold as a bear), influenced by the word *bird*. **Birdean, Birdeen, Berdyne.**

BIZELLA   American: Contemporary.

BLENDA   American: Contemporary, modeled after Glenda (pure one).

BOAHINMAA   Ghana. Ewe: "an expatriate."

BOBBETTE   English. German: "bright with fame." **Bobette.**

BOBBIE   English. German: "bright with fame." Originally a pet form of Roberta.

BOJANA   American: Contemporary.

BOLADE   Nigeria. Yoruba: "honor arrives."

BOLANILE   Nigeria. Yoruba: "she is the wealth of this house; she is our treasure."

BONNIA   American. Scottish: "beautiful; good-natured and cheerful."

BONNIE   Scottish: "beautiful; good-natured and cheerful."

BOZENA   Slavic: "Christmas child."

BRANDENNE   American: Contemporary, based on Brandy (brandy, a type of liquor). **Brandeen, Brandene, Brandine. Brandi, Brandie, Brandy.**

BRANDY   American: "brandy, a liquor distilled from wine or fermented fruit juice." Brandy Norwood, singer and actress.

BRAYNA   American: Contemporary.

BREE   Irish: "hill." **Breea.**

BRENDA   Celtic: Meaning uncertain. Some believe it is from *brandr* (the blade of a sword). Other popular definitions include "firebrand" and "flaming sword." **Brinda.**

BREQLYNN   American: Contemporary. **Breqlyne.**

BREZINA   Czech: "from the place of birch trees."

BRIANNE   Irish: "strength." **Breann, Breanna, Breanne, Briana, Brianna, Brieann, Brieanna, Brieanne, Brienne.**

BRIDEY   Scottish: "strength." **Bridie.**

BRITTANICA   English: "British, of Britain."

BRITTANY   France: "a Breton, from Brittany." **Britany, Britney, Britni, Brittainy, Brittanee, Brittney, Brittny. Britt.**

BROOKLYN   American: After the New York City borough of the same name. **Brooklin, Brooklinn, Brooklynn.**

BRYNAE   American: Contemporary.

BUNMI   Nigeria. Yoruba: "my gift."

BURNETIA   American: Contemporary, probably based on Bernice (bringer of victory).

BUSEJE   Malawi. Yao: "ask me."

BUTHANAYA   Arabic: "having a beautiful body."

CACHAY   American: Contemporary, probably based on the French cachet (distinction, prestige).

CALANDRA   Greek: "beautiful one." **Calandrah, Kalandra, Kalandrah. Calli, Callie, Kalli, Kallie.**

CALLA   Latin: "lily, a type of plant." **Calah, Callah.**

CALLIE   American: Originally a pet form of any name beginning with *Cal-*. **Calee, Caleigh, Callee, Calleigh, Calli, Cally.**

CAMBRIA   Welsh: After the Cambrian Mountains. American: After the place-name Cambria, a county in Pennsylvania that was first settled by the Welsh.

CAMELA   American: Contemporary, based on Pamela.

CAMELIA   Spanish. Latin: "virgin of unblemished character." **Camelea. Cami.**

CAMEO   American. Italiann: "a carving in relief on certain gems or shells; a small but well-defined theatrical role."

CAMIKA   American: Contemporary.

CAMILLA   Latin: "virgin of unblemished character." **Camille. Cami, Milli, Millie, Milly.** Camille Cosby, philanthropist. Camille Billops, sculptor. Camille Yarbrough, actress.

CAMIRIA Spanish: Borrowed from a type of tree.

CANDACE Latin: "white, pure, sincere."

CANDACY American: Contemporary, possibly influenced by Candace (white, pure, sincere).

CANDLE English: "a candle."

CANDRA Sanskrit: "the moon." Latin: "luminescent."

CANDRIA Latin: "luminescent." **Candrea**.

CANDYSE American. Latin: "white, pure, sincere." **Candice, Candise, Kandace, Kandase, Kandice, Kandise, Kandyse. Candi, Candie, Candy, Kandi, Kandie, Kandy**.

CAPREA Latin: "a roe deer."

CAPRENIA American: Contemporary, possibly influenced by the Latin *caprinus* (relating to a goat).

CAPRI Italiann. Latin: "goat." Capri is the name of an island in the Bay of Naples.

CAPRICE American. French: "a whim, whimsical."

CARDISS American: Contemporary. Cardiss Collins, U.S. representative and first woman to chair the Congressional Black Caucus.

CARESSE French: "beloved."

CARILLA American: Contemporary.

CARLA English: "woman, freewoman, peasant." **Karla**.

CARLANE American: Contemporary.

CARLEEN Irish: "full-grown, a woman." A feminine form of Charles. **Carlene**.

CARLEN English: "woman, freewoman, peasant." **Karlen**.

CARLEY English: "woman, freewoman, peasant." **Carlee, Carleigh, Carli, Carlie, Carly, Karlee, Karli, Karlie**.

CARMEL Hebrew: "orchard, garden, vineyard." **Carmela, Karmel, Karmela**.

CARMEN Spanish. Hebrew: "orchard, garden, vineyard." Carmen de Lavallade, dancer.

CARMIYA Hebrew: "vineyard of the Lord."

CARNELIA Spanish. Latin: "horn." **Carnella**.

CAROL English: "full-grown; joyous song, a carol." Carol Woods, singer and actress.

CAROLINE German: "full-grown, womanly." **Carol. Caro, Carrie**.

CARTELIA American: Contemporary. **Cartie**.

CARTIE American: Contemporary. **Carti**.

CASEY English. Greek: Short form of Cassandra. **Casie, Kacey, Kacie, Kasey, Kasi, Kaycee, Kaycey, Kaycie, Kaycy**.

CASSANDRA Greek: Meaning uncertain. In Greek mythology, Cassandra had the gift of prophecy, but unfortunately, no one ever believed her. **CaSandra, Casaundra, Cassondra, Cassaundra, KaSandra, Kasandra, Kasaundra, Kassaundra. Cass, Cassie, Cassy, Kass, Kassie, Kassy**. Cassandra Wilson, singer.

CASSIA Greek: "cinnamon." **Cass, Cassi, Cassie.**

CASSIETTA American: Contemporary.

CASTANA Spanish. Latin: "pure."

CATALINA Spanish. Greek: "pure, unsullied." A form of Catherine.

CATHELLA American: Possibly a blending of Catherine (pure, unsullied) and Ella (light).

CATHERINE Greek: "pure." **Katherine. Cass, Cassie, Cathie, Cathy, Kate, Kathie, Kathy, Katie, Katy.**

CATHY English. Greek: "pure, unsullied, virtuous."

CATIN French. Greek: "pure, unsullied, virtuous."

CEALY American: Contemporary, probably a variant spelling of the French Celie (heaven).

CEARA American. Irish: "Black-haired one."

CEDONIA Spanish. Greek: "a swallow." **Sadonia.**

CELESTE French: "celestial, heavenly." **Celestia.**

CELIA Latin: "heaven." Celia Cruz, singer.

CELINA Spanish. Greek: "the moon." **Celena, Salena, Selena, Selenia, Selina.**

CELINDA Spanish. Greek: "the moon." **Celenda, Selenda, Selinda.**

CELITA American: Contemporary.

CENITHA American: Contemporary.

CERACIA American: Contemporary.

CERELIA English. Latin: "springlike, blossoming." **Cerelie.**

CERISE French: "cherry, cherry-flavored."

CEYLON American: Borrowed from the former name of Sri Lanka, the country off the coast of Indian.

CHAHNA India: "love; light."

CHAINNIE American: Contemporary, possibly influenced by Janie.

CHALESE American: Contemporary. **Chalees, Chalise, Chalyse, Shalees, Shalese, Shalise, Shalyse.**

CHALISA American: Contemporary.

CHALMETTE American. French: Taken from a Louisiana place-name.

CHAMIQUE American: Contemporary.

CHANA Hebrew: "grace, mercy."

CHANDA American: Contemporary, based on element Chan-.

CHANDAA Sanskrit: "the moon."

CHANDANI Sanskrit: "moonlight."

CHANDELL French: "candle." **Chandelle. Chan.**

CHANDNI Sanskrit: "moonlight."

CHANDRA Sanskrit: "the moon, shining." **Chandrah. Chan.**

CHANDREE Sanskrit: "moonlight."

CHANDRIA American: Contemporary, perhaps based on the Sanskrit Chandree (moonlight). **Chandreea.**

CHANELLE American: Contemporary, based on the French surname Chanel (channel, irrigation ditch). **Channell, Channelle, Shanell, Shanelle, Shannell, Shannelle.**

CHANEY English: "dweller near the oak wood."

CHANNIE American: Contemporary.

CHANTAL French: "stone, boulder." **Chantall.**

CHANTÉ American: Contemporary, possibly influenced by the French *enchanté* (enchanted). **Chantae, Chantay, Chante, Chantee.** Chanté Moore, singer.

CHANTEL American. French: "stone, boulder." **Chantale, Chantele, Chantelle.**

CHANTERELLE French: "drinking cup shaped like a mushroom." **Chantrel, Chantrell, Chantrelle, Shanterell, Shanterelle, Shantrel, Shantrell, Shantrelle. Chan, Shan.**

CHAONAINE Malawi. Ngoni: "it has seen me."

CHARANNE American: Contemporary. **Charann, Charenn.**

CHARENE American: Contemporary. **Chareen, Chareene.**

CHARISMA English: "a charming and inspiring personality."

CHARISSA Greek: "grace." **Charis, Charisse, Karis, Karissa, Karisse, Kharis, Kharissa, Kharisse.**

CHARLAYNE American. English: "woman, freewoman, peasant." **Charlain, Charlaine, Charlane, Sharlain, Sharlaine, Sharlayn, Sharlayne. Charlie.** Charlaine Woodard, actress.

CHARLENE English: "a woman, freewoman, peasant." **Charline, Cherlene, Cherline, Sharleen, Sharlene. Charli, Charlie.**

CHARLESETTA American. English: "a woman, freewoman, peasant."

CHARLETTE American. English: "a woman, freewoman, peasant."

CHARLISE American. English: "a woman, freewoman, peasant."

CHARLOTTE French: "a woman, freewoman, peasant." Charlotte originated as a feminine form of Charles. **Charlette.** Charlotte L. Forten, author and poet.

CHARMAINE American. French: "a song, verse, chant." **Charmain, Charmayne, Sharmain, Sharmaine, Sharmayn, Sharmayne.**

CHARMANEY American: Contemporary, probably influenced by Charmaine (song) and Harmony (pleasing, order). **Charmony.**

CHARMIAN English. Greek: "joy, delight." **Charmyan, Sharman, Sharmeian, Sharmian.**

CHARMIN American: Contemporary.

CHARNETTE American: Contemporary.

CHARON Greek: Meaning uncertain. In Greek mythology, Charon was the name of the boatman who ferried souls of the dead across the river Styx. **Charron.**

CHARQUINTA American: Hispanic coinage.

CHARRON American: Contemporary.

CHATEYA American: Contemporary.

CHAUNCEY English: "chancellor, secretary." **Chauncee, Chaunsee, Chaunsie.**

CHAUNDRA American: Contemporary, based on Saundra (mankind).

CHAUNTEL American: Contemporary, probably influenced by the French Chantal (boulder, stone).

CHAUSIKU Swahili: "born at night."

CHAVELLE Spanish. Hebrew: "God is my oath." Chavelle is a pet form of Isabela.

CHAVONDA American: Contemporary.

CHAYNI American: Contemporary variant of Chaney (dweller near the oak wood).

CHAZMIN American: Contemporary, based on Jasmine (the jasmine bush).

CHEBRÉE American: Contemporary. **Chebrae, Chebree, Chebrey.**

CHEIRON American: Modern variant of Sharon.

CHELLE American and English: A shortened form of any of the names containing this element.

CHELSEA English: "a port of ships." **Chealsea, Chelsie.** Chelsie Smith, Miss Universe. Chelsea Brown, actress.

CHENEY English. French: "from the oak wood."

CHENILLE American. French: "hairy caterpillar." The name was probably used in reference to the fabric of the same name. **Shanille, Shanyll, Shenille.**

CHENZIRA African: "born while parents are on a journey."

CHEREE American: Contemporary, a phonetic spelling of the French *chérie* (darling).

CHERELLE American: Modern variant of Cheryl. **Sharol.**

CHERENE American: Contemporary. **Chereen, Chereene, Cherine, Cheryne.**

CHERIE American: Contemporary, from the French *chérie* (darling). Also, a variant spelling of Sherry (a fortified wine).

CHERIKA American: Contemporary.

CHERISE American. French: "cherry, cherry-flavored." **Chereese, Cherrise.**

CHERISH English: "treasured, cherished, beloved."

CHERLEY American: Contemporary variant of Shirley (from the bright meadow). **Cherlee, Cherli, Cherlie, Cherly.**

CHERLYN American: Contemporary.

CHERMONA Hebrew: "sacred mountains."

CHERON American: Contemporary variant of Sharon (a plain, a flat area).

CHERRY English. French: "darling, sweetheart." The name Cherry is now usually associated with the fruit.

CHERRYMAE American: Blending of the names Cherry (darling; a cherry) and Mae (May).

CHERYL American and English: Twentieth-century coinage, possibly formed by combining Cherry and Beryl. **Cheril, Cherril, Cherrill, Sherill, Sherril, Sherrill, Sherryl, Sheryl.** Cheryl Miller, Olympic gold medal winner, sports announcer, and inductee into the Basketball Hall of Fame. Sheryl Lee Randolph, singer and actress.

CHEVELLE American: Contemporary, probably influenced by the car of the same name.

CHEVONNE English. Irish: "God is gracious." **Chevon, Chevonn, Shevon, Shevonn, Shevonne.**

CHEVONTE American: Contemporary, based on Chevonne (God is gracious). **Chevontae, Chevonté.**

CHEYENNE Native American. Sioux: "unintelligible speakers."

CHIFFONAH American: Contemporary, possibly influenced by *chiffon* (a sheer, lightweight fabric). **Chiffona, Chiffonae, Chiffonay, Chiffonée, Chiffonna, Chiffonnah.**

CHIKA Nigeria. Ibo: "Chi is supreme."

CHIKU Swahili: "chatterer."

CHINAKA Nigeria. Ibo: "Chi decides."

CHINARA Nigeria. Ibo: "Chi receives."

CHINEYE Nigeria. Ibo: "Chi gives."

CHINUE Nigeria. Ibo: "blessings of Chi." In Ibo religion, Chi is a personal god who stays with a person from conception until death.

CHINYERE Nigeria. Ibo: "Chi is the giver."

CHIQUITA Spanish: "little one."

CHLEO American: Modern spelling of Cleo (glory).

CHLOE Greek: "verdant, blooming, green." **Chloë.**

CHLORA Greek: "pale green."

CHOTSANI Malawi. Yao: "take it away." This type of name is used to trick the ancestors into thinking the child is not worthy, so they will not take it away.

CHRISTEAN American: Modern variant of Christine (a Christian). **Chris, Christie, Christy.**

CHRISTEL American: Modern variant of Crystal (clear quartz, glass). **Chrystel, Crystel, Khristel, Khrystel, Krystel.**

CHRISTINA Greek: "a follower of Christ." **Christine. Chris, Chrissy, Christie, Christy.**

CHRITIE American: Contemporary.

CHRYSTELLE American: Contemporary, based on Crystal (clear quartz, brilliant glass). **Chrys.**

CHYLESE American: Contemporary.

CHYREL American: Contemporary. **Chyrell, Shyrel, Shyrell.**

CIANA Italiann. Hebrew: "God is gracious." American: Contemporary, modeled after Diana (divine). **Cianna.**

CIARA Irish: "black-haired one."

CICELY English: "blind, dim-sighted." **Cicily.** Cicely Tyson, actress.

CINDY English: Short form of Cynthia (from Kynthos). **Cindee, Cindie, Sindee,**

Sindie, Sindy. Cindy Blackman, jazz drummer.

CINNAMON   English: from the spice of the same name.

CLAIRE   French: "bright, famous, clear." **Clare.**

CLAIRETTE   American. French: "little Claire." **Clairetta, Claretta, Clarette.**

CLARADINE   American: Elaboration of Clara (bright, clear, famous). Also, a blending of Clara (bright, clear, famous) and Dean (a dean). **Claradean, Claradeen.**

CLARETHA   American: elaboration of Clare (bright, clear; famous).

CLARICE   English. Latin: "bright; famous; clear." **Claricia, Clarisa, Clarise, Clarissa, Clarisse, Clarissia, Clarrice, Clarrisa, Clarrissa, Clarrisse, Klarisa, Klarise, Klarissa, Klarisse, Klarrissia.**

CLATONIA   American: Contemporary.

CLAUDETTE   French.   Latin: "little Claude."

CLAUDIA   Latin: "lame."

CLAYLEE   American: Contemporary.

CLELA   American: Coinage, perhaps influenced by the Latin Clelia (client).

CLELAMAE   American: Blending of the names Clela and Mae (May).

CLEMENCIA   Spanish. Latin: "mild, gentle."

CLEON   Greek: "glory." **Cleona, Cleone.**

CLÉOPHA   French. Greek: "famous."

CLEVIA   American: Coinage, possibly a feminine form of Clive (cliff, bank of a river).

CLODENE   American. Spanish. German: "great in fame."

CLODINA   Spanish. German: "great in fame."

CLOREAN   American: Perhaps inspired by the word *chlorine* (a chemical element).

CLOTENE   American: Contemporary.

CLOVER   English: From the plant of the same name.

COLANDA   American: Contemporary name, probably based on the name Yolanda. **Colandah, Kolanda, Kolandah.**

COLETTE   French: "victory of the people." Colette originated as a short form of Nicolette. **Collette.**

CONDEE   American: Contemporary, possibly influenced by the French surname Condé (the confluence).

CONDOLA   American: Contemporary.

CONDOLEEZA   American: Contemporary. Condoleeza Rice, provost of Stanford University and Soviet affairs expert.

CONSTANCE   English. Latin: "constant, standing together." **Connie.**

COPPELIA   American: Coinage, possibly influenced by names such as Cordelia (jewel of the sea) or Cornelia (horn).

CORA   English. Greek: "maiden." **Kora. Cori, Kori.**

CORAL English: "coral." The word refers to the skeletons of certain marine animals. It is a popular jewelry material. **Koral.**

CORALIE English: Variation of the names Coral and Cora (maiden), or a blending of Cora and Lee (a wood, meadow). **Coralee. Cori, Kori.**

CORBY Scottish: "from Cor's settlement." **Corbi, Korbi, Korby.**

CORDEAN American: Possible blending of Cora or Corinne (maiden) and Dean (a dean).

CORDELIA Celtic: "jewel of the sea, daughter of the sea."

CORDELLE French: "rope."

CORENA American. Greek: "maiden." **Korena.**

CORETTA American. Greek: "little maiden." Coretta Scott King, civil rights activist, widow of Dr. Martin Luther King, Jr.

CORINNA English. Greek: "maiden." **Corine, Corinne, Corrina, Corrine, Corynne. Cori, Corri, Cory.**

CORLISS English: "cheerful, kindhearted."

CORNELIA Latin: "horn." **Cornelya.**

COVA American: Contemporary.

COZETTE American: "cozy, warm, snug."

CREE American: Denotes a member of an Algonquian Indiann tribe and their language. Cree Summer, actress.

CREMOLIA American: Contemporary.

CREZETTE American: Coinage, perhaps influenced by Cozette.

CRIMSON American: "deep red."

CRYSTAL English: "crystal, clear." **Chrystal, Khrystal, Krystal.**

CRYSTALYN American: Blending of Crystal (crystal, clear) and Lynn (lake).

CULLIE REE American: "at the woodland."

CURTISENE American. French: "courteous." A feminine form of Curtis.

CYDNEY American. French: "follower of St. Denis; dweller near the wide, wet land." **Cidnee, Cidney, Cidny, Cydny.**

CYMA Greek: "flourishing, growing."

CYNARA Greek: "thistle." **Cyna.**

CYNTHIA Latin and Greek: "from Kynthos, a mountain on the island of Delos." Kynthia was another name of Artemus, the goddess of the moon. Therefore, many give the meaning of "moon" to the name. **Cinthia. Cindi, Cindy, Cyndee, Cyndi.**

CYRICE American: Contemporary, perhaps influenced by Cherise (cherry, cherry-flavored).

DACIA Greek: "from Dacia (an ancient kingdom on the Danube River)."

DAHINDA Native American. Ojibway: "bullfrog."

DAHLIA Swedish: "valley." Taken from the name of the dahlia flower, which is named for Swedish botanist Anders Dahl. **Dalia.**

DAIDRA American: Contemporary, perhaps influenced by Deidre (young girl).

DAINNESE American: Contemporary variant of Denise (of Dionysus). **Dainnyse.**

DAISY English: "day's eye." Used in reference to the daisy flower. **Daisey.**

DAJANA American: Contemporary.

DAJUANA American. Spanish: "God is gracious." A modern variation of Juana. **Da Juana, D'juana, Djuana.**

DA'JUNE American: Modern variation of June (the sixth month; Juno, the Roman mythological goddess of marriage).

DALENNA American: Contemporary.

DALIA Swahili: "gentle."

DALIENNE American: Contemporary, influenced by the French language.

DALILA American. Hebrew: "delicate." Swahili: "gentle."

DALILI Swahili: "sign, omen."

DALINDA American: Modern variation of Linda (beautiful).

DALMAR African: "versatile."

DAMACIA Spanish. Greek: "tamer."

DAMEEKA American: Contemporary. **Dahmeeka, Dameekah.**

DAMEESHA American: Contemporary. **Damisha, Damishah, Damysha, Damyshah.**

DAMIANA Spanish. Greek: "tame."

DAMICIO American: Contemporary, possibly based on Damacia (tamer).

DAMIETTA American. Greek: "tame." Damietta is also the name of an Egyptian city in the Nile Delta.

DAMITA Spanish: "little noble lady."

DANA Hebrew: "judge." Dana Owens, actress and rap artist known as Queen Latifah.

DANACIA American: Contemporary.

DANAE Greek: Meaning unknown. In Greek mythology, Danae was the daughter of Acrisius and the mother of Perseus.

DANALEE American: Blending of the names Dana (judge) and Lee (meadow, clearing, woods).

DANEAN American: Contemporary.

DANELLA American. Hebrew: "God is my judge."

DANETTE American. Hebrew: "judge."

DANICA Slavic: "morning star." **Danika, Danikka.**

DANIELA Hebrew: "God is my judge." **Daniele, Daniella, Danielle, Danniel, Danniela, Danniele, Danniella, Danielle, Danyel, Danyell, Danyella, Danyelle, Danylle. Dani, Danie.**

DANITA Spanish: "little Daniella (God is my judge)."

DANLYS American: Contemporary.

DANNETTE American: Contemporary, possibly influenced by Annette (little Anne), or a feminine form of Dan (judge).

DANNISE American: Contemporary, influenced by Denise (of Dionysos). **Daneece, Daneese, Danice, Danise.**

DAPHNE Greek: "laurel tree, bay tree." In Greek myth, Daphne was a nymph who was transformed into a laurel tree in her attempt to escape the attentions of Apollo.

DARAH American: Contemporary.

DAREECE American. Persian: "queenly." **Darees, Dareese.**

DARENDA American: Contemporary. **Darendah, Derenda, Derendah.**

DARIEN American: Contemporary, possibly borrowed from the Gulf of Darien, in the Caribbean. **Darrien, Darriun, Darryen.**

DARLA American: "darling."

DARLENE English: "darling." **Darleen, Darleena, Darlina, Darline.**

D'ARLINE American: Modern variation of Arline, undoubtedly influenced by Darlene (darling).

DARLONNA American: Contemporary name, possibly originating as a blending of Darla (darling) and Donna (world ruler).

DARLWIN American: Contemporary.

DARMANDA American: Contemporary name, possibly originating as a blending of Darla (darling) and Amanda (lovable).

DARNEICE American: Contemporary, influenced by Denise (of Dionysus) and Darlene (darling).

DARNELL English: "from the hidden nook." Darnell Martin, filmmaker.

DARRENE English: Feminine form of Darren.

DARSHELLE American: Contemporary. **Darchell, Darchella, Darchelle, Darshella, Darshellea.**

DARTHULIUA American: Contemporary.

DASHAY American: Contemporary. **Dashae, Dashay, Dashaye, D'Shae, D'Shay, D'Shaye.**

DASIA Hebrew: "faith in God." American: Possible variant of Dacia (from Dacia).

DAVETTA American. Hebrew: "beloved." **Davette.**

DAVINA Scottish. Hebrew: "beloved." **Davenia, Davinia.**

DAWN English: "daybreak, dawn."

DAWNITA American: "little dawn."

DAYA Hebrew: "a bird, a bird of prey."

DAYAA Hindi: "compassion."

DAYANA American: Contemporary, possibly modeled after Diana (divine).

DAYANITA Hindi: "tender."

DAYELI American: Contemporary.

DAYNA American: Modern variation of the name Dana (judge).

DAYO Nigeria. Yoruba: "joy arrives."

DEANDRA American. Greek: "woman, womanly." **D'Andra, De Andra. Dee.**

DEASHUNDA American: Contemporary.

DEBARA American: Contemporary, influenced by Deborah (a bee).

DEBORAH Hebrew: "a bee." **Debora, Debra, Debrah. Deb, Debbi, Debbie, Debby.**

DEBORRAH American: Contemporary form of Deborah (a bee).

DEBRENA American: Contemporary.

DEBRY American: Contemporary.

DEEANNA American: A blending of the names Dee and Anna (gracious, full of grace) or a variant of Dianna (divine). **Deeann, Deeanne. Dee, Dee Dee.**

DEELVA American: Contemporary.

DEIANIRA Latin and Greek: From classical mythology, the daughter of Oeneus and wife of Hercules (Heracles). She accidentally killed her husband by giving him a cloak smeared with the blood of Nessus.

DEIRDRE Irish: Uncertain meaning, perhaps "young girl" or "fear." **Deedra, Deedrah, Deedre, Deidra, Deirdra. Dee, Dee Dee.**

DEJANA American: Contemporary, based on Jana (God is gracious). **DeJana, DeJanna, Dejanna, DeJannah, Dejannah.**

DEKA Somali: "pleaser."

DELANI American: Contemporary. **Delanee, Delanni.**

DELAWN American: Contemporary.

DELEANNA American: Contemporary, based on Leanna (sun; dweller by the wood or clearing; grace, mercy).

DELEENA American: Contemporary. **Deleenah, Delina, Delyna.**

DELEESA American: Contemporary.

DELIA English. Celtic: "daughter of the sea." Greek: "from the island of Delos." **Dehlia. Dee, Dee Dee.**

DELICIA Latin: "delight." **Daleesha, Dalicia, Dalisha, Dalisia, Dalysha, Dalysia, Delecia, Deleesha, Delisha, Delisia, Delysha, Delysia.**

DELIGHT American: "pleasure, enjoyment."

DELILAH Hebrew: "delicate." **Delila.**

DELINDA American: Contemporary form of Linda (beautiful).

DELISA American: Modern elaboration of Lisa (God is my oath).

DELISA Spanish. Latin: "delight." **Delissa, Delyssa.**

DELLA English: "a small valley, a dell." German: "nobility." **Dellah.**

DELMA Spanish: "of the sea." American: Possibly a variant of Elma (pleasant).

DELMI American: Contemporary.

DELORA Latin: "from the seashore."

DELORES English. Spanish: "sorrows." **Dalores, Deloris.**

DELORIOUS American: Contemporary form of Delores (sorrows).

DELPHIA Greek: "of Delphi." **Delphie.**

DELPHNIE American. Greek: "of Delphi."

DELPHYNNE American. Greek: "of Delphi." **Delphine. Delphie.**

DELSY American: Possible variant of Elsie (God is my oath).

DELVONDA American: Contemporary.

DELYNN American: Contemporary. De-Linn, Delinn, Delynn, DeLynne, De-lynne.

DELYSE American: Contemporary. De-leese, Deliis, Deliise, D'Lyse.

DELYTH Welsh: "pretty."

DEMEISHA American: Contemporary. De-meesha, Demisha, Demishah.

DEMENI American: Contemporary.

DEMERI American. French: "dweller near the sea."

DEMIKA American: Contemporary. De-meeka, Dameka.

DENA English: "a dean." Hebrew: "judged." Deana, Deena.

DENEISHA American: Contemporary. De-neesha, Denisha, Denishah, Denysha.

DENELL American: Contemporary. De-nella, Denelle.

DENIKA American: Contemporary. De-neeka, Deneka.

DENISE English. American. Greek: "a follower of the god Dionysos." Danice, Dan-ise, Denice, Deniece, Deniese, Dennise, Dennyse, Denyce, Denys, Denyse, D'Neese.

DENISHE American: Contemporary. Den-isha.

DENITA American: Variant of Donita (little lady).

DEONDRAY American: Contemporary, in-fluenced by the male names Deon (god, of Zeus) and André (mankind). Deondré, Deondrey, Diondray, Diondré, Diondrey.

DEONNA American: Contemporary, based on Donna (world ruler; lady).

DERAE American: Contemporary. Derée, Deray.

DEREVA American: Contemporary.

DEREXA American: Contemporary.

DERHONDA American: Contemporary variant of Rhonda (good lance).

DERRAIL American: Contemporary, pos-sibly influenced by Darryl (from Airelle).

DERRIANN American: Contemporary.

DERRYALE American: Contemporary.

DESHANDA American: Contemporary. Deeshanda, Deeshandah, Deshandah.

DESHANDRA American: Contemporary. Deeshandra, Deeshandrah, Deshandra.

DESHAWNA American: Contemporary. Deshaana, Deshauna, Deshonna.

DESIRAE American. French: "desired, be-loved." Desirae, Desiray, Desiree, Dési-rée, Desirey, Desiri, Deziray, Deziree, Dezirey.

DESIRÉE French. Latin: "desired, beloved."

DESMA Greek: "pledge, bond."

DES'REE American: Contemporary form of Desirée (desired). Dez'ree. Des'ree, record-ing artist.

DESSA RAE American: Contemporary, possibly modeled after the phonetics of De-sirée (desired).

DESTINA Spanish: "destiny, fate."

DESTINY American: "destiny, fate." **Destanee, Destani, Destany, Desteny, Destiney, Destini, Destinni, Destinny.**

DEVA Hindi: "a god."

DEVANEE Sanskrit: "divine."

DEVINI American: Contemporary, possibly influenced by Devanee (divine). **Devinee, Devinie, Deviny.**

DEVONA Irish: "a poet." **Devan, Devin, Devona, Devonia, Devyn, Devynn.**

DEWANDA American: Contemporary.

DEYANIRA Spanish. Latin and Greek: From classical mythology, the daughter of Oeneus and wife of Hercules.

DEYSI American: Contemporary form of Daisy (day's eye). **Dayzee, Deisy, Deysie, Deyzee.**

DEZIE LEE American: Contemporary.

DHARANA Sanskrit: "she who supports."

DIADRA American: Contemporary.

DIAMANTINA Spanish. Greek: "indomitable." **Diamentina, Diamintina. Tina.**

DIAMOND English: "a diamond." **Diamonda, Diamonde.**

DIAMONIQUE American: Contemporary, possibly a combination of Diamond (a diamond) and the French Monique (meaning unknown), an elaboration of Diamond (a diamond), or borrowed from the trade name of a line of faux-diamond jewelry.

DIANA Latin: "divine." **Dianna.** Diana Ross, singer. Diana Sands, actress.

DIANE French. Latin: "divine." **Dianne.** Dianne Reeves, singer.

DIANTHE Greek: "flower of God." **Diantha.**

DIELCIE American: Contemporary.

DIJA American. Arabic: "premature baby."

DILMA American: Contemporary, probably influenced by Wilma (resolute guardian).

DINA Hebrew: "judged." **Dinah.**

DINISHA American: Contemporary. **Dineesha.**

DINORAH Aramaic: "causing light."

DIONETTE American: "little Dionne (divine)." **Dionetta. Didi, Netti.**

DIONNE Greek: "divine; of Dionysus." In classical mythology, Dione was the mother of Venus. **Deionna, Deionne, Dion, Diona, Dione, Dionn, Dionna.** Dionne Warwick, singer.

DIVANNA American. Latin: "divine."

DIVETTE American: Contemporary.

DIVINE English: "divine, wonderful, celestial."

DIVONAH Hebrew: "south." **Divona, Divonna.**

DIZA Hebrew: "joy."

DJENNÉ African: A borrowing of the name of a city in Mali.

DMITRIA American. Greek: "of Demeter."

DOCIA American: Contemporary.

DOE American: "female deer."

DOFI Ghana. Ewe: "second child after twins."

DOMINIQUE French. Latin: "belonging to God, belonging to a lord." Dominique Dawes, Olympic medal–winning gymnast.

DONALDA Scottish. Gaelic: "world ruler." **Donelda.**

DONDI American: Contemporary.

DONDRA American: Contemporary.

DONELL American: Contemporary. **Donella.**

DONETTA American. Spanish: "little lady."

DONIA American: Contemporary.

DONILA American: "little Donna (lady; world ruler)." **Donnila.**

DONITA Spanish: "little lady." **Donetta.**

DONNA English. Gaelic: "world ruler." Latin: "lady." **D'onna.** Donna Summer, singer.

DONNAGENE American: Modern blending of the names Donna (world ruler; lady) and Gene (well-born).

DONNELTA American: Contemporary.

DONZALEIGH American: Contemporary.

DORAINE American. Irish: "little Dora (gift)." **Dorayne.**

DOREEN Irish: "little Dora (gift)." **Dorene, Dorine. Dori, Dorie, Dory.**

DORELLE American: Contemporary, possibly an elaboration of Dora (gift). **Dorella.**

DORETHA Scandinavian. Greek: "gift of God."

DORIA English. Greek: "gift; Dorian woman." **Dorea, Dorya.**

DORLISHA American: Contemporary.

DOROTHEA Greek: "gift of God."

DOROTHY English. Greek: "gift of God." **Doretha, Dorothee, Dorthee, Dorthy. Dolli, Dollie, Dolly, Dora, Dori, Dorie, Dory, Dot, Dotti, Dottie.** Dr. Dorothy Height, President and CEO of the National Council of Negro Women.

DORRISSENSE American: Contemporary.

DOVIE American: "little dove."

DREE American. German. Greek: "manly."

DRUSILLA Latin: Meaning unknown. **Drucilla. Dru.**

DUANN American: Contemporary.

DUCHESS English: "the wife of a duke, a woman with the rank of a duke."

DUELLA Spanish. Latin: "sorrow."

DUETTE American. Latin: "two."

DULCIE American. Latin: "sweet, agreeable." **Dulcee, Dulci, Dulcy.**

DUTCHESS American: Variant spelling of Duchess (a woman with the rank of a duke).

DWAYLA American: Contemporary.

DYHANN American: Contemporary variant of Dianne (divine). **Diahann, Dienn, Dienna, Dienne, Diyan, Diyann, Di-**

yanna, Diyanne, Dyana, Dyane, Dyann, Dyanna, Dyanne. Diahann Carroll, actress.

DYMOND American: Contemporary variant of Diamond (a diamond). **Dymonda, Dymonde**.

DYVETTE American: Contemporary, possibly modeled after Yvette (little archer). **Divett, Divette, Dyvett**.

DZIDZO African: "happiness."

DZIKO South Africa. Nguni: "the world."

EARLENE English: "nobleman, warrior." **Earleen, Earline, Erleen, Erlene, Erline**.

EARTHA American: "the earth." Eartha Kitt, singer.

EBONY English: "ebony, black." **Eboné, Eboni, Ebonii**.

EBUN Nigeria. Yoruba: "gift."

EDANNA American: Contemporary. **Edannah**.

EDEN Hebrew: "delight." The name is associated with the Garden of Eden, the biblical paradise where Adam and Eve lived. Thus "paradise" is a popular definition of the name.

EDENAUSEGBOYE Nigeria. Benin: "good deeds and kindness are remembered."

EDESSA Latin: The name of a Macedonian town.

EDITH English: "prosperous in war." **Edyth, Edythe**.

EDORIS American: Variant form of Doris (gift) or Eudora (good gift).

EDREA English: "wealthy, powerful." **Edra**.

EDWINA English: "prosperous friend." **Edweena, Edwena, Edwyna**.

EFAY American: Contemporary.

EFIA Ghana. Fante: "born on Friday." **Efea, Efeah, Effiah, Efyah**.

EGYPT English: A borrowing of the name of the African country.

ELAINE French. Greek: "light, torch, bright."

ELAINIA American. French. Greek: "light, torch, bright." **Elainya, Ilainia, Ilainya, Ylainia**.

ELDYNE American: Contemporary. **Eldeen, Eldene, Eldine**.

ELEE Sanskrit: "intelligent."

ELEIN American. French. Greek: "light, torch, bright."

ELENITA Spanish. Greek: "light." **Leni, Nelly, Nina, Nita**.

ELEONDRA American: An elaboration of **Leondra** (lion woman).

ELGEREE American: Contemporary.

ELICIA American. French: "noble one." **Elisia, Elycia, Elysha**.

ELIESSE American: Contemporary form of Elise (God is my oath).

ELIKA Sanskrit: "intelligent."

ELINDA American: Contemporary form of Linda (beautiful; tender, soft; wait).

ELIORA Hebrew: "my Lord is light." **Eleora**.

ELISA English. Hebrew: "God is my oath." A short form of Elisabeth. **Alees, Alisa, Alise, Aliza, Elees, Elise, Eliza.**

ELISSA Latin: From Roman mythology, another name for Dido, the founder and queen of Carthage. **Elisa.**

ELIZABETH English. Hebrew: "God is my oath." **Elisabeth, Lisabeth, Lisbeth, Lizabeth, Lizbeth. Beth, Betsy, Bett, Betty, Elsie, Lizzie, Lizzy.** Elizabeth Catlett, artist.

ELLA English. Greek: "light, bright." Ella Joyce, actress.

ELLEN English. Greek: "light, bright." **Ellie.** Ellen Tarry, author. Ellen Cleghorne, actress.

ELLISHA American: Variant of Alicia (noble one).

ELODIE American. Latin: "a water plant."

ELON African: "God loves me."

ELORA American: Possibly a variant of Eliora (my Lord is light) or Lora (laurel).

ELRAE American: Contemporary. **El Raye.**

ELSIE English. Hebrew: "God is my oath." **Elzie.**

ELTINA American: Contemporary.

ELTRIA American: Contemporary.

ELVIRA Spanish. German: "amiable, friendly." **Elvera.**

ELWILMA American: Blending of Eldon (Ella's hill) and Wilma (resolute protector).

ELZINA American: Contemporary. **Elsie, Elzie.**

ELZONIA American: Contemporary.

EMERALD English: "emerald gemstone." **Emarald, Emmarald, Emmerald. Merl.**

EMESE American: Contemporary.

ENEIDA Spanish. Greek: "praise."

ENRIQUA Spanish. German: "home ruler." **Enrequeta, Enrequette, Enrica, Enricetta, Henriqua, Henriquetta. Ricki, Riqueta.**

ENVI American: "envy."

ENYONYAM Ghana. Ewe: "she is good for me."

EOLA American: Probably a variant of Iola (violet-colored dawn).

EPHYRA Latin: The ancient name of Corinth.

EREMITA Spanish. Latin: "desert."

ERIKA Scandinavian: "honorable ruler." **Erica, Eryca, Eryka.** Erika Alexander, actress.

ERIN Nigeria. Yoruba: "elephant." English: "Ireland."

ERISHA Sanskrit: "speech."

ERLINDA American: Contemporary.

ERNESTINE American. German: "earnest."

ERVEOLIVA American: Contemporary.

ESELYN American: Contemporary, possibly modeled after Evelyn.

ESETTIA American: Contemporary.

ESHANA Sanskrit: "desire."

ESHAUN American: Contemporary, possibly based on the Irish Shaun (God is gracious).

ESHE Swahili: "life."

ESI Ghana. Fante: "born on Sunday."

ESIVIRA American: Contemporary.

ESPECIAL Spanish: "special."

ESSELIE American: Contemporary.

ESTELLA Spanish. Latin: "star." **Estela, Estelae, Estell, Estelle.**

ESTHER Persian: "star." Hebrew: "myrtle."

ETHELYN American: Blending of the names Ethel (noble) and Evelyn.

ETIENNETTE French. Greek: "crown, garland."

ETRELLE American: Contemporary.

EUCLEA Greek: "fair glory."

EUDORA Greek: "good gift." **Edora.**

EUGENIA Greek: "well-born." **Eugenie. Genie.** Eugenia Charles, former prime minister of Dominica.

EUJANIE American. Greek: "well-born."

EULA American: Probably a short form of Eulalia (fair speech).

EULAJEAN American: Blending of the names Eula and Jean (God is gracious).

EULALIA Greek: "fair speech."

EULOGIA Latin: "the Eucharist, blessed bread given at Communion."

EUMELIA Spanish. Greek: "fair singer."

EUNICE English. Greek: "fair victory."

EURLYNE American: Contemporary, based on the name Earlene (noblewoman).

EVADNE Greek: "well-pleasing." In Greek mythology, Evadne was the wife of Capaneus, one of the Seven who fought against Thebes. **Evadney.**

EVAE American: Contemporary, possibly a phonetic spelling of Ewe, an African tribe and language.

EVANGELINE English. Latin: "good news, the gospel." **Evie.**

EVE English. Hebrew: "life." In the Bible, Eve is the first woman and mother.

EVELIA Hebrew: "life." **Evilia.**

EVELYN English. French: Meaning uncertain. Evelyn Ashford, Olympic gold medal–winning runner.

EXIE American: Contemporary.

FABAYO Nigeria. Yoruba: "a lucky birth is joy."

FABIENNE French. Latin: "a bean."

FAHIMA Arabic: "intelligent." **Fahimah.**

FAHNDELIA American: Contemporary. **Faandelia, Fawndelia. Delia, Faan, Fahn, Fawn.**

FAITH English: "unquestioning belief, complete trust." Faith Ringgold, multimedia artist. Faith Evans, singer.

FAIZAH Arabic: "victorious."

FANA Ethiopia. Amharic: "light."

FANCHETTE American: Coinage containing the French diminutive suffix *-ette*.

FANCHON French: "free."

FANNY English. French: "a Frank." **Fanee, Fannee.**

FARAH Arabic: "happiness."

FARIDAH Arabic: "unique, precious." **Farida.**

FARIMAH American: Contemporary.

FARRAH English: "beautiful, fair, pleasant." **Fara, Farah, Farra, Ferra, Ferrah.**

FASINA Nigeria. Yoruba: "the god Ifa has opened a way."

FATIA African. Arabic: "abstainer from forbidden things; she who weans an infant."

FATIMA Arabic: "abstainer from forbidden things; she who weans an infant." Fatima was the name of the Prophet Muhammad's favorite daughter. **Fatemeh, Fatimah.**

FATINA Arabic: "charming." **Fatinah.**

FAUSTINA Spanish. Latin: "bringer of good luck." **Faustena, Faustia, Faustiana, Faustine.**

FAWN American: "baby deer."

FAWNDELLA American: A blending of the names Fawn (baby deer) and Della (a small valley).

FAWNIAH American: An elaboration of the name Fawn (baby deer).

FAY English: "fairy." **Fae, Faye.**

FAYELEECIA American: Contemporary, influenced by Felicia (lucky).

FAYNA American: Contemporary.

FAYOLA Nigeria. Yoruba: "lucky; good fortune walks with honor."

FELICIA Latin: "lucky, happy." **Felecia.** Felecia Bell, actress.

FELICITY English: "happiness." **Felicitee, Felicitie.**

FELISA American: Variant spelling of Felicia (lucky).

FEMI Nigeria. Yoruba: "love me."

FERREN American: Contemporary.

FIDELIA Spanish: "faithful, trusty." **Fedelia, Fedila, Fideila, Fidylia.**

FIONA Irish: "fair, white, clear."

FLEURETTE French: "little flower."

FLORENCE English. Latin: "blooming, flourishing." **Flo, Florrie, Flossie.** Florence Griffith-Joyner, Olympic gold medal-winning track star.

FLORIDALMA Spanish: Blending of the names Florida (abounding in flowers) and Alma (soul).

FOLA Nigeria. Yoruba: "honorable."

FOLADE Nigeria. Yoruba: "honor arrives."

FOLAMI Nigeria. Yoruba: "honor and respect me."

FOLASHADE Nigeria. Yoruba: "honor bestows a crown."

FOLAWN American: Contemporary, possibly a variant of Folayan (she walks in dignity).

FOLAYAN Nigeria. Yoruba: "she walks in dignity."

FOLUKE Nigeria. Yoruba: "placed in God's care."

FORESTYNE American. English: "of the forest."

FRANCES French: "a Frank, from the Frankish Empire." Frances Cress Welsing, noted psychiatrist.

FRANISHA American: Contemporary.

FRANZETTA American: Contemporary.

FREDA English: "elf of great strength." **Freeda.**

FREDERICA English. German: "peaceful ruler." **Fredericka, Frederycka, Frederyka. Freddi, Freddie.**

FREEDOSHIA American: Contemporary.

FRONDA American: Contemporary.

FUJO Swahili: "born after the parents separated."

FUKAYNA Arabic: "knowledgeable."

GABRIELA Hebrew: "God is my strength." **Gabriella, Gavriela, Gavriella. Gabi, Gaby.**

GAEL American: Contemporary variant of Gail (father of exaltation).

GAIL English. Hebrew: "father of exaltation." **Gale, Gayle.** Gail Devers, track star.

GALENE Greek: "calm."

GALVESTA American: Contemporary, perhaps influenced by the city of Galveston, Texas.

GARCELLE French: "little spear." Garcelle Beauvais, model and actress.

GARNECIA American: Contemporary.

GARNET English: "deep red gemstone." **Garnett.**

GAYATRI American: Contemporary.

GAYLENE American: Contemporary form of Galene (calm).

GAYLYNN American: Blending of the names Gay (happy, cheerful) and Lynn (lake).

GEANELITA American: Contemporary.

GEARALDINE American: Variant of Geraldine (spear ruler). **Gearaldeen, Gearaldina.**

GEINA American: Variant of Gina (earthworker). **Geena, Geenah, Geinah.**

GENEACE American: Contemporary form of Janice (God is gracious). **Geneece, Geneese.**

GENENE American: Contemporary form of Janine (God is gracious). **Genean, Geneen, Geneene, Ghenine.**

GENERIA American: Contemporary, perhaps based on the word *generic* (referring to a whole kind or class).

GENEVA English. French: "juniper berry." Celtic: "tribal woman." **Genevia, Geniva.**

GENEVIEVE French. Celtic: Meaning uncertain. The elements of the name might translate into "tribal woman." **Geneviève. Genni, Gennie, Genny.**

GENIKWA American: Contemporary. **Geneekua, Geneekwa, Geneequa, Janeekua, Janeekwa, Janeequa, Jeneekua, Jeneekwa, Jeneequa.**

GEORGEANNE English: Blending of George (earthworker) and Anne (grace, mercy). **Georgiana, Georgiann, Georgianna, Georgianne. Georgi, Georgie.**

GEORGETTE French. Greek: "earthworker, farmer." **Georgetta. Georgi, Georgie.**

GEORGIA Greek: "earthworker, farmer." **Georgi, Georgie.** Georgia Douglas Johnson (1886–1966), poet.

GERALDINE English. German: "spear ruler." **Geri, Gerri, Gerrie, Gerry.** Geraldine McCullough, sculptor.

GERI English. German: "spear ruler." **Geree, Gerie, Gerree, Gerri, Gerrie, Gerry.** Geri Allen, jazz pianist.

GERLENA American: Contemporary.

GERMAINE French. Latin: "brother."

GESNA American: Possible variant of the Slavic Chesna (peaceful).

GESTINE American: Contemporary spelling of Justine (just, proper). **Gestyne.**

GEULAH American: Coinage, most likely influenced by Beulah (married).

GEVONNA American: Contemporary, possibly modeled after the Italian Giovanna (God is gracious).

GHALIYA Arabic: "fragrant." **Ghaliyah.**

GINANNE American: Contemporary.

GINETTE American: Contemporary spelling of Jeanette (God is gracious).

GLENDA Welsh: "pure one, holy one."

GLENNETTE American. Scottish: "mountain valley." Glennette Tilly Turner, author.

GLINDA American. Welsh: "pure one, holy one." **Glynda.**

GLORETHA American: Coinage, probably based on Glory (exalted praise).

GLORIA Latin: "glory." Dr. Gloria Randle Scott, president of Bennett College. Gloria Naylor, award-winning writer. Gloria Foster, actress.

GLORIANNA American: Blending of Glory (exalted praise) and Anna (grace, full of grace). **Gloriann, Glorianne, Gloryann, Gloryanna, Gloryanne.**

GLORY American. Latin: "exalted praise."

GRACE English: "favor, kindness, mercy." Grace Jones, actress and singer.

GRANVANETTA American: Contemporary.

GUSSTEAN American: Contemporary.

GUSTAVIA Scandinavian: "noble staff, staff of the Goths."

GWENDOLYN Welsh: "fair browed." **Gwendolen, Gwendolin, Gwendoline, Gwendolynn, Gwendolynne. Gwen.** Gwendolyn Brooks, Pulitzer prize–winning poet. Gwen Torrence Waller, Olympic gold medal–winning sprinter.

GWIN   American: Welsh: "fair, blessed."

HABIBA   Arabic: "beloved." **Habibah.**

HADIYA   Swahili: "present, gift." **Hadiyah.**

HAFSAH   Arabic: Pre-Islamic name of uncertain meaning. Hafsah was the name of a wife of the Prophet Muhammad. She became the guardian of the sole written copy of the Koran after Muhammad's death. **Hafsa, Hafza, Hafzah.**

HAIDEE   English: Coinage of Byron for a character in his poem *Don Juan*.

HALI   American: Possible variant spelling of Hayley (dweller in the remote valley) or Halley (dweller at the gathering place meadow). **Haleigh.**

HALIMA   Arabic: "gentle." Halima was the name of the Prophet Muhammad's nurse. **Halimah.**

HALINA   Swahili. Arabic: "gentle." **Halinah.**

HALLEY   English: "dweller at the gathering-place meadow." **Halle, Hallee, Halli, Hallie, Hally.** Halle Berry, actress.

HAMIDA   Arabic: "to praise." **Hameeda, Hameedah, Hamidah.**

HANDIA   American: Contemporary.

HANELLE   German. Hebrew: "grace, mercy." **Hannele, Hannelle.**

HANIFA   Arabic: "a true believer of Islam." **Haneefa, Hanifah.**

HANNAH   Hebrew: "gracious, full of grace."

HAQIKAH   Arabic: "truthful."

HARIKA   Turkish: "beautiful."

HARMONY   English: "agreeable, pleasing, orderly."

HAROLYNNE   American: Blending of Harold (ruler of an army) and Lynne (lake). **Harolynn.**

HASANATI   Swahili: "good."

HASINA   Swahili: "good." **Hasinah, Hasine.**

HATTIE   English. French: "ruler of an estate."

HAWA   Swahili: "longing."

HAWNA   American. German: "dweller at the sign of the rooster." Also, a coinage influenced by Dawna (daybreak, dawn).

HAYDEE   American: Contemporary.

HAYLEY   English: "dweller in the remote valley." **Haley, Haylie.**

HAZEL   English: "hazelnut tree." Hazel Rollins O'Leary, first woman and first Black Secretary of Energy.

HAZIE   American: "little Hazel (hazelnut tree); hazy, misty, unclear."

HEKIMA   American: Contemporary.

HELENE   Greek: "light, bright." **Helena.** Dr. Helena Mitchell, chief of the Emergency Alert System.

HELIANA   American. Greek: "woman of the sun."

HENRIETTE   French: "ruler of an estate." **Henretta, Henrietta. Hattie, Hettie.**

HERMIONE Greek: Meaning uncertain. In legend, Hermione is the daughter of King Menelaus of Sparta and Helen of Troy.

HILARY English. Latin: "cheerful, merry." **Hillary, Hilleri, Hillery.**

HOLLY English: "the holly tree." **Hollee, Holli, Hollie.** Holly Robinson, actress.

HONEY English: "honey; sweetheart."

HONNA American: Contemporary, possibly influenced by the European and Caribbean pronunciation of Hannah (grace, mercy).

HUSNIYA Arabic: "beauty." **Husniyah.**

IAMAR Arabic: "moon."

IANTHE Greek: "violet-colored flower." In classical mythology, Ianthe was a sea nymph. **Ianthia, Ianthina.**

IBERIA American: After the peninsula of the same name comprising Spain and Portugal.

IDA German: "work, labor." Ida B. Wells (1862–1931), anti-lynching crusader and author.

IDRIYA Hebrew: "a duck."

IDUVINA American: Contemporary.

IEESHA American. Arabic: "life; alive and well." From the name Aisha. **Iisha, Iyisha, Iyishah.**

IFAMA Nigeria. Ibo: "everything is fine."

IFE Nigeria. Yoruba: "love."

IFEOMA Nigeria. Ibo: "a good thing."

IFETAYO Nigeria. Yoruba: "love brings happiness."

IJOMA African: "travel safely."

IKUSEGHAN Nigeria. Benin: "peace is better than war." **Ikusegham.**

ILAISAANE American: Contemporary.

ILANA Hebrew: "a tree." **Elana.**

ILEANDRA American. Greek: "lion woman." **Ileondra.**

ILESHA Sanskrit: "lord of the earth." **Ileshaa.**

ILIONA Latin: Meaning unknown. In Roman mythology, Iliona is the daughter of Priam.

ILIZZIBET American: Contemporary form of Elizabeth (God is my oath).

ILLEANA American: Contemporary, possibly based on Iliona (meaning unknown).

IMAN Arabic: "faith, belief in God." Iman, supermodel.

IMANI Swahili. Arabic: "faith, belief in God." **Imanee.**

IMOGENE English. Celtic: "girl, maiden." **Imogen.**

INDIA English: Borrowing of the name of the Asian subcontinent.

INDIANA Latin: "of India."

INELL American. Greek: "light, torch."

INEZ Spanish. Latin: "pure." **Enés, Enez, Inés.**

INFINITY American: "without end."

IOLA Greek: "violet-colored dawn." **Iolie.**

IONIA   Greek: Borrowing of the name of a region in ancient western Asia Minor.

IRAIANA   American: Contemporary variant of Irene (peace). **Iraina, Irayana, Irayna.**

IRISHA   American: Contemporary. **Ireesha, Irishia, Irysha.**

ISABELLA   Spanish. Hebrew: "God is my oath." **Isabel, Isabela, Isabell, Isabelle, Izabell, Izabella, Izabelle. Bell, Bella, Belle, Izzie, Izzy.** Isabel Wilkerson, Pulitzer prize—winning journalist. Isabel Sanford, actress.

ISOKE   Nigeria. Benin: "a satisfying gift from God."

ISSA   Swahili. Hebrew: "the Lord is salvation."

ISSIA   American: Fanciful spelling of Aisha (life).

ITHALEEN   American: Contemporary. **Ithalean, Ithalene.**

IVA LEA   American: Combination name.

IVEKA   American: Contemporary.

IVEREM   Nigeria. Tiv: "blessings and favor."

IVONNE   American. French: "archer." **Evonne.**

IVY   English: "ivy, climbing vine." **Ivee, Ivey, Ivi, Ivie.**

IYANLA   American: Contemporary.

IZEGBE   Nigeria. Benin: "long-awaited child."

IZZY   English. Spanish: "God is my oath." **Izzi, Izzie.**

JAAMINI   Sanskrit: "night."

JACINTA   Spanish: "hyacinth." **Jacinda, Jasenta, Jasinta.**

JACKIE   English. Hebrew: "God is gracious." **Jackee, Jacki.** Jackie "Moms" Mabley (1897–1975), comedienne, born Loretta Mary Aiken.

JACKLIN   English. Hebrew: "God is gracious." **Jacklyn. Jackee, Jacki, Jackie.**

JACQUA   American. Hebrew: "God is gracious."

JACQUÉ   French. Hebrew: "God is gracious." **Jacquee, Jacqui, Jacquie.**

JACQUELINE   French. Hebrew: "God is gracious." **Jacquelyn. Jacqui.**

JACQUETTE   American. Hebrew: "God is gracious." **Jacqui, Jacquie.**

JACQUEWYN   American: Contemporary, modeled after Jacqueline (God is gracious).

JACY   American: Contemporary, possibly modeled after Lacy, or an elaboration of the initials J and C. **Jacee, Jaycee, Jayci, Jaycie.**

JACYNTA   American. Spanish: "hyacinth."

JADE   English. Spanish: "jade, stone of the side (from the belief that it cured pains in the side)." **Jada.** Jada Pinkett, actress.

JADINE   American: Contemporary, based on Jade (the jade stone) or Dean (a dean, an official). **Jadean, Jadeane, Jadeen, Jadeene, Jadyne.**

JAHA   Swahili: "dignity."

JAHNAUI   American: Contemporary.

JAKEISHA American: Contemporary. **Jakeesha, Jakiesha, Jakisha, Jakysha.**

JAKIYA American: Contemporary, influenced by Zakiya (intelligent; pure).

JAKODI American: Contemporary. **Jacodi.**

JALEE American: Contemporary.

JALEESA American: Contemporary, based on Leesa (God is my oath). **JaLeesa, Jalicia, JaLisa, Jalisa.**

JALILA Arabic: "illustrious." **Jalilah.**

JALINDA American: Contemporary, based on Linda (beautiful). **Jalynda.**

JALINI Sanskrit: "water dweller."

JAMAE American: Contemporary. **JaMae, JaMai, Jamai, JaMay, Jamay, JaMaye, Jamaye.**

JAMAICA American: Borrowing of the name of the Caribbean country.

JAMAIIA American: Contemporary.

JAMAINE American: Contemporary, influenced by Jermaine (brother). **Jamain, Jamayn, Jamayne.**

JAMARA American: Contemporary, influenced by Tamara (a date palm) or the male name Jamar.

JAMARI American: Contemporary.

JAMEEKA American: Contemporary. **Jameika, Jamieka, Jamika, Jamikah.**

JAMEESHA American: Contemporary. **Jameisha, Jamiesha, Jamisha, Jamishah, Jamyshah.**

JAMESETTA Scottish. Hebrew: "supplanting, seizing by the heel."

JAMESINA Scottish. Hebrew: "supplanting, seizing by the heel."

JAMIE English. Hebrew: "supplanting." **Jaime, Jaimee, Jaimie, Jaimy, Jamee, Jayme, Jaymee, Jaymie.**

JAMILA Arabic: "beautiful, graceful." **Jameela, Jameelah, Jamilah.**

JAMYMA American. English. Hebrew: "dove." **Jamima, Jamimah, Jamymia.**

JAN Scandinavian. Hebrew: "God is gracious." Jan is a cognate of John. Dr. Jan Hutchinson, noted pediatrician and psychiatrist.

JANAAN American: Contemporary.

JANACE American: Variant of Janice (God is gracious). **Jannas, Jannase.**

JANAE American: Contemporary, possibly modeled after the name Danae. **Janay, Janea, Janee, Jenae, Jenea, Jenee. Jan, Jen.**

JANAI American: Contemporary. **Ja'nai, Janei.**

JANANEE Sanskrit: "mother."

JANAYA American: Contemporary. **Jenaya. Jan, Jen.**

JANDELLYN American: Contemporary.

JANE English. Hebrew: "God is gracious." **Jain, Jayn, Jayne. Janie, Janey.**

JANEAL American: Contemporary, possibly influenced by Janelle (God is gracious) or Neal (chief). **Janeale, Janeel, Janeil, Janeile, Janeill, Janeille. Jan, Janey, Janie.**

JANELLE English. Hebrew: "God is gracious." **Janel, Janell, Janella, Jannell. Jan, Janey, Janie.**

JANESSA American: Contemporary, probably modeled after Vanessa. **Jenessa. Jan, Jen, Jenni, Jennie, Jenny.**

JANET English. Hebrew: "God is gracious." **Ja'net, Janett, Janette, Jannette. Jan.** Janet Jackson, singer and actress.

JANICE English. Hebrew: "God is gracious." **Janis, Janiss, Janyce, Janys, Janyse. Jan, Jannie.**

JANIECE American: A modern variant of Janice (God is gracious). **Janeece, Janeese. Jan.**

JANIEL American: Contemporary, possibly based on the male name Daniel (God is my judge).

JANIKA Sanskrit: "mother." **Janikaa.**

JANINE English. Hebrew: "God is gracious." **Janina, Janeen, Janyne, Jeneen, Jenina, Jenine, Jenneen, Jennine. Jan, Janey, Janie, Jen, Jenni, Jennie, Jenny.**

JANIQUE American: Contemporary. **Janeeke, Janike, Janyk, Janyke.**

JANISHA American: Contemporary. **Janeesha, Janeisha, Janiesha.**

JANISHRA American: Contemporary. **Janeeshra.**

JANIVA American: Possible variation of the name Geneva (juniper berry). **Janeeva, Janeevah, Janieva, Janievah.**

JANNIE English: Pet form of Jan, Janet, etc.

JANNIKE Scandinavian: "little Jan (God is gracious)."

JANUARY American: After the first month of the calendar year. **Jan.**

JANUS American: Contemporary form of Janice (God is gracious). Latin: "gated, arched passageway." In Roman mythology, Janus was the two-faced god of beginnings and endings and the guardian of portals.

JAPERA Zimbabwe. Shona: "offer thanks, we are finished."

JAPHIA Hebrew: "splendid."

JAREE American: Contemporary. **Jaree.**

JARIENNE American: Contemporary.

JARUTHA American: Possibly a variant of the Hebrew Jerusha (married).

JASMIN Persian: "jasmine." **Jasmine, Jazmin, Jazmine.** Jasmin Guy, actress.

JAUNICE American: Contemporary.

JAVONA American: Contemporary.

JAVONNA American: Contemporary, possibly influenced by the Italian Giovanna (God is gracious). **Javonnah.**

JAXINE American: Contemporary, modeled after Maxine (greatest).

JAYA Hindi: "victory."

JAYDEE American: Contemporary, possibly based on the letters J and D. **Jaedee, Jaydii.**

JAYE English: Originating from names beginning with the letter J. **Jae.**

JAYLEEN American: Contemporary, based on Jay. **Jayeleen, Jayelene, Jayeline, Jaylene.**

JAYLYNN American: Contemporary, possibly a combination of Jay and Lynn (a lake). **Jaylin, Jaylinn, Jaylyn, Jaylynne.**

JEAN French. Hebrew: "God is gracious." **Jeanne.** Jean Toomer (1894–1967), novelist and poet.

JEANERIA American: Contemporary, possibly modeled after Generia (generic).

JEANETTE French. Hebrew: "God is gracious." **Jeanett, Jenett, Jenette. Jeanie, Jenni, Jennie, Jenny.**

JEHLANI Swahili: "strong, mighty."

JEMILA American. Arabic: "beautiful, elegant." **Jemilah.**

JEMIMA English. Hebrew: "dove." **Jemimah.**

JENA Sanskrit: "patience."

JENCIA American: Contemporary.

JENDAYI Zimbabwe. Shona: "offer thanks."

JENÉE American: Contemporary, probably modeled after Renée (rebirth). **Jenae, Jenai, Jenay.**

JENEVIA American: Contemporary.

JENNAL American: Contemporary.

JENNIANNE American: A blending of the names Jenni and Anne (gracious, full of grace). **Jenniann, Jennyann, Jennyanne. Jenni, Jennie, Jenny.**

JENNIFER Cornish. Welsh: "fair lady." **Jenifer, Jenyfer. Jen, Jenni, Jennie, Jenny.** Jenifer Lewis, actress. Jennifer Holiday, singer and actress.

JENNYFFER American. Welsh: "fair lady." **Genifer, Geniffer, Gennifer, Genniffer, Gennyfer, Gennyffer, Genyfer, Jennipher, Jennyfer, Jennypher.**

JENYNE American: Contemporary spelling of Janine (God is gracious).

JERUSHAH Hebrew: "a possession." **Jerusha.**

JESSICA English. Hebrew: "God is gracious; gift." **Jessaca, Jessaka, Jesseca, Jesseka, Jessika, Jessyca, Jessyka. Jess, Jessi, Jessie.**

JESSIE English. Hebrew: "God is gracious; gift." **Jessee, Jessey, Jessy, Jessye. Jess.** Jessye Norman, opera diva. Jessie Redmon Faust, novelist.

JESSILYNN English: Blending of Jessie (God is gracious; gift) and Lynn (lake). **Jessilinn, Jessilyn, Jessilynne.**

JESSYCIA American: Contemporary variant of Jessica (gift; God is gracious).

JETTE English: "jet." Jet is a lustrous black variety of lignite used in jewelry making. **Jett, Jetta.**

JEVETTA American: Contemporary. **Jevette.**

JEVON American: Contemporary, modeled after Devon, an English place-name.

JEVRILYN American: Contemporary, perhaps influenced by Marilyn (sea of bitterness; lake).

JEWEL English: "gem." **Jewell, Jewelle.** Jewell Jackson McCabe, founder of the National Coalition of 100 Black Women.

JHANEL American: Contemporary.

JILANN American: Blending of Jill (youth) and Ann (grace, mercy). **Jilanne.**

JILL English. Latin: "youth, downybearded."

JIYA American: Contemporary, possibly a phonetic spelling of Jie, the name of an African tribe from Uganda.

JO English: Originating as a short form of several names beginning with *Jo-*, such as Josephine and Joanna.

JOAN English. Hebrew: "God is gracious." Joan Armatrading, singer-songwriter.

JOBINA English. Hebrew: "tormented." **Jobena, Jobyna.**

JOCASTA Latin: "cheerful."

JOCELYN English. German: "of the Gauts tribe." **Jocelin, Joceline, Joscelin, Josceline, Joycelin, Joyceline, Joycelyn.** Joycelyn Elders, first black surgeon general.

JOCINDA American: Blending of Jo and Lucinda (light).

JODEEN American: Contemporary, perhaps inspired by the name Jody or Jo.

JODILYNN American: Blending of Jody (praise) and Lynn (lake). **Jodilin, Jodilinn, Jodilyn, Jodilynne, Jodylin, Jodylinn, Jodylynn, Jodylynne.**

JODY English. Hebrew: "praised." **Jodee, Jodey, Jodi, Jodie.** Jody Watley, singer.

JOEDRECKA American: Contemporary.

JOETTA American. Hebrew: "he shall add."

JOHARA Arabic: "jewel." **Joharra.**

JOHNNA English. Hebrew: "God is gracious."

JOKINA American: Coinage, possibly a condensed form of Jakobina (supplanted) or a variant of the Spanish Joaquina (God gives strength). **Joakina.**

JOLANDA American: Contemporary, probably based on the name Yolanda. **Jolandah.**

JOLANE American: Contemporary. **Jolain, Jolaine, Jolayne. Jo.**

JOLEETA American: Contemporary.

JOLYEN American: Contemporary.

JOLYNN American: Blending of Jo and Lynn (lake). **Johlyn, Jolinn, Jolyn, Jolynne. Jo.**

JONAVÁ American: Contemporary. **Jonavay, Jonavée.**

JONELL American. Hebrew: "God is gracious." **Jonelle, Jonnell, Jonnelle. Jonni, Jonnie.** Jonelle Allen, actress.

JONETTE American. Hebrew: "God is gracious." **Johnette. Johnni, Jonni, Jonnie.**

JONICA American: Contemporary.

JONICIA American: Contemporary, based on Jon (God is gracious). **Johnisha, Jonisha. Johnni, Johnnie, Jonni, Jonnie.**

JONIQUE American: Contemporary, based on Jon (God is gracious). **Johnique. Johnni, Johnnie, Jonni, Jonnie.**

JONNETTE American: Contemporary, based on Jeannette (God is gracious). **Johnnett, Johnetta, Johnnetta, Johnnette, Jonett, Jonette. Johnni, Johnnie, Jonni, Jonnie.** Johnnetta B. Cole, president of Spelman College.

JORJA American: Phonetic variation of Georgia (farmer, earthworker).

JOSAH American: Contemporary.

JOSANIE American: Contemporary. **Jozanie. Jo.**

JOSÉE French. Hebrew: "God will add."

JOSELLE American: Contemporary. **Jozelle. Jo.**

JOSEPHINE French. Hebrew: "God will add." **Josie.** Josephine Baker (1906–1975), stage performer.

JOSETTE French: "little Josée (God will add)."

JOSIANN American: Blending of Josie (God will add) and Ann (grace, mercy). **Josiane, Josianne.**

JOSIE English. Hebrew: "God will add." **Josee.**

JOSLYN American: Contemporary.

JOVANNA American: Contemporary, probably based on the Italian Giovanna (God is gracious) or Joviana (Jove, Jupiter).

JOVIANA Spanish. Greek: "Jove, Jupiter." **Jovana, Jovenia.**

JOY English: "joy, delight."

JOYCE English. Latin: "merry, happy, jovial." Dr. Joyce Ladner, sociologist.

JOYCENA American: Contemporary, based on Joy (joy, delight).

JUANA Spanish. Hebrew: "God is gracious." **Juanna.**

JUANITA Spanish. Hebrew: "God is gracious."

JUBA Ghana. Ashanti: "born on Monday."

JUBILEE English. Hebrew: "a celebration held every fifty years; a ram's horn used to announce the sabbatical year."

JUDITH English. Hebrew: "he will be praised; from Judah." **Judeth Judyth. Judi, Judie, Judy.** Judith Jamison, dancer and head of the Jamison Project.

JUDY English. Hebrew: "he will be praised; from Judah." **Judee, Judi, Judie.** Judy Pace, actress.

JULEAH American. Latin: "youth." Jualeah.

JULIA Latin: "youth." **Julie.** Julie Dash, filmmaker.

JUMANA Arabic: "a pearl." **Jumanah.**

JUMOKE Nigeria. Yoruba: "loved by everyone."

JUNE English. Latin: "Juno, the mythological goddess of marriage." June Jordan, poet and novelist.

JURIDELL American: Contemporary.

JUSSICA American: Modern elaboration of Jessica (God is gracious; gift).

JUSTINE English. Latin: "just, proper." **Justina, Justyna, Justyne.**

KAAREN American: Danish. Greek: "pure, unsullied."

KAARINA American: Contemporary.

KACIA American: Contemporary. **Kaisha, Kaisia, Kasha, Kasia, Kaycia, Kaysha, Kaysia.**

KAERINSA American: Contemporary.

KAHANA Hawaiian: "turning point."

KAI Hawaiian: "the sea." American: Contemporary spelling of Kay. African: "lovable."

KAIMAIE American: Contemporary.

KAIRA American: Contemporary. **Kairah, Kaireh.**

KAISA American: Contemporary. **Kaisah, Kaiseh.**

KAIT American: Contemporary spelling of Kate (pure, unsullied).

KAIYA American: Contemporary.

KALAIN American: Contemporary.

KALI Sanskrit: "the black one." Another name for the goddess Durga. **Kalee.**

KALIDA Greek: "most beautiful."

KALIEMAH American. Arabic: "speaker, orator." **Kalyma.**

KALIFA Arabic: "holy girl." **Kalifah.**

KALILA Arabic: "beloved."

KALIMA Arabic: "speaker, orator." **Kaleema.**

KALINA Polish: From the name of a flower. **Kaleen, Kaleena, Kaline.**

KALINDA American: Contemporary. Hindu: "sun."

KALINDI Hindi: The name of a river.

KALLISTA American. Greek: "she that is most beautiful." **Kalista.**

KALYCA Greek: "bud, pod, rosebud." **Kalika.**

KAMA Hindu: "one who brings about love."

KAMALEI Hawaiian: "beloved child."

KAMANI Hawaiian: A type of tree.

KAMANIA Swahili: "like the moon."

KAMARIA Swahili: "like the moon."

KAMBA African: "tortoise."

KAMEESHA American: Contemporary.

KAMELIA Hawaiian. Hebrew: "vineyard, orchard."

KAMIKA American: Contemporary.

KAMILAH Arabic: "perfect." Hindi: A type of tree. **Kameela, Kameelah, Kamila.**

KANATINIA American: Contemporary.

KANDI English. Latin: "pure, sincere." **Kandee.**

KANEESHA American: Contemporary. **Kaneisha, Kanisha.**

KANIKA Kenya. Mwera: "black cloth."

KANIQUA American: Contemporary, perhaps influenced by Kanika (black cloth). **Kaneekwa, Kaneequa, Kanikwa.**

KANTHI American: Contemporary, possibly a blending of Kandi (pure) and Kathi (pure).

KANYKA American: Contemporary, possibly influenced by Kanika (black cloth). **Kaneeka, Kaneekah.**

KARA Latin: "beloved, dear." African: After the Kara River in Togo.

KARANZA American: Contemporary.

KAREN Danish. Greek: "pure, unsullied." **Caren, Carena, Carin, Caryn, Karan, Karena, Karin, Karina, Karon, Karrin, Karron, Karyn.** Karen Briggs, violinist. Karyn Parsons, actress.

KARIMA Arabic: "generous; noble." **Karimah.**

KARINA Italian. Latin: "beloved, dear." **Karine, Karinna.**

KARLYNN American: Blending of Karl (freeman) and Lynn (lake). **Karlinn, Karlyn, Karlynne.**

KARNETTE American: Contemporary. **Karnetta.**

KARON American: Modern form of Karen (pure, unsullied).

KASIAH American: Contemporary form of Cassia (cinnamon).

KASTLE American: "castle."

KATHERINE English. Greek: "pure, unsullied." **Catherine, Catheryn, Catheryne, Katheryn, Katheryne. Cass, Cassi, Cassie, Cathi, Cathie, Cathy, Kass, Kassi, Kassie, Kassy, Kathi, Kathie, Kathy, Kit, Kitty.** Katheryn Hall, founder of the Birthing Project. Katherine Dunham, dance pioneer.

KATHERLEEN American: Blending of Katherine (pure, unsullied) and Kathleen (pure, unsullied). **Katherlean. Kathi.**

KATHERLYNN American: Blending of Katherine (pure, unsullied) and Lynn (lake). **Katherlin, Katherlinn, Katherlyn, Katherlynne. Kathi.**

KATHLEEN Irish. Greek: "pure, unsullied." Kathleen Battle, singer. **Kathi.**

KATHURA American: Contemporary.

KATIAH American: Contemporary.

KATREEA American: Contemporary, possibly based on Katrina (pure, unsullied).

KATRENIA American: Contemporary, probably influenced by Katrina (pure, unsullied).

KATRESHA American: Contemporary.

KATRINA Dutch and German: "pure, unsullied." A cognate of Katherine.

KATSINA African: A borrowing of the name of a city in Nigerian. **Kat.**

KAUCYILA American: Contemporary.

KAUSIWA Malawi. Yao: "poor one."

KAY English: Originated from various names beginning with K. **Kae.**

KAYANNA American: Combination of Kay and Anna (grace, mercy). **Kaeann, Kaeanna, Kaeanne, Kayana, Kayann, Kayanne.**

KAYLA American: Contemporary.

KAYLYNN American: Blending of Kay and Lynn (lake). **Kaelyn, Kaelynn, Kaelynne, Kailyn, Kailynne, Kaylyn, Kaylynne.**

KAYRENE American: Contemporary, probably a blending of Kay and Irene (peace).

KECIA American: Contemporary, possibly a variant of Keisha.

KEDMA Hebrew: "east."

KEDRA American: Contemporary.

KEELEY English. Irish: "slender." **Keeleigh, Keeli, Keely, Keighlee, Keighli, Keighly.**

KEENA American: Contemporary.

KEFIRA Hebrew: "young lioness."

KEFLYN American: Contemporary.

KEHINDE Nigeria. Yoruba: "second-born of twins."

KEILA American: Contemporary. **Keela.**

KEINYATA American. African: "musician."

KEISHA American: Contemporary. **Keesha, Kesha, Keshia, Kiesha.** Keshia Knight Pulliam, actress.

KEISLA American: Contemporary.

KEITHA Scottish: "the wind, wood."

KELBY English. Scandinavian: "dweller at the farm by the spring; from Kell's (sacrificial cauldron) homestead." **Kelbi.**

KELILAH Hebrew: "laurel, crown." **Kelila.**

KELINDE Nigeria. Yoruba: "second of twins."

KENBRA American: Contemporary, probably a blending of Ken (chief, high) and Debra (a bee).

KENDRA English. Welsh: "chief hero; high summit." Scottish: "son of Henry." Old English: "royal rule." **Kendrah.**

KENETHA American: Contemporary, based on Ken.

KENIKA American: Contemporary, possibly a variant of Kanika (black cloth).

KENISHA American: Contemporary. **Keneesha, Keneeshah, Keneisha, Kenneesha, Kenneisha, Kenniesha.**

KENITRA American: Contemporary. Also, the name of a Moroccan city.

KENNA Scottish: "born of fire; comely, pretty."

KENYA African: A borrowing of the name of the East African nation.

KENYATTA African: "musician." **Kenyata, Kenyeta, Kenyetta, Kenyette.**

KEREN Hebrew: "horn."

KESHAWNA American: Contemporary, based on Shawn (God is gracious).

KESHIKA Hindi: "woman with beautiful hair."

KESI Swahili: "born when the father was having difficulties."

KESIA African: "favorite." **Keshia.**

KESSEY American: Possibly influenced by Kesia (favorite) or Kessie (born fat).

KESSIE Ghana. Fante: "born fat."

KETIFA Arabic: "to pick (a piece of fruit)."

KETURA Hebrew: "incense." **Kethura, Keturah**.

KEVA Hindi: "lotus."

KEVLYN American: Contemporary, probably a blending of Kevin (comely) and Evelyn.

KEVONNA American: Contemporary. **Kevonnah**.

KEZIAH English. Hebrew: "cassia, cinnamon." In the Bible, Keziah was one of the three beautiful daughters of Job. **Kezia. Kizzi, Kizzie, Kizzy**.

KHADIJA Arabic: "premature baby." Khadija was the first wife of the Prophet Muhammad and the mother of his children. **Kadija. Dija**.

KHALIFA Arabic: "holy." **Kalifa, Kalifah, Khalifah**.

KHALILA Arabic: "best friend." **Kaleela, Kaleelah, Kalila, Khalilah**.

KHANA American: Contemporary.

KHASYA American: Contemporary, possibly a variant of Cassia (cinnamon).

KHAYSA American: Contemporary.

KHYLA American: Contemporary. A feminine form of Kyle (from the narrow channel).

KIA American: Contemporary, possibly a variant of Kiah (beginning of the season).

KIAH African: "beginning of the season."

KIANA American: Contemporary. **Kianna, Kyana, Kyanna**.

KIARA American: Contemporary.

KIBIBI Swahili: "little lady."

KIERA English. Irish: "little dark one."

KIERAN American. Irish: "little black-haired one."

KIESLA American: Contemporary.

KIFIMBO Swahili: "twig; a very thin child."

KIHRY American: Contemporary.

KIJAKAZI Swahili: "your life is owed to us."

KIMANA Native American. Shoshone: "butterfly."

KIMBERELY English: "dweller in the meadow." **Kimberlee, Kimberleigh, Kimberli, Kimberly, Kymberely, Kymberly. Kim, Kimmie, Kym, Kymmie**. Kim Fields, actress.

KIMBRA English: Contemporary, possibly blending Kim (dweller in the meadow) and Debra (a bee). **Kim, Kimmie**.

KIMELA American: Contemporary.

KIMIKA American: Contemporary.

KINA American: Contemporary. Also, a short form of the Scottish Alickina (defender of mankind).

KINSHASA African: A borrowing of the name of the capital of the Democratic Republic of Congo (Zaire). **Kinshasha, Kinshasta**.

KISAMA African: Borrowed from the name of an African city.

KISHI   American: Contemporary.

KISSA   Uganda. Luganda: "born after twins." **Kizza.**

KITAUNIA   American: Contemporary.

KITTY   English: "a kitten." Greek: "pure, unsullied." **Kit.**

KIZUWANDA   Tanzania. Zaramo: "last-born child."

KIZZY   English. Hebrew: "cassia, cinnamon." **Kizzee, Kizzie.**

KLARNISSA   American: Contemporary, perhaps influenced by the name Klarissa.

KLEANDRIA   American: Contemporary.

KNESHIA   American: Contemporary.

KOKUMO   Nigeria. Yoruba: "this one will not die."

KOREL   American: Variant spelling of Coral (sea coral).

KRISTIN   European. Latin and Greek: "a Christian, a follower of Christ." **Kristinn, Kristyn, Kristynn. Kris, Kristi, Kristie, Kristy.**

KRITEESA   American: Contemporary.

KRYSTALYNN   American: Blending of Krystal (a crystal) and Lynn (lake). **Krystalin, Krystalinn, Krystalyn, Krystalynne. Krys, Krysti, Krystie, Krysty.**

K'SEA   American: Fanciful spelling of the name Kasey or the initials *K* and *C*.

KUTILDA   American: Contemporary.

KWANIESHA   American: Contemporary.

KWANIKA   American: Contemporary.

KYALAMBOKA   Tanzania. Nyakyusa: "God save me."

KYESHA   American: Contemporary, possibly influenced by Ayesha (life; alive and well). **Kaiesha, Kyeesha, Kyeeshah, Kyiesha, Kyisha, Kyishah.**

KYLIE   American. Scottish: "from the narrow channel." **Khylie, Kyli.**

KYMECHA   American: Contemporary.

KYRA   American: Contemporary.

LABABA   American: Contemporary.

L'ABANA   American: Contemporary, possibly an elaboration of the biblical name Abana (stony).

LACERINE   American: Contemporary.

LACHELL   American: Contemporary. **Lachell, Lachelle, Lashell, Lashella, Lashelle.**

LACONDRA   American: Contemporary.

LACY   American. French: "from the town of Lacy." The name is now commonly associated with the word *lacy*. **Lacee, Lacey, Laci, Lacie.**

LADAWN   American: "daybreak, dawn." **Ladawn, Ladawna.**

LADEAN   American. English: "a dean." **Ladean, LaDeen, Ladeen, LaDena, Ladena.**

LADEANE   American: Contemporary. **Ladeana, Ladeeana.**

LADELLE   American: An elaboration of Delle (dweller in the remote valley). **LaDell, Ladell, LaDella, Ladella.**

LaDONNA American. English: "world ruler." Italian: "lady." **Ladonna, Ladonnah.**

LaDORIS American. Greek: "Dorian woman."

LA'DRENNA American: Contemporary.

LAFESCA American: Contemporary.

LAHUE American: Contemporary.

LAIYA American: Contemporary.

LaKEISHA American: An elaboration of the name Keisha. **LaKeesha, Lakeesha, Lakeisha, Lakesha, Lakeshah, LaKisha, Lakisha, Laquesha, Laquisha, LeKeesha, Lekeesha, LeKisha, Lekisha, Lequesha, Lequisha.**

LAKENDRA American: Contemporary, based on Kendra (chief hero; royal rule; son of Henry). **Lakendrah.**

LAKEYIA American: Contemporary, possibly influenced by Zakiya (intelligent, pure). **Lakiya, Lakeeya.**

LAKIMBA American: Contemporary.

LAKIMREE American: Contemporary.

LaLEE American: Contemporary, based on Lee (a wood, clearing, meadow).

LALITA Hindi: "beautiful." Spanish: "of the sorrows."

LAMARTINE American: Coinage based on Lamar (famous across the land).

LAMAYA American: Contemporary, based on Maya (the Greek goddess of increase; illusion). **Lamaea, Lamaia, Lamaiah, Lamayah.**

LAMEESA American: Contemporary. **Lamiisa, Lamysah.**

LAMETRIA American: Contemporary.

LANAI Hawaiian: "veranda, porch."

LANAYA American: Contemporary, possibly based on Linnea (from the name of Swedish botanist Karl von Linné (Linnaeus 1707–1778).

LaNEECE American: Contemporary.

LaNEESHA American: Contemporary. **Laneesha, LaNeisha, Laneisha, Lanisha, LeNeesha, Leneesha, LeNeisha, Leneisha.**

LANEI American: Contemporary. Lanei Chapman, actress.

LANELLE American: Contemporary. **Lannell, Lannelle.**

LaNEVA Spanish: "the snow."

LANI Hawaiian: "the heavens." **Lanie.** Lanie Guinier, University of Pennsylvania law professor.

LANITA American: Contemporary. **Lannita, Lanyta.**

LANNETTE French: "from the small lane." American: Contemporary, modeled after Annette (little Anne). **Lanette.**

LaQUANANISHA American: Contemporary. **Quana.**

LAQUESHA American: Contemporary. **Lakqueesha, Lakweesha, Lakweisha, Lakwiesha, Laqueesha, Laquisha.**

LAQUINTA American. Latin: "the fifth child."

LAQUITA American: Contemporary. **Lakweeta, Lakweetah, Lakwyta, Laqueeta, Laqueetah.**

LARAINE American: Contemporary, possibly a variant of Lorraine (territory of Lothar). **LaRayne.**

LAREE American: Contemporary. **LaRee, L'Ree.**

LARISA Russian: Meaning uncertain, possibly "cheerful." **Laressa, Larissa.**

LARK English: "a lark, a songbird."

LARONDA American: Contemporary, based on Rhonda (good lance). **LaRhonda, Larhonda, LaRonda.**

LAROUX French: "red-haired."

LARRA American: Variant of Laura (laurel).

LARRICE American: Contemporary.

LARSHELL American: Contemporary. **Larchell, Larchelle, Larshelle.**

LARUTH American. Hebrew: "friend, companion."

LASHAN American: Contemporary.

LASHANDA American: Contemporary. **Lashanda, Lashandah.**

LASHANDRA American: Contemporary. **LaShandra, LaShandrah, Lashandrah. Shan, Shandy.**

LASHANNA American: Hebrew: "rose, lily."

LASHAUNA American. Irish: "God is gracious." Shauna is an Irish form of Jane. **LaSeana, LaShawna, Lashauna, La-**shawna, LaShon, Lashon, LaShonna, Lashonna, LaShonnah, Lashonnah.

LASHAUNDA American. Irish: "God is gracious." **LaShawnda, Lashawnda, Lashaunda, LaShonda, Lashonda.**

LASHAWN American. Irish. Hebrew: "God is gracious."

LASHERYL American: Contemporary.

LASHOA American: Contemporary.

LASONYA American. Russian. Greek: "wisdom."

LATANYA American: Modern elaboration of the Russian Tanya, a short form of Tatiana (uncertain derivation). The folk definition of Tatiana is "fairy queen." **LaTania, Latiana, Latanya, LaTonya, Latonya.**

LATASHA American. Russian: "natal day, Christmas." From the name Natasha.

LATASHIA American: Contemporary, influenced by Tasha (natal day) and Letitia (happiness).

LATAWNYA American: "tawny." **LaTaunya, Lataunya, LaTawnia, Latawnia.**

LATESHIA American. Latin: "happiness." **LaTeesha, Lateesha, LaTicia, LaTisha, Latisha. Teesha, Ticia, Tisha.**

LATIANA American: Contemporary, based on the Russian Tatiana (fairy queen). **Latyana.**

LATIFA Arabic: "gentle, kind." Hebrew: "caress." **Lateefa, Lateefah, Latifah.**

LATIFATU Nigeria. Yoruba. Arabic: "gentle, kind."

LATIKA Hindi: The name of a plant.

LATONA Latin: Meaning unknown. In classical mythology, Latona was the mother of Apollo and Diana.

LATONDRA American: Contemporary.

LATONIA Latin: "sacred to Latona." **Lationa.**

LATOSHA American: Contemporary.

LATOYA Spanish. Greek: "victory." **LaToiya.** La Toya Jackson, singer.

LAVELLE American: Contemporary.

LATRENA American: Contemporary. **Latreena, Latrina. Treena, Trina.**

LATRISHA American: Contemporary. **Latreesha, Latricia. Tricia, Trish, Trisha.**

LAUFEIA Scandinavian: "leafy island." In Norse mythology, the mother of the god Loki. **Laufee, Laufey.**

LAURA Latin: "laurel." **Lora. Lauri, Laurie, Lori, Lorie.**

LAUREEN American. Latin: "laurel." **Laureene, Lareen, Lareene.**

LAUREL Latin: "laurel, an evergreen shrub." **Laurell. Lauri, Laurie.**

LAUREN English. Latin: "from Laurentum." **Lauryn.**

LAURIANA American: Blending of Laura (laurel) and Ana (grace, mercy). **Laurianah, Laurianna, Lauriannah, Laurianne.**

LAURICE American. Latin: "laurel." **Lauri, Laurie.**

LAURIEL American. Latin: "laurel." **Lauri, Laurie.**

LAURILL American. Latin: "laurel." **Lauril, Laurille, Lauryl, Lauryll, Laurylle.**

LAURINDA American. Latin: "laurel."

LAURNETTA American. Latin: "laurel." **Lauri, Laurie.**

LAURONDA American: Contemporary, probably a blending of Laura (laurel) and Rhonda (lance).

LAUVENA American: Contemporary.

LAVALINA American: Contemporary.

LAVEDA English. Latin: "purified, cleansed." **Lavada.**

LAVERNA English. French: "springlike." **LaVerna.**

LAVERNE French: "springlike." **LaVern, Lavern, LaVerne.**

LAVET American: Contemporary.

LAVINIA Spanish. Latin: "from Latium." Latium was the area surrounding ancient Rome. **Lavina, Levina, Levinia, Livina, Livinia, Luvena, Luvenia, Luvina, Luvinia.**

LAVITA American. Latin: "life."

LAVOICE American: Contemporary, based on the word *voice* (utterance, oral sound).

LAVON American: Contemporary.

LAVONA Hebrew: "frankincense." **Lavonna.**

LAVONDA American: Contemporary. **Lavonda, Lavondah.**

LAVONNE American: Contemporary, possibly influenced by Yvonne (yew; archer).

L'AWAN American: Contemporary.

LAWANDA American: Contemporary. **Lawandah.**

LAWANDRA American: Contemporary.

LAWNLIA American: Contemporary.

LAYIA African. Arabic: "night, born at night."

LAYNE English: "dweller near the lane." Also a shortened form of Elaine (light). **Laine.**

L'CORINE American. Greek: "maiden." **L'Corrine, L'Corrinn, L'Corrinne.**

LEAH Hebrew: "weary." **Lea.**

LEANDRA Greek: "lion woman." **Leondra.**

LEATTA American: Contemporary.

LEBRA American: Variant of Libra (balance, a pair of scales), or possibly modeled after Debra (a bee).

LECOLE American: Contemporary, modeled after Nicole (victory of the people). **Lecola.**

LEDA Greek: Meaning unknown. In Greek mythology, Leda was a queen of Sparta and the mother of Clytemnestra. **Leeda.**

LEEAMBER American: Blending of Lee (woods, meadow) and Amber (a fossilized resin; the sky).

LEENA Hindi: "devoted."

LEILA Arabic: "dark beauty, night." **Laila,** Lailah, Layla, Leela, Leilah, Leilia, Lela, Leyla. Lela Rochon, actress.

LEISHA American: Contemporary. **Leecia, Leesha, Leeshah, Leeshia, Leishah, Licia, Liesha, Lisha.**

LEMURIA American: Contemporary.

LENA Hebrew: "dwelling, place of lodging." English. Greek: "light." Lena Horne, singer and actress.

LENICE American: Contemporary, probably modeled after Denice. **LaNeece, LaNeese, Laneese, LaNiece, Laniece, Laniese, LeNeece, LeNeese.**

LENNIA American: Contemporary, possibly based on Linnae, from Swedish botanist Karl von Linné (Linnaeus) 1707–1778).

LEOLA German: "deer."

LEOMA English: "light, bright."

LEONA French: "lion." Leona Mitchell, soprano.

LEONETTE French: "little lion."

LEONORE English. Greek: "light, bright." **Lennora, Lennorah, Lennore, Lenora, Lenore, Leonora.** Lenora Fulani, leader of the New Alliance Party.

LEONTINE American. Latin: "lion." **Leonteen, Leontyne.** Bishop Leontine Kelly, first black woman elected bishop in the United Methodist Church. Leontyne Price, opera diva, recipient of the Presidential Freedom Medal.

LEORA Hebrew: "light." **Liora.**

LERATO Botswana. Tswana: "love."

LEREEN American: Possible variant of Lorraine (territory of the people of Lothar).

LERLENE American. German: "ambush cliff." **Lerlean, Lerleen, Lerline.**

LERMA American: Possible elaboration of Erma (strength).

LERNIECE American: Contemporary.

LESLIE Scottish: "small clearing, small meadow." **Leslee, Lesley, Lesli.** Leslie Uggans, singer and actress.

LETHA English. Greek: "oblivion, forgetfulness." **Litha.**

LETHA MAE American: Compound of the names Letha (oblivion, forgetfulness) and Mae (the Greek goddess of increase; the month of May).

LETHIA English. Greek: "oblivion, forgetfulness." **Leethia, Leithea.**

LETITIA English. Latin: "happiness." **Laeticia, Latecia, Laticia, Latitia, Leticia. Ticia, Tisha.**

LETONYA American: Contemporary.

LETUANA American: Contemporary.

LEUMI Hebrew: "my nationality."

LEVANNAH South African: Contemporary, based on Levana (moon; light).

LEVONNE American: Contemporary, based on the name Yvonne (archer).

LIANA English. French. Latin: "the sun."

LIBYA Latin: "from Libya." Libya is a country in North Africa. **Libia.**

LILA Persian: "lilac." **Lilah.**

LILANE American: Contemporary.

LILKENYNNA American: Contemporary.

LILLIAN English. Latin: "lily." **Lilian. Lil, Lilli, Lillie, Lilly, Lily.**

LILLYBELLE American: A blending of Lilly (lily) and Belle (beautiful). **Lillybell, Lilybel, Lilybell, Lilybelle, Lylybel, Lylybell, Lylybelle. Lili, Lilli, Lillie, Lilly, Lily.**

LILY English. Latin: "lily." Often bestowed in reference to the flower, which represents purity and perfection. **Lilee, Lili, Lilly, Lillye.**

LIMBA Nigeria. Tiv: "joy, joyfulness." **Limbe.**

LIMBER American: "limber, flexible." Nigeria. Tiv: "joyfulness."

LINDA Spanish: "beautiful." German: "tender, soft." South Africa. Xhosa: "wait."

LINDALEE American: Blending of Linda (beautiful) and Lee (meadow, woods). **Lindalea, Lindaleigh.**

LINDIWE South Africa. Xhosa: "I have waited."

LINIKA Hindi: "dedicated."

LINITA American: Contemporary.

LINNEA Swedish: From the name of Swedish botanist Karl von Linné (Linnaeus, 1707–1778). **Linea, Linnae, Linnaea, Linnay, Lynnay, Lynnae.**

LINNELL American: Contemporary.

LINZA American: Contemporary, probably influenced by Linda (beautiful).

LIRETTE   English. Greek: "little lyrical one."

LISA   English. Hebrew: "God is my oath." **Leesa, Leesah, Leeza, Leisa, Liesa, Liza.** Lisa Bonet, actress.

LISETTE   German. Hebrew: "God is my oath." **Lise.**

LISHAN   Ethiopia. Amharic: "award."

LISHANNA   American: Contemporary.

LISSA   American. Greek: "a bee." A shortened form of Melissa.

LIVANA   Hebrew: "moon; light." **Levana, Livona.**

LIZBETH   English. Hebrew: "God is my oath." **Lisbet, Lisbeth, Lisbett, Lizbet, Lizbett. Lizzi, Lizzie, Lizzy.**

LIZIUZAYANI   Malawi. Yao: "tell somebody." **Lizi, Zayani.**

L'NAYIM   American: Contemporary.

LOANDA   African: Borrowed from the name of an African city.

LODIS   American: Coinage, possibly influenced by Lotus (the lotus flower).

LOFIA   American: Contemporary. **Lofya, Lophia, Lophya.**

LOIS   Greek: Meaning uncertain. Lois Alexander, founder and director of the Black Fashion Museum in Harlem. Lois Samuels, model.

LOLA   Spanish: Originated as a nickname of several names. Lola Falana, singer.

LOLEAN   American: Probably originated as a blending of two names.

LOLITA   Spanish: A common diminutive of Dolores (sorrows) and Dorotea (gift of God). **Loleta.**

LONNETTE   American: Contemporary. **Lonette.**

LORANDA   American: Contemporary.

LOREEN   English. Latin: "laurel." **Lorena, Lorene. Lori.** Lorene Cary, author.

LORENA   Spanish. French: "from Lorraine, the territory of the people of Lothar." **Lorenya.**

LORENDA   American: Contemporary, possibly an elaboration of Lorena (from Lorraine). **Lorinda.**

LORETTA   English. Latin: "laurel." Loretta Devine, actress.

LORIS   American: Possibly borrowed from *loris* (a small nocturnal lemur) or a variant of Chloris (green).

LORITA   Spanish. Latin: "laurel."

LORNA   English: A nineteenth-century coinage by novelist R. D. Blackmore. Lorna Simpson, multimedia artist.

LORRAINE   English. French: "territory of the people of Lothar." **Laraine, Larraine, Loraine, Lorayne, Loreen, Lorein, Loreine, Lorraina, Lorrainna, Lorrainne, Lorrine. Lori, Lorie, Lorri, Lorrie.** Lorraine Hansberry, dramatist.

LORYNN   American: Contemporary, possibly based on the male name Loren (laurel).

LOSSEN   American: Contemporary.

LOTUS   Greek: Borrowed from the plant of the same name. In legend, the fruit of the lotus plant induced forgetfulness and a dreamy languor.

LOUBERTHA American: Blending of Lou (famous in war) and Bertha (shining, bright).

LOUDEAN American: Blending of Lou (famous in war) and Dean (valley; a dean).

LOUETHA American: Probably originated as a variant of Louisa (famous in war).

LOUISA English. French. German: "famous in war."

LOUISE French. German: "famous in war." Louise Meriwether, novelist.

LOUISIANA American: Borrowed from the name of the southern state.

LOURIA Spanish. Latin: "laurel."

LOUVENIA American. Latin: In Roman mythology, the mother of the Roman people. **Levenia.**

LOVE American: "love, affection."

LOVERINE American: Contemporary.

LUANDA African: Borrowed from the name of the capital of Angola in southwestern Africa. **Loanda.**

LUBA Congolese: The name of an agricultural tribe in southern Democratic Republic of Congo (Zaire) and their language.

LUCILLE French. Latin: "light." **Lucile.** Lucille Clifton, poet.

LUCINDA English. Latin: "light." Coined by Miguel Cervantes for a character in *Don Quixote* (1605). **Loucinda.**

LUCYNA American: Contemporary.

LUETISHA American: Contemporary, based on Leticia (happiness). **Luticha.**

LUEVESTA American: Contemporary.

LUISAH American. French. German: "famous in war."

LUJAYN Arabic: "silver."

LULAVA Hebrew: "palm frond."

LULICIOUS American: Contemporary, possibly based on the word *delicious* (having a wonderful flavor).

LULU Swahili: "a pearl, precious."

LUMUSI Ghana. Ewe: "born facedown."

LURENNA American: Contemporary.

LURLEEN German: A variant of Lorelei (ambush cliff). In legend, Lorelei was a siren who sat upon a rock in the Rhine River and lured sailors to shipwreck. **Lurlean, Lurlene, Lurline.**

LUVENIA Spanish. Latin: In Roman mythology, the daughter of King Latinus and mother of the Roman people. **Lavinia, Luvenuia.**

LUVERTA American: Contemporary.

LUVETTA American: Contemporary.

LUWANNA American: Contemporary.

LYAH American: Variant of Leah (weary).

LYDGIA American: Contemporary.

LYDIA Greek: "Lydian woman." Lydia was the name of an ancient kingdom in western Asia Minor. **Lidia, Lidya, Lydya.**

LYNAE American. Swedish: From botanist Karl von Linné ([Linnaeus] 1707–1778).

LYNETTE   English. Welsh: "shapely; lake." French: "flaxen-haired." **Linnett, Linnette, Lynett, Lynnett, Lynnette. Linn, Lyn, Lynn.**

LYNN   English. Welsh: "lake." **Linn, Lyne, Lynne.** Lynn Whitfield, actress. Lyn Vaughn, anchorwoman.

MAACHA   Hebrew: "to press, to squeeze."

MACIE   English: "from Macey (Matheus' estate). American: Variant of Maisie (pearl).

MADELEINE   French. Hebrew: "woman from Magdala." **Madeline, Madelyn, Madelyne, Madolyne. Maddi, Maddie.**

MADGALYN   American: Variation of Magdalene (woman of Magdala).

MADISON   English: "Mad's son." Mad was a pet form of Matthew (gift of God), commonly used during the Middle Ages. **Maddi, Maddie.**

MADONNA   Italian: "my lady."

MAEDELL   America: A blending of Mae (May) and Dell (valley).

MAGNOLIA   American: From a type of tree or shrub that bears large, fragrant flowers. **Magnoliah. Maggi, Maggie.**

MAHALIA   Aramaic: "marrow, fat." Hebrew: "woman, tenderness." Mahalia Jackson (1911–1972), gospel singer.

MAHVAHNA   American: Contemporary.

MAIA   Greek: In Greek mythology, the goddess of increase. In Roman mythology, an earth goddess sometimes associated with the Greek Maia. **Maiya.**

MAIEOSIA   American: Contemporary.

MAISHA   Swahili: "life."

MAISIE   Scottish: "a pearl." Originated as a pet form of Margaret.

MAIZAH   Arabic: "discerning."

MAKAYLA   American. Hebrew: "Who is like God?"

MAKEDA   Ethiopian. Amharic: "beautiful armrest."

MAKENA   Kenya. Kikuyu: "the happy one."

MALAAK   American: Contemporary.

MALAIKA   Swahili: "an angel."

MALANA   Hawaiian: "light, buoyant."

MALEA   Hawaiian: Hawaiian form of Maria (sea of bitterness). **Maleia, Malia.**

MALENE   African: "tower."

MALIKA   Hindi: "queen." Arabic: "queen." Swahili: "angel."

MALINDA   English: "gentle."

MALINDI   African: A borrowing of the name of a city in Kenya.

MALKIA   Swahili: "queen."

MANDISA   South Africa. Xhosa: "sweet."

MANDOLIN   American: A stringed musical instrument.

MANGENA   Hebrew: "song, melody." **Mangina.**

MANGENI   Uganda. Musamia: "fish."

MANYA   Russian. Hebrew: "sea of bitterness." A Russian nickname of Maria.

MARA   Swahili: "a time." Hebrew: "bitter."

MARAE American: Contemporary.

MARAIS French: "dweller near the marsh."

MARASHELL American: Contemporary.

MARCELLA Italian. Latin: "of Mars." **Marcelle, Marchella, Marchelle.**

MARCHÉ French: "market, bargain."

MARCIA Latin: "warlike, of the god Mars." **Marsha, Marshia. Marcie, Marcy.**

MARDI American. French: "Tuesday." Also, a variant spelling of Marty (of Mars, warlike).

MARDINE American: Contemporary.

MARGARET English. Greek: "a pearl." **Margeret, Margret. Maggie, Margi, Margie, Meg, Peg, Peggy.** Margaret Walker Alexander, poet.

MARGO American. French. Greek: "a pearl." **Margeau, Margeaux.**

MARGOT French. Greek: "a pearl." Margot originated as a pet form of Marguerite.

MARGUERITE French. Greek: "a pearl."

MARIAH American: Variant of Maria (sea of bitterness) or Moriah (teacher). Mariah Carey, pop singer.

MARIAHADESSA American: Probable blending of Maria (sea of bitterness) and Hadassah (myrtle tree).

MARIAM Arabic. Hebrew: "sea of bitterness."

MARIAMA Swahili. Hebrew: "sea of bitterness."

MARIAN French. Hebrew: "sea of bitterness." From the name Miryam. **Marion, Maryan, Maryon.** Marian Wright Edelman, founder of the Children's Defense Fund and the Black Community Crusade for Children.

MARICE American: Possibly a variant of Maris (of the sea).

MARICELIA Spanish: Blending of Maria (sea of bitterness) and Celia (heaven).

MARIKA Slavic. Hebrew: "sea of bitterness."

MARILEE English: Blending of Mary (sea of bitterness) and Lee (woods, clearing). **Marilea, Marileigh, Marily, Maryleah, Marylee, Maryleigh.**

MARILOUISE American: Compound of the names Mari (sea of bitterness) and Louise (famous in war).

MARILYN English: Blending of Mary (sea of bitterness) and Lyn (lake). **Maralyn, Maralynn, Marilinn, Marilynn, Marylin, Marylyn, Marylynn, Meralin, Meralinn, Meralyn, Meralynn.**

MARINELLA American: Contemporary.

MARIQUILLA Spanish: A pet form of Maria (sea of bitterness).

MARIS English. Latin: "of the sea."

MARISOL Spanish: Combination of Maria (sea of bitterness) and Soledad (solitude).

MARISSA English. Hebrew: "sea of bitterness." **Marisa.**

MARJANI Swahili: "coral."

MARKEA American: Contemporary. **Marquia**.

MARKEESHA American: Contemporary. **Marquesha**.

MARKETA Czech. Greek: "a pearl." The Czech form of Margaret.

MARLAJO American: Contemporary. **Marlejo**.

MARLEAH American: Contemporary, probably a blending of any of the names beginning with *Mar-* and Leah (weary; wild cow, gazelle).

MARLENE German: Contraction of the name Mary Magdalene. **Marlain, Marlaine, Marlane, Marlayn, Marlayne, Marleen, Marleena, Marlena. Marlie**.

MARLISSA American: Contemporary.

MARLYTA American: Contemporary.

MARNESHA American: Contemporary.

MARNI Hebrew: "rejoice."

MARQUEELAH American: Contemporary.

MARQUITA French: "awning, canopy." **Marquite, Marquitta**.

MARRAKESH African: Borrowed from the Moroccan city. **Marrakech**.

MARSHAE American: Contemporary, probably a variant of Marché (market, bargain). **Marshay, Marshaye**.

MARSHELL American: Contemporary. **Marchel, Marchell, Marchelle, Marshel, Marshelle**.

MARTHA Aramaic: "lady." **Marthe**.

MARVA English. Welsh: "sea hill." French: "worthy of awe." Hebrew: "a plant of the mint family." Marva Collins, founder of Chicago's Westside Preparatory School and advocate for underprivileged children.

MARVELLE English: "from Marvell (pleasant, open country)." **Marvell**.

MARVLYNN American: Blending of the names Marva (sea hill) and Lynn (lake). **Marvlin, Marvlinn, Marvlyn, Marvlynne**.

MARY English. Hebrew: "sea of bitterness, sea of sorrow." Mary Frances Berry, appointee to the U.S. Commission on Civil Rights.

MARYCELA American: Contemporary, possibly influenced by Marcella (Mars).

MARYLON American: Fanciful spelling of Marilyn (sea of bitterness/lake).

MARYOMA American: Contemporary.

MARYSE American: Contemporary. Maryse Condé, award-winning author.

MARZELLE American: Contemporary. **Marzella**.

MARZETTE American: Contemporary.

MASANI Uganda. Luganda: "a gap between the teeth."

MASHAMA African: "she is a surprise."

MASHAUVA American: Possibly a variant of Mashavu (chubby cheeks).

MASHAVU Swahili: "cheeks, chubby cheeks."

MASHAWNA American: Contemporary.

MASHENA Hebrew: "a place of rest."

MASIKA Swahili: "born during the rainy season."

MASKINI Swahili: "poor."

MATISSE French: After the French painter Henri Matisse (1869–1954). **Mattisse.**

MAUDELL American: Variant of Maude (battle maid).

MAUDISA South Africa. Xhosa: "sweet one."

MAULANA Hawaiian: "constantly floating, ever buoyant."

MAULIDI Swahili: "born during the Islamic month of Maulidi (mawlid)."

MAURA Latin: "Moorish, dark-skinned."

MAURECIA Latin: "Moorish, dark-skinned."

MAUREEN English. Irish. Hebrew: "sea of bitterness."

MAURISSA American: Blending of Maureen (sea of bitterness) and Melissa (a bee). Also used as a variant of Marissa (sea of bitterness).

MAVIS English: "song thrush, a small songbird." **Mavie.**

MAWIYAH Arabic: "the essence of life."

MAWUSI Ghana. Ewe: "in the hands of God."

MAXIMIANA Spanish. Latin: "greatest."

MAY English: A pet form of Mary and Margaret, as well as a name taken from the month of May. **Mae.**

MAYA Spanish. Greek: From Maia, the name of the mythological goddess of increase. Hindu: "illusion." Maya Angelou, author and actress.

MAYBRY American: Contemporary.

MAYCIE American: Possibly a variant of Mazie (a pearl).

MAYLEN American: Contemporary, possibly a variant of Maylynn.

MAYLYNN American: Blending of May (the month of May) and Lynn (lake). **Mailin, Mailinn, Mailynn, Mailynne, Maylin, Maylinn, Maylynne.**

MAYRLYS American: Contemporary, likely influenced by the flower amaryllis.

MAYSA Arabic: "walking with a proud and swinging gait."

MAZALA Hebrew: "star; good luck."

MAZIE American. Scottish: "a pearl." **Maicie, Maicy, Maisey, Maisy.**

MBEKE Nigeria. Ibo: "born on the last day of the week."

MCKAYLA American: Fanciful spelling of Michaela (Who is like God?). **Micaela.**

MEHIRA Hebrew: "energetic."

MEIRA Hebrew: "light." **Meera.**

MEISHA American: Contemporary. **Meesha, Miisha, Mysha.**

MELANA Greek: "black, dark."

MELANIE English. Greek: "black, dark." **Melany, Mellanie, Melony.**

MELBA Australian: After a type of thin toast originating in Melbourne. Melba Moore, singer and actress.

MELEANNA American: Combination of Mel- and Anna (grace, mercy). **Meleannah.**

MELIA Hawaiian: "the plumeria tree." The flowers of the plumeria tree are commonly used in leis.

MELIBEA Spanish. Greek: "to care for." **Meli.**

MELIKA American: Contemporary, possibly influenced by the male name Malik (prince, king).

MELISSA Greek: "a bee." **Melisa, Melisah, Melissah, Mellisa, Mellisah, Mellissa, Mellissah.**

MELODY English: "melody, song." **Melodee, Melodie, Mellodee, Mellodie, Mellody.**

MELORA Greek: "golden apple."

MELVA Latin: "sweet friend."

MELVEN American. Gaelic: "chief."

MELVINA Latin: "sweet friend."

MELYSSA American. Greek: "a bee." **Melisah, Melissah, Mellisa, Mellisah, Melissah, Melyssah.**

MENDY American: Contemporary, modeled after Wendy or influenced by Mindy.

MEORAH Hebrew: "light." **Meora.**

MERCEDES Spanish. Latin: "mercy." **Marcedes, Mersedes.**

MERDIA American: Contemporary.

MEREDA American: Contemporary.

MERIAM American: Variant of Mariam (sea of bitterness).

MERIPAT American: Blending of Meri (merry, happy) and Pat (a patrician).

MERLINDA American: Contemporary, influenced by Merlin (sea fortress) and Linda (beautiful).

MERYLAND American: A fanciful spelling of Maryland.

ME'SHELL American: Modern fanciful spelling of Michelle (Who is like God?). **Mechell, Mechelle, Mischelle, Mishell, Mishelle, Mychell, Myshelle.**

MESI Malawi. Yao: "water."

MEXIE American: Contemporary.

MHONUM Nigeria. Tiv: "mercifulness."

MIA Hebrew: "Who is like God?" Italian: "mine." **Miya.**

MIATA American: Contemporary, its use influenced by a popular sports car of the same name.

MICHAELA Hebrew: "Who is like God?"

MICHELAY American. Hebrew: "Who is like God?" **Michelée.**

MICHELLE French. Hebrew: "Who is like God?" **Michèle, Michele.** Michele Wallace, professor and feminist author.

MICHI American: Contemporary.

MICOLE American: Contemporary, based on Nicole (victory of the people).

MIEKA American: Contemporary.

MIGNON American. French: "delicate, dainty, petite."

MIKAELA Swedish. Hebrew: "Who is like God?" **Mikala**.

MILLISIA American: Contemporary. Perhaps a variant form of the Greek Melissa (a bee). **Milli, Millie, Milly**.

MILLY English: Originating as a short form of any name beginning with *Mil-*. **Milee, Mili, Milie, Mille, Millee, Milli, Mily**.

MILYA Russian. Greek: "dark, black."

MINCHA Hebrew: "gift."

MINEOLA Native American. Sioux: "much water."

MINERVA Latin: "wisdom." In classical mythology, the goddess of learning and handicrafts.

MINNA American: Contemporary. Also, a borrowing of the name of a Nigerian city.

MINOCA American: Contemporary.

MINOLA American: Contemporary, possibly a variant of Mineola (much water).

MINTIE American: "minty." **Mintee**.

MIRA Spanish. Latin: "wonderful."

MIREYA Spanish. Hebrew: "God has spoken."

MIRSADA American: Contemporary.

MIRYAM Hebrew: "sea of bitterness, sea of sorrow." **Marium, Miriam**.

MISCHA Russian. Hebrew: "Who is like God?"

MISCHAL American: Contemporary, probably a variant of Michelle (Who is like God?).

MISHAILA American: Contemporary, based on Michelle (Who is like God?). **Mishayla**.

MISHAY American: Contemporary. **Michae, Michay, Mishae, Mishaye**.

MISKAELA American: Contemporary, based on Michaela (Who is like God?).

MISLYNNE American: Contemporary.

MIVAHN American: Contemporary.

MIYA American: Variant of Mia (Who is like God?; mine).

MIZURA American: Contemporary, possibly influenced by regional pronunciation of Missouri.

MKIWA Swahili: "orphaned child."

MOEESHA American: Contemporary. **Moesha, Moweesha, Mowesha**.

MONA Arabic: "hope."

MONAE American: Contemporary, possibly a phonetic spelling of Monet.

MONEE English: Contemporary.

MONET American: After the French painter Claude Monet (1840–1926).

MONICA A name of uncertain etymology and meaning. It is thought to be African, Phoenician, or Latin. Monica was the name of the mother of Saint Augustine.

MONIFA Nigeria. Yoruba: "I am lucky."

MONIKA Hindi: "quiet."

MONIQUE French: The French form of Monica. The name is of uncertain derivation and meaning.

MONISHA American: Contemporary.

MONTERIA American: Contemporary.

MONTSHO Botswana. Tswana: "black."

MOORÉA Polynesian: Borrowed from a South Pacific island of the same name.

MORGAN Welsh: "sea circle, sea bright, white seas."

MORGHANN American. Welsh: "sea circle, sea bright, white seas." **Morghan**.

MORIAH Hebrew: "teacher." **Moriyah**.

MOROWA Ghana. Akan: "queen."

MOSI Swahili: "firstborn."

MUDIWA Zimbabwe. Shona: "beloved."

MUMINAH Arabic: "pious, true believer."

MUNIRAH Arabic: "enlightener." **Munira**.

MURIEL English. Irish: "bright seas." **Merial, Meriel, Miriel, Murial**.

MUTETELI Rwanda. Rwandan: "dainty."

MWAJUMA Swahili: "born on Friday."

MWANAHAMISI Swahili: "born on Thursday."

MWANAJUMA Swahili: "born on Friday."

MWANAWA Tanzania. Zaramo: "firstborn."

MYIESHA American: Contemporary, probably influenced by Aisha (life). **Miesha, Mieshah, Myeesha, Myeeshah, Myisha**.

MYNELL American: Contemporary.

MYNKA American: Contemporary, possibly a variant of the male name Minkah (justice).

MYRA Latin: "wonderful."

MYRIA Spanish. Latin: "wonderful." **Myreah**.

MYRLEE American. French: "blackbird." **Myrlee, Myrlie**. Myrlie Evers-Williams, chairperson of the NAACP.

MYRTELLA American: "myrtle wood."

MYRTICE American: "myrtle wood."

MYSTIQUE French: "intriguing, mystical." **Mistique**.

NAAMAH Hebrew: "beautiful, pleasant." **Naama**.

NAAMANAH Hebrew: "pleasant." **Naamana**.

NAAVAH Hebrew: "delightful, pleasing." **Naava**.

NABIHA Arabic: "intelligent."

NABILA Arabic: "noble, an honorable person." **Nabeela, Nabeelah, Nabilah**.

NADEAH American. Russian: "hope." Arabic: "full of dew."

NADEEN American: An alternative spelling of Nadine (hope). **Na Dean, Nadeen, Nadina, Nadine**.

NADEZHDA Russian: "hope."

NADIA Russian: "hope." Sudan. Arabic: "full of dew." **Nadiya, Nadya**.

NADIDA Arabic: "equal, a peer." **Nadeeda, Nadidah.**

NADIFA Somali: "born between two seasons."

NADINE French. Russian: "hope." **Nadina.**

NADIRA Swahili: "rare." Hindu: "pinnacle."

NAFULA Uganda. Abaluhya: "born during the rainy season."

NAIDA Spanish. Greek: "pertaining to Zeus." A short form of Zenaida.

NAILA Arabic: "successful." **Nailah.**

NAIMA Arabic: "happy, content." **Naeemah, Naimah.**

NAIROBI African: Borrowed from the name of the capital of Kenya.

NAJA Arabic: "to confide in; success."

NAJLA Arabic: "having large beautiful eyes."

NAJUMA Swahili: "abounding in joy."

NAKARI American: Contemporary.

NAKI Ghana. Adangbe: "first female child."

NAKIA American: Contemporary. **Naekia, Naekiah, Nakiah.**

NALIAKA Kenya. Luya: "a wedding."

NALO African: "beloved."

NAMBI Uganda: The wife of Kintu, legendary first king of Uganda.

NAMEENA American: Contemporary.

NAMONO Uganda. Luganda: "younger of twins."

NANA English. Hebrew: "grace, mercy." Ghana: "mother of the earth."

NANCY English. Hebrew: "full of grace, mercy." **Nanci. Nan.** Nancy Wilson, jazz singer.

NANGILA Kenya. Luya: "born while parents are on a journey."

NANYAMKA Ghana. Ewe: "God's gift."

NAOMI Hebrew: "pleasant, my delight." Naomi Sims, supermodel. Naomi Campbell, supermodel.

NARA English: "near."

NARAH Hebrew: "child of the Lord."

NARVA American: Contemporary.

NASEEM Hindi: "morning breeze."

NA'SHEEMA American: Contemporary.

NASHIRA Hindi: "star."

NASICHE Uganda. Musoga: "born during the locust season." **Nasike.**

NASRIN Persian: "wild rose." **Nasreen.**

NASSRA American. Arabic: "victory."

NASYA Hebrew: "miracle of the Lord." **Nasia, Nasiah, Nasiya.**

NATALIE Latin: "natal day, Christmas." **Natalee. Nat.** Natalie Cole, singer.

NATARSHA American: Contemporary, influenced by Natasha (natal day, Christmas).

NATASHA Russian. Latin: "natal day, Christmas." **Natascha**.

NATHIFA Arabic: "clean, pure." **Nateefa, Nateefah, Nathifah, Natifa, Natifah**.

NATIMA American: Contemporary.

NATOSHA American: Variant of Natasha (natal day, Christmas).

NATRA American: Contemporary.

NAVA Hebrew: "beautiful."

NAVANI Hindi: "young, modern."

NAWAL Arabic: "gift, present."

NAYANA Hindi: "beautiful eyes."

NAYIKA Hindi: "beautiful."

NAYO Nigeria. Yoruba: "we have joy."

NAZIHAH Arabic: "honest."

NAZIRA Arabic: "equal." **Nazirah**.

NBUSHE Swahili: "the godly one." **N'Bushe**. N'Bushe Wright, actress.

NECHAMA Hebrew: "comfort."

NEDA Slavic: "born on Sunday." **Nedda**.

NEDIRA Arabic: "rare."

NEDRA Slavic: "born on Sunday."

NEEDARA Hebrew: "glorified."

NEEMA Swahili: "born during a prosperous time."

NEEMANA Hebrew: "truthful."

NEESHA American: Contemporary. **Neisha, Niesha, Nisha, Nysha**.

NEFERTITI Egypt: After the fourteenth-century B.C. queen and wife of Ikhnaton. **Nefertete, Nefhertiti**. Nefertiti, actress and rap musician.

NEHANDA Zimbabwe. Zezuru: "strong."

NEHEDARA Hebrew: "beautiful."

NEKIA American: Contemporary.

NELCINA American: Contemporary, possibly a variant of the Swedish Nilsine (victory of the people). **Nelcine, Nelsene, Nelsina**.

NELL English. Greek: "light." **Nelli, Nellie, Nelly**. Nell Carter, actress.

NELSIE American: Elaboration of Nell (light) and Elsie (God is my oath).

NELVOLIA American: Contemporary.

NEOFITA Spanish: "neophyte, novice, new convert."

NEOSHA Native American. Osage: "cold clear water."

NEQUAI American: Contemporary.

NERISSA English. Latin: "sea snail." **Narissa, Nerisa, Nerrisa, Nerrissa**.

NESHA American: Contemporary.

NESHAMA Hebrew: "soul."

NESHANDA American: Contemporary.

NESHANDRA American: Contemporary.

NESHE American. Norse: "headland, promontory."

NESHOBA Native American. Choctaw: "wolf."

NESICHA Hebrew: "princess."

NESSA Norse: "headland, promontory."

NEVA Spanish: "snow."

NEVARA Spanish: "snow." The name implies purity.

NEVONA Hebrew: "intelligent."

NGOZI Nigeria. Ibo: "blessing."

NGULINGA Malawi. Ngoni: "weeping."

NIA American: Contemporary. Swahili: "resolve."

NIAMBY African: "the song is heard."

NIAMEY African: Borrowed from the capital of Niger.

NIARA American: Contemporary. Hindi: "nebula, mist." Dr. Niara Sudarkasa, president of Lincoln University.

NICHELLE American: Contemporary, based on Michelle (Who is like God?). **NaChelle, Nichella.** Nichelle Nichols, actress.

NICHOEL American: Modern variant spelling of Nicole (victory of the people). **Niccole, Nickole, Nicol, Nikkole, Nikole. Nicki, Nickie, Niki, Nikki, Nikkie.**

NICHOLENE American: Contemporary variant of Nicole (victory of the people). **Nickolene.**

NICOLE French. Greek: "victory of the people." **Nicola.**

NIESHA American: Contemporary.

NIKA English. Greek: "victory." Also, a short form of Dominika (belonging to the Lord).

NIKEESHA American: Contemporary. **Niceesha, Nickeesha, Nickisha, Nickysha, Nicquisha, Nikisha, Nikkisha, Nikysha, Niquisha. Nici, Nicki, Niki, Nikki.**

NIKETA American: Contemporary, most likely influenced by Nikita (excellent; unconquered).

NIKITA Hindi: "excellent." Russian. Greek: "unconquered."

NIKKI American. Greek: "victory." **Nicki, Nickie, Nicky, Nikkee, Nikkie.** Nikki Giovanni, poet.

NIKOLIA Greek: "victory of the people." **Nicolia. Nicki, Niki, Nikki.**

NILAY Hindi: "home."

NILISHA Hindi: "the blue god."

NIMAH Arabic: "blessing." **Neema.**

NINA Russian. Hebrew: "grace, mercy." Originated as a pet form of Anna. Nina Simone, jazz singer and pianist.

NIOBE Greek: Meaning uncertain. In Greek mythology, Niobe was a queen of Thebes who was turned into stone while weeping for her slain children.

NISHA Hindi: "night."

NISHAN Ethiopia. Amharic: "award."

NISSA Hebrew: "to test."

NITZA Hebrew: "a flower bud." **Nitzah.**

NIVIERA American: Contemporary, possibly based on Riviera (a stream, river).

NIYA   American: Contemporary.

NIZANA   Hebrew: "a flower bud."

NJEMILE   Malawi. Yao: "upstanding."

NKECHI   Nigeria. Ibo: "loyal."

NKEKA   Nigeria. Ibo: "tenderness."

NKOSAZANA   South Africa. Xhosa: "princess."

NNEKA   Nigeria. Ibo: "her mother is supreme."

NNENIA   Nigeria. Ibo: "the likeness of her grandmother."

NOBANTU   South Africa. Xhosa: "popular."

NOBANZI   South Africa. Xhosa: "width."

NOEL   French: "Christmas."

NOELANI   Hawaiian: "heavenly mist."

NOLA   Latin: "little bell."

NOLITA   Italian. Latin: "unwilling." **Noleta.**

NOMALANGA   South Africa. Zulu: "sunny."

NOMBEKO   South Africa. Xhosa: "respect."

NOMBESE   Nigeria. Benin: "wonderful child."

NOMBLE   South Africa. Xhosa: "beauty."

NOMUSA   Zimbabwe. Ndebele: "merciful."

NONA   Latin: "ninth." Nona Gaye, singer.

NONI   African: "gift of God."

NONYAMEKO   South Africa. Xhosa: "patience."

NORALEEN   Irish: "little Nora (light)."

NORMA   English: "northern woman."

NORMALYNN   American: Blending of Norma (northern woman) and Lynn (lake). **Normalinn, Normalyn, Normalynne.**

NORMARENE   American: Blending of Norma (northern woman) and Irene (peace).

NORVELLA   English. French: "from the northern town."

NOURA   Arabic: "light."

NOURBESE   Nigeria. Benin: "a wonderful child."

NOVA   Latin: "new."

NOVALYNE   American: Contemporary.

NOVELETTE   American: "a short novel."

NOVIA   Italian. Latin: "new."

NOYA   Hebrew: "beautiful, ornamented." **Noia.**

NURU   East Africa. Swahili: "in the daylight."

NYANA   American: Contemporary, modeled after Dyana (divine).

NYKESHA   American: Contemporary, possibly influenced by the Russian Nikita (unconquered). **Nikeesha, Nikesha, Nikeisha, Nykeesha, Nykesha, Nykeisha. Nikki, Nykki.**

NYLA   American: Contemporary. **Nylah.**

NYSSA Greek: After a city where Bacchus, the god of wine and revelry, was believed to have been reared.

NZINGHA African: "beautiful and courageous."

OANCEA American: Contemporary, an anagram of Oceana (the sea).

OBAX Somali: "flower."

OBIOMA Nigeria. Ibo: "kind."

OCEANA English: "the ocean, the sea."

OCTAVIA Latin: "eight." Octavia E. Butler, award-winning science-fiction writer.

ODELIA Hebrew: "I praise Jehovah." Teutonic: "wealthy."

ODESSA Greek: "odyssey." **Odessia.**

ODESSIAMAE American: Blending of Odessia (the *Odyssey*) and Mae (May). **Odessa Mae, Odessamae, Odessia Mae.**

ODESTA American: Coinage, possibly influenced by Odessa (the *Odyssey*).

ODIENNE African: A borrowing of the name of a city in Côte d'Ivoire.

OLABISI Nigeria. Yoruba: "joy is multiplied."

OLANIYI Nigeria. Yoruba: "there is joy in wealth."

OLETHA English. Scandinavian: "nimble." **Oleta.** Oleta Adams, singer.

OLEVIA Spanish. Latin: "olive tree."

OLINDA Spanish. Latin: "from Olinda." Teutonic: "gentle."

OLIVE English. Latin: "olive tree." **Oliva. Liv, Livvie.**

OLIVIA Latin: "olive tree." **Olevia. Liv, Livvie.**

OLOKUN Nigeria. Yoruba: "Owner of the sea." In mythology, Olokun is the goddess of the sea and of marshes.

OLUBAYO Nigeria. Yoruba: "supreme joy."

OLUFEMI Nigeria. Yoruba: "God loves me."

OLUREMI Nigeria. Yoruba: "God consoles me."

OLYMPIA Greek: "of Olympus." In Greek mythology Mount Olympus was the home of the gods.

OMEGA Greek: "large." The last letter of the Greek alphabet.

OMOLARA Nigeria. Benin: "born at the right time."

OMOROSE Nigeria. Benin: "my beautiful child."

ONAEDO Nigeria. Ibo: "gold."

ONDREA American: Variant of Andrea (womanly).

ONEIDA Native American. Iroquois: "standing rock." **Oneda, Onida, Onyda.**

ONI Nigeria. Benin: "desired."

OPELINE American: "a translucent, milky type of glass." **Opelene.**

OPHELIA Greek: "help, succor." The name was coined by the Italian poet Jacopo Sannazaro in 1504. **Ofelia, Opheelia.**

OPHIRA   Hebrew: Taken from the name of a region famous for its gold.

OPHRAH   Hebrew: "a fawn." **Ofra, Ofrah, Ophra, Oprah.** Oprah Winfrey, actress and philanthropist.

ORDELLA   American: Coinage, perhaps inspired by the Latin Orela (a divine announcement).

ORIANA   English: Medieval literary coinage found in the Spanish romance *Amadís de Gaula.* It is possibly derived from the Latin *oriri* (to rise) or the French *or* (gold). **Orianna.**

ORIEL   English: Of debated origin. Perhaps from the Latin Aurelius (golden) or the Middle English *oriel* (bay window).

ORIENA   American: Variant form of Oriana. **Oriene, Orienna, Orienne.**

ORIOLE   English. Latin: "gold." A reference to orioles, birds that are chiefly yellow and black.

ORLAIN   American: Contemporary, perhaps influenced by Arlene. **Orlaine, Orlane, Orlayne.**

ORLINDA   American: Contemporary.

ORNETTE   American: Contemporary. **Ornetta.**

OSCEOLA   Native American Creek: "black drink crier." Osceola Archer, actress. Osceola Davis, soprano.

OSHUN   Nigeria. Yoruba: Goddess of the Oshun River and wife of Shango, god of the thunderbolt.

OUIDA   American: Contemporary.

OVALENE   American: Coinage, possibly based on *ova* (eggs) and utilizing the Irish diminutive *-lene.*

OYA   Nigeria. Yoruba: Goddess of the Niger River and a wife of Shango, god of the thunderbolt.

OZELLE   American: Contemporary. **Ozella.**

PACIFICA   Spanish. Latin: "to make peace."

PAISLEY   American: From the design, which consists of an elaborate pattern of intricate figures.

PALLAS   Greek: "wisdom, knowledge." In Greek mythology, another name for Athena, the goddess of wisdom.

PALMINA   American: "little palm tree."

PALOMA   Spanish: "dove."

PAMEITHIA   American: Contemporary.

PAMELA   English: A sixteenth-century coinage by the poet Sir Philip Sidney. **Pamila.**

PAMELJA   American: Variant of Pamela.

PANACEA   American. Latin: "cure-all, remedy."

PANYA   Swahili: "mouse; a tiny baby."

PARALEE   American: Contemporary.

PARTHENA   American: Contemporary.

PARTICIA   American: Contemporary, probably influenced by Patricia (a patrician).

PASUA   Swahili: "born by cesarean section."

PATRICIA Latin: "a patrician, an aristocrat." **Pat, Patsy, Patti, Patty, Tricia.** Patricia Roberts Harris, secretary of housing and urban development, first African-American woman cabinet member. Dr. Patricia Cowings, NASA behavioral psychologist.

PATRISIA English. Latin: "a patrician, an aristocrat." **Patrice, Patrika. Pat, Patsy, Patti, Patty, Trisia.**

PAULA Latin: "small." Paula Giddings, author.

PAULE French. Latin: "small." Paule Marshall, novelist.

PAULETTE American: "little Paula; small one."

PAULINE English. Latin: "small."

PEARL English: "a pearl." Pearl Bailey, singer.

PEARLINE American: "a pearl." **Pearlean, Pearleen, Pearlene.**

PENDA Swahili: "beloved."

PENOLA Australian: After a city of the same name.

PERVIA Latin: "thoroughfare, passage."

PETRA Latin: "a rock."

PHEDRA Greek: "bright." **Phaedra.**

PHILADELPHIA American. Greek: "brotherly love." **Delphia, Delphie, Phillie.**

PHILANA Greek: "lover of mankind." American: Blending of Phil (loving) and Ana (grace, mercy).

PHILANTHA Greek: "lover of flowers."

PHILATHEA American. Greek: "lover of God." **Phillie, Thea.**

PHILLISE American: Contemporary, influenced by Phyllis (a leaf).

PHILOMELA Latin. Greek: "lover of song."

PHOMESIA American: Contemporary, perhaps influenced by Phoenicia, an ancient region of the Mediterranean.

PHYLEA American. Greek: "tribe."

PHYLICIA American: Contemporary reworking of Felicia (lucky). Phylicia Rashad, actress and dancer.

PHYLLA American: Contemporary, perhaps influenced by Phyllis (a leaf) or Philip (lover of horses). **Philla.**

PHYLLIS Greek: "a leaf." **Phillis, Phylis.** Phyllis Yvonne Stickney, actress. Phyllis Hyman, singer and actress.

PIA Latin: "pious."

PILETTE American: Contemporary.

PILI Swahili: "second born." Hebrew: "miraculous."

PORTIA English. Latin: "pig, hog." **Porche, Porsche.**

PRECILLA American. Latin: "ancient."

PRECIOUS English: "of great value."

PRENTELLA American: Contemporary.

PRINCELLA American: Coinage, perhaps a blending of Princess and Priscilla (ancient).

PRINCESS English: "princess, daughter of a queen or king."

PRISCILLA English. Latin: "ancient." **Priscella. Prisca.**

QAMAR Arabic: "the moon."

QUANDA English: "queenly." Spanish: Variant of Wanda.

QUBILAH Arabic: "concord, harmony." **Qubila.**

QUEENA English: "queenly." **Queenie.**

QUEENETTA American: "queenly."

QUESTA English. French: "a quest."

QUILLA Gaelic: "a cub."

RAANANA Hebrew: "beautiful, fresh." **Ranana, Rananah.**

RAASHIDA American. Arabic: "rightly guided." **Raasheeda, Raasheedah, Raashidah.**

RABIAH Arabic: "spring." **Rabia.**

RACHEL Latin and Greek. Hebrew: "ewe." **Rachael.**

RACHELL English. Hebrew: "ewe." **Rachelle, Rachella, Rochell, Rochelle, Roschelle, Roshelle.** Rachelle Ferrell, singer.

RADHIYA Swahili: "agreeable."

RADIANCE American: "brightness, radiance."

RAE English. German: "wise protection." **Raye.**

RAEA American. German: "wise protection." **Raia, Raya, Rhaea, Rhaia, Rhaya.**

RAEDENA American: Blending of Rae (wise protection) and Dena (a dean; judged).

RAELEEN American: An elaboration of Rae (wise protection). **Raeleena, Raeleene, Raelina, Raeline, Rayeleen, Rayleen, Rayline.**

RAHANA American: Contemporary, possibly influenced by Rihana (sweet basil).

RAIDAH Arabic: "leader."

RAINE American: "rain." **Rayne.**

RAINEY Scottish. German: "ruler of judgment."

RAKEISHA American: A modern coinage. **Ra Keesha, Rakeesha, Rakisha, Rakishah.**

RALINA American: Contemporary, possibly a variant of Raelina.

RAMA Hebrew: "exalted."

RAMANA Hindi: "beautiful."

RAMIA African: "prophet."

RAMLA Swahili: "fortune-teller."

RAMONA Spanish. German: "wise protection."

RANA Arabic: "a beautiful object, that which catches the eye." Hindu: "queenly, royal."

RANCE American: Possibly originated as a shortened form of Laurence (man from Laurentum).

RANDA Arabic: Borrowed from the name of a sweet-smelling tree.

RANDELLE American. German: "shield wolf."

RANEE Hindi: "queenly." **Rani.**

RANIELLE American: Contemporary.

RAPONSICA American: Contemporary.

RASHA Arabic: "a young gazelle."

RASHANDA American: Contemporary. **Rashandah.**

RASHIDA Arabic: "rightly guided." **Rasheeda, Rasheedah, Rashidah.**

RASIDA Swahili. Arabic: "rightly guided."

RAVEN American: "raven, crow." **Raivan, Raiven, Rayven.**

RAWIYA Arabic: "storyteller."

RAYA Hebrew: "friend."

RAYANNE American: Blending of Ray (wise protection) and Anne (grace, mercy). **Raeann, Raeanne, Rayan, Rayann.**

RAYELLE American: Contemporary. **Rayell.**

RAYLEE American: A blending of Ray (wise protection) and Lee (dweller by the meadow). **Raelee, Raely, Railee, Railie, Raylie, Rayly.**

RAYMELLE American: Contemporary. **Raemell, Raemelle, Rayemell, Rayemelle. Mell, Rae, Ray, Raye.**

RAYNA Hebrew: "song of the Lord." **Raina.**

RAYNELL American: Blending of Ray (wise protection) and Nell (light). **Raenell, Raenelle, Rayenell, Rayenelle, Raynelle. Nell, Rae, Ray, Raye.**

RAYSHAL American. Hebrew: "ewe."

RAZILI Hebrew: "my secret."

RAZIYA Arabic: "sweet, agreeable." **Raziyah.**

RAZZY American: Contemporary.

REBA Hebrew: "young girl."

REGINA Latin: "queen." **Reginia.** Regina King, actress.

REHEMA Swahili: "compassion."

REICHANA Hebrew: "sweet-smelling." **Rechana.**

REISHA American: Contemporary.

REJANE American: Contemporary, possibly influenced by Regina (queen).

REMEGIA American: Contemporary. **Remejia.**

REMELEEN American: Contemporary.

REMELL American: Contemporary.

REMITHA American: Contemporary.

RENANA Hebrew: "joy."

RENÉ French. Latin: "reborn."

RENEDA American: Contemporary.

RENEE American. French. Latin: "reborn." **Renae, Renai, Rennay, Rennea, Rhenae, Rhennae, Rhennay, Rinae, Rinée, Rinay.**

RENISE American: Contemporary, modeled after Denise (of Dionysus).

RENISHA American: Contemporary.

RENITA American: Possible variant of Renata (reborn). English. Latin: "rebel."

RENNY English. German: "strong judgment." Originated as a pet form of Reynard. **Renni, Rennie.**

RENYE   American: Contemporary, possibly an alternate spelling of Renny (strong judgment).

REOLA   American: Contemporary.

RESEDA   English. Latin: "to rest, to sit down."

RESHAM   Hindi: "silk."

REVA   English. Latin: "restored to health." Hebrew: "young girl." Hindu: Another name for the Narmada River.

REVAYA   Hebrew: "satisfied."

REVEDA   American: Contemporary.

REVEE   American: Contemporary.

REVOYDA   American: Contempoary.

REYNA   Spanish. Latin: "queen."

REZINA   American: Contemporary.

RHAMAH   Swahili: "my sweetness, my delight."

RHAPSODY   American: "great delight."

RHAXMA   Somali: "sweet."

RHEA   Greek: "flowing." In Greek mythology, Rhea was the mother of Zeus.

RHIANNON   Welsh: "great queen."

RHODESIA   African: The former name of the region in southern Africa which is now Zambia and Zimbabwe. The area was named for Cecil John Rhodes, a British financier and colonial administrator.

RHODIA   Greek: "garland of roses." **Rhoda**.

RHONDA   Welsh: "good lance." **Randa, Ronda, Rondah**.

RHONDALYN   American: Blending of Rhonda (good lance) and Lynn (lake). **Rhondalin, Rhondalinn, Rhondalynn, Rhondalynne, Rondalin, Rondalinn, Rondalyn, Rondalynn, Rondalynne**.

RHONDELLA   American: A blending of Rhonda (good lance) and Della (small valley; nobility). **Rhondell, Rhondella, Rhondelle, Rondell, Rondelle, Rondella**.

RIA   Scandinavian: Short form of Maria (sea of bitterness). Spanish: "river."

RIANA   American: Contemporary. **Reeana, Reeanna, Rianah, Rianna, Riannah**.

RICHELLE   American: Contemporary, possibly a melding of Richard (stern king) and Michelle (Who is like God?).

RIDA   Arabic: "contentment." **Radeya, Radeyah, Radhiya**.

RIHANA   Arabic: "sweet basil." **Rihanna, Rihannah**.

RIISA   American: Contemporary, possibly influenced by the Russian Raisa (rose).

RIKKI   English: "strong king." **Rikkee**.

RILEC   American: Contemporary.

RILLA   German: "stream, brook."

RIMONA   Hebrew: "pomegranate."

RINA   English: Originated as a short form of names ending in -rina, such as Sabrina or Katherina.

RISHONA   Hebrew: "first."

RITA   Spanish. Greek: "a pearl." The name originated as a short form of Margarita.

Hindu: "divine law." Rita Dove, former U.S. poet laureate.

ROBERTA German: "bright fame." **Robertah. Bobbi, Bobbie, Robbi, Robbie.** Roberta Flack, Grammy-winning singer. Roberta Alexander, soprano.

ROBIN English. German: "bright with fame." **Robyn. Robbi, Robbie.** Robin Givens, actress.

ROCHANA Hindi: "beautiful." *Rochani.*

ROCHELLE American: A modern form of Rachel (ewe). **Rochell, Roshel, Roshell, Roshelle.**

ROCQUINA American: Contemporary.

RODERICA English. German: "famous ruler."

ROHANA Hindi: "sandalwood."

ROLANDA English. German: "famous land." **Ro Landa, Rolandah.**

ROLEAN American. German: "famous land." **Rolene, Rollene.**

ROLONDA American. German: "famous land." **Rolondah.** Rolonda Watts, talk show host.

ROMA Latin: "from Rome."

ROMAE American: Contemporary.

ROMANA Spanish: "from Rome."

ROMELIA Spanish. German: "glorious heroine." **Ramelia, Romellia.**

RONDI American: Contemporary.

RONEEKA American: Contemporary. **Roneekah.**

RONIKA American: Contemporary, possibly a shortened form of Veronica (bringer of victory).

RONNA Scottish: "wise ruler." **Rohna.**

RONNELL American. Scandinavian: "ruler of judgment." **Ronell, Ronelle, Ronnel, Ronnelle. Roni, Ronni, Ronnie.**

RONNELLA American: A combination of Ron (ruler of judgment) and Ella (light). Scandinavian: "ruler of judgment."

RONNESHA American: Contemporary.

RONNETTE American. Scandinavian: "ruler of judgment."

ROSA Spanish: "a rose." Rosa Parks, civil rights pioneer. Rosa Guy, author.

ROSALBA Spanish: "white rose." **Rosa.**

ROSALIND German: "gentle horse; gentle fame." Spanish: "beautiful rose." **Rosaleen, Rosalin, Rosaline, Rosalyn, Roslyn, Roslynn, Rozalin, Rozlin, Rozalyn, Rozalynn. Roz.** Rosalind Cash, actress.

ROSAMIRA Spanish: "wonderful rose." **Rosa.**

ROSEANNA English: Blending of Rose (a rose) and Anna (grace, mercy). **Rosanna, Rosannah, Rosanne, Roseann, Roseannah, Roseanne. Rosie.**

ROSELYNN American: A blending of Rose (a rose) and Lynn (lake). **Roselyn, Roselynne. Rose, Rosie.**

ROSETTA Italian and Spanish: "little rose." **Rose, Rosie.** Rosetta LeNoire, actress.

ROSILLA Spanish. Latin: "feast of roses."

ROSSALENE   American: Contemporary.

ROTHA   German: "red, red-haired."

ROWANNA   American: Variant of Rowena (famous friend; joyful fame; blessed spear).

ROWENA   English: Perhaps "famous friend," "joyful fame," or "blessed spear." **Winnie.**

ROXANE   Greek. Persian: "dawn of day." **Roxann, Roxanna, Roxanne. Roxi, Roxie, Roxy.**

ROZANDA   American: Contemporary. **Rosanda, Rosandah, Rozandah. Rosie, Rozie.** Rozanda Thomas, singer with the group TLC.

ROZOLIA   Spanish. Latin: "feast of roses."

RUBY   English: "ruby gemstone." Ruby Dee, actress.

RUCHAMA   Hebrew: "compassion."

RUDY   English: "little Rudolph (fame wolf)." **Rudee, Rudi, Rudie.**

RUFARO   Zimbabwe. Shona: "happiness."

RUKIYA   Swahili: "she rises up."

RUQAYYA   Arabic: "ascent, rising up." **Rukaiyah, Ruqayah, Ruqayyah.**

RUSHANE   American: Contemporary.

RUSHIA   American: Contemporary.

RUSHINDA   American: Contemporary.

RUSTINE   American: "red-haired."

RUTH   Hebrew: "companion, friend." Dr. Ruth J. Simmons, president of Smith College. Ruth Pointer, singer.

RYLEE   American: Contemporary, likely based on Riley (dweller near the rye field). **Rilee.**

SAADA   Swahili: "help."

SABAH   Arabic: "morning." **Saba.**

SABINA   Latin: "Sabine woman."

SABRA   Spanish. Latin: "Sabine woman." Arabic: "thorny cactus."

SABRINA   Celtic: Of uncertain meaning. The name is borne in Celtic mythology by a daughter of the Welsh king Locrine. The name of the river Severn is said to have evolved from the name Sabrina.

SABRIYYA   Arabic: "patience." **Sabriyyah.**

SADE   Nigeria. Yoruba: Short form of Folashade (honor bestows a crown). Popularized by singer Sade.

SADELLE   American. Hebrew: "little princess."

SADIE   American. Hebrew: "princess." Sadie originated as a pet form of Sarah. **Saidie, Sady.** Sadie Tanner Mossell Alexander, first Black to receive a doctorate in economics and first Black to practice law in Pennsylvania.

SADIKA   Arabic: "truthful, faithful." **Sadeeka, Sadeekah, Sadikah, Sadiqa, Sadiqah.**

SADIRA   Arabic: "an ostrich returning from water." Hebrew: "organized."

SADRIA   Persian: "lotus tree."

SAFIA   Swahili: "clean, pure."

SAFIYYA   Arabic: "confidante." **Safiyyah.**

SAGIRA Arabic: "short, little one." **Sagirah.**

SAHAR Arabic: "dawn, sunrise."

SAHARA Arabic: "a desert." Hebrew: "moon."

SAIDA Arabic: "lucky, happy." Swahili: "helper." **Saidah.**

SAKINA Hindi: "a friend."

SALAMA Swahili: "peace."

SALETHIA American: Contemporary.

SALIHA Arabic: "virtuous, correct." **Salihah.**

SALINA Greek: "salty." American: Variant spelling of Selena (the moon).

SALMA Arabic: "safe, healthy." **Salmah.**

SALOME Hebrew: "peace." In the Bible, Salome was the daughter of Herodias. Her dancing led Herod to grant her request: the head of John the Baptist.

SALOMEA Spanish. Hebrew: "peace." **Saloma, Salomé.**

SALONA American: Contemporary, possibly influenced by *salon* (parlor, gallery, room).

SALONI Hindi: "beautiful."

SALONIKA American: Possibly borrowed from the gulf and seaport of the same name in Greece.

SAMANTHA American: A nineteenth-century feminine form of Samuel (name of God). Aramaic: "the listener." **Samanthe. Sam, Sammi, Sammie.**

SAMARA Hebrew: "a guardian, a protector; from Samaria." **Sam, Sami, Sammi.**

SAMIEL American: Contemporary.

SAMIR Arabic: "a companion in evening conversations."

SAMIRA Arabic: "a companion in evening conversations." **Sameera, Sameerah, Samirah.**

SAMISHA American: Contemporary. **Sameesha, Sameeshah, Samishah.**

SAMONE American: Contemporary variant of Simone (heard).

SAMYA Arabic: "elevated." **Samia, Samiah, Samiya, Samiyah.**

SANA Arabic: "to gaze upon, to look at." **Sanna.**

SANDRA Greek: A short form of Cassandra and Alexandra (defender of mankind). **Sandrah, Saundra, Saundrah. Sandi, Sandie, Sandy.**

SANDREEA American: Contemporary.

SANIYYA Arabic: "radiant, brillant."

SANTI Italian. "little saint."

SANURA Swahili: "kittenlike."

SAPHIRA Hebrew: "the sapphire gemstone."

SAPPHIRE English: "the sapphire gemstone."

SARAH Hebrew: "princess." **Sara, Sera, Serah. Sadie, Sally, Sarie.**

SARAN Guinea: "joy."

SARANI American: Contemporary.

SAREE Arabic: "noble, distinguished."

SARICE Hebrew: "princess."

SARIKA Hindi: "a thrush, a kind of bird."

SARINA American: Variant of Serena (calm, serene).

SARISSA American: Contemporary.

SARITA Spanish: "little Sara (princess)." Hindi: "river."

SARJANA Hindi: "creation."

SARLA Hindi: "honest."

SARONDA American: Contemporary. **Sarondah.**

SARONNA American: Contemporary.

SASHA Russian. Greek: "helper or defender of mankind." Originated as a pet form of Aleksandra.

SASHEEN American: Contemporary.

SASONA Hebrew: "bliss, joy."

SAUDA Swahili: "dark-complexioned, black."

SAUDIA Arabic: "dark-complexioned, black."

SAUNDRA Scottish. Greek: "defender of mankind." Saundra Quarterman, actress.

SAVANNAH Spanish: "a savannah, a treeless plain." **Savanna, Sevannah.**

SAVASIA American: Contemporary. **Savasseah, Savassia.**

SAWNDRA American: Contemporary. **Sawndrah.**

SCHAWANNAH American: Contemporary.

SEBREENIKA American: Contemporary.

SEDALIA American: Contemporary.

SEDRA American: Contemporary. **Sedrah.**

SEKAI Zimbabwean. Shona: "laughter."

SEKELAGA Tanzanian. Nyakyusa: "rejoice."

SELENE Greek: "the moon, moonlight." **Selena, Selina.**

SELETHA American: Contemporary.

SELIMA Hebrew: "peaceful." **Selimah.**

SELMA Arabic: "secure." Celtic: "fair one."

SEMEICHA Hebrew: "happy."

SENAIDA Spanish. Greek: "pertaining to Zeus."

SENIA American: Contemporary.

SENORA Spanish. Italian: "young lady."

SENOVIA Spanish. Latin: "pertaining to Zeus."

SERENA Latin: "calm, peaceful, serene."

SERETHA American: Contemporary.

SERWA Ghana. Ewe: "noble woman."

SESSION American: "meeting, assembly."

SEVATHEDA American: Contemporary.

SHAANANA Hebrew: "tranquil, peaceful."

SHABONNAH American: Contemporary.

SHADEL American: Contemporary.

SHADIE American: Contemporary, probably influenced by the word shady.

SHADIYA Arabic: "singer." **Shadya.**

SHADOWNA American: Contemporary.

SHAELYN American: Contemporary.

SHAENA American. Yiddish: "beautiful."

SHAFIQA Arabic: "sympathetic." **Shafeeka, Shafeekah, Shafeka, Shafekah, Shafiqah.**

SHAHAR Arabic: "the moon."

SHAILA Hindi: "a small mountain."

SHAILESHA Hindi: "king of the mountain."

SHAINA Yiddish: "beautiful." **Shayna.**

SHAKEISHA American: Contemporary. **Shakeesha, Shakisha, Shakysha.**

SHAKIETHA American: Contemporary. **Shakeetha, Shakeitha, Shakytha.**

SHAKILA Hindi: "beautiful."

SHAKIYA American. Variant of Zakiya (intelligent) or Zakiyya (pure, righteous).

SHAKONDA American: Contemporary.

SHALA American: Contemporary.

SHALAINE American: Contemporary, based on Elaine (light). **Shalaene, Shalane, Shalayne.**

SHALALA American: Contemporary.

SHALANDA American: Contemporary.

SHALEEKA American: Contemporary. **Shaleekah, Shalika, Shalikah.**

SHALENE American: Contemporary.

SHALETA American: Contemporary.

SHALIKA Hindi: "bird."

SHALISA Hebrew: Borrowed from a place-name. American: Contemporary, based on Lisa (God is my oath). **Shaleesa, Shaleisa, Shalisah, Shalysa, Shalysah.**

SHALONDA American: Contemporary. **Shalondah.**

SHALVIYA Hebrew: "the peace of God." **Shalvi.**

SHAMA Hindi: "candle, flame."

SHAMAHNEEA American: Contemporary. **Shamahnia.**

SHAMARRA American: Contemporary. **Shamara, Shamarah, Shamarrah.**

SHAMBALA American: Contemporary.

SHAMEEKA American: Contemporary. **Shameekah, Shameka, Shamekah, Shamika, Shamikah, Shamyka, Shamykah.**

SHAMEENA Hindi: "beautiful."

SHAMEESHA American: Contemporary. **Shameeshah, Shamisha, Shamishah, Shamysha.**

SHAMEETA American: Contemporary. **Shameetah, Shamita, Shamitah, Shamyta.**

SHAMEILLE American: Contemporary.

SHAMFA Swahili: "sunshine."

SHAMIMA American: Contemporary. **Shameema.**

SHAMIRA Hebrew: "defender." **Shamirah.**

SHAMONISE American: Contemporary. **Shamoneece, Shamoneese.**

SHAMS Arabic: "the sun."

SHAN Welsh. Hebrew: "God is gracious." **Shanee.**

SHANAY American: Contemporary. **Shanae, Shanai, Shanaye.**

SHANAYNAH American: Contemporary. **Shanayna.**

SHANDA American: Contemporary.

SHANDELLE American. French: "candle." **Shandel, Shandell, Shandella. Shan, Shani.**

SHANDRA American: Contemporary variant of Sandra (defender of mankind). **Shandrah.**

SHANEE American: Contemporary.

SHANEEZA American: Contemporary.

SHANELLE American: Contemporary, modeled after the French surname Chanel (channel, irrigation ditch).

SHANGALEZA American: Contemporary.

SHANGELA American: Blending of Shan (God is gracious) and Angela (angel). **Shangella. Shan.**

SHANI Swahili: "wonderful, marvelous."

SHANIMA American: Contemporary. **Shanyma.**

SHANINE American: Contemporary. **Shaneen, Shaneene, Shanyne, Sheneen, Shenine, Shenyne, Shineen, Shineene, Shinine, Shinyne.**

SHANIQUA American: Contemporary. **Shaneekqua, Shaneekwa, Shaneekwah, Shaneequa, Shanykqua, Shanykwa, Shanykwah.**

SHANIQUE American: Contemporary. **Shaneek, Shaneeka, Shaneekah, Shaneeke, Shaneeque, Shanika, Shanikah, Shanike, Shannyke, Shanyke, Shanyque.**

SHANIS American: Contemporary, possibly modeled after Janis (God is gracious).

SHANISE American: Contemporary, possibly based on Denise (of Dionysus). **Shaneece, Shaneese, Shanice, Shaniece, Shanyse.**

SHANIYA American: Contemporary. **Shaneea, Shaneeah, Shaniyah.**

SHANNAH Hebrew: "lily; rose." **Shanna.**

SHANNON Irish: "old, wise." **Shannan.**

SHANTA Hindi: "quiet, calm, peaceful."

SHANTAL American: Contemporary, influenced by the French Chantal (boulder, stone). **Shahntahl, Shantaul, Shantell, Shauntal.**

SHANTAY American: Contemporary. **Shantae, Shantaye.**

SHANTELLA American: Contemporary.

SHANTICIA American: Contemporary.

SHANTISA American: Contemporary.

SHANYGNE American: Fanciful spelling of Shanine.

SHARAI Hebrew: "princess."

SHARANEE Hindi: "protector."

SHAREE American: Contemporary, based on the name Sherry.

SHAREESE American: Variant of Cerise (cherry, cherry-flavored). **Shareece, Sharhyse, Sharise.**

SHARIFA Arabic: "noble." **Shareefa, Shareefah, Sharifah, Sharufa, Sherifa, Sherifah.**

SHARLA American: Contemporary, probably modeled after Darla. **Charla.**

SHARLEESA American: Contemporary. **Sharleesah, Sharlisa, Sharlysa.**

SHARLINDA American: Contemporary, based on Linda (beautiful).

SHARLON American: Contemporary.

SHARMA American: Contemporary.

SHARMEE American: Contemporary.

SHARMILA Hindi: "happy; modest."

SHARNA Hindi: "protection."

SHA-RON American: Contemporary.

SHARON Hebrew: "a plain, a flat area." In biblical times, Sharon was the name of a fertile coastal area of Palestine. **Sheron.** Sharon Monplaisir, Olympic fencer.

SHARONDA American: Contemporary. **ShaRhonda, Sharhonda, ShaRonda.**

SHARRA American: Contemporary.

SHARRAN American. Hebrew: From Sharon (a plain, a flat area). **ShaRon, Sharona, Sharron, Sharrona, Sheron, Sherron, Sheryn.**

SHARREE American: Contemporary, likely influenced by Sherry (a Spanish wine; darling).

SHARRELL American: Contemporary, possibly based on Cheryl. **ShaRell, Sherelle, Sherrelle.**

SHARRIS American: Contemporary.

SHARRISSA American: Contemporary. **Sharisa, Sharissa, Sharrisa.**

SHARVELLE American: Contemporary.

SHARYL American: Reworking of the name Cheryl.

SHARYN American. Hebrew: "a plain, a flat area." **Sheryn.**

SHASHAWNEE American: Contemporary, possibly influenced by the Native American Shawnee (southern people) or the Hebrew Shoshannah (lily, rose).

SHASTA Native American: Meaning uncertain. Shasta is borrowed from the name of a mountain in northern California.

SHAUMITA American: Contemporary.

SHAUNA Irish. Hebrew: "God is gracious." Shauna is an Irish form of Jane.

SHAUNDA American: Contemporary, based on Shauna (God is gracious). **Shaundah, Shawnda, Shawndah, Shonda, Shondah, Shonnda, Shonndah.**

SHAUNDRA American: Contemporary, modeled after Saundra (mankind) and Shauna (God is gracious).

SHAUNITA American: Contemporary, based on Shaun (God is gracious).

SHAUNTA American: Contemporary.

SHAUNTAVIA American: Probably a blending of Shaun (God is gracious) and Octavia (eight).

SHAVANNA American: Contemporary, influenced by Savanna (a treeless plain).

SHAVEENA American: Contemporary.

SHAVONDA American: Contemporary.

SHAVONNA American: Contemporary. **Shavonne.**

SHAWANDELE American: Contemporary.

SHAWANDELIA American: Contemporary.

SHAWANIKA American: Contemporary. **Shawaneeka, Shawaneekah, Shawanikah.**

SHAWANNAH American: Contemporary. **Shawana, Shawanah, Shawanna.**

SHAWNA American. Irish. Hebrew: "God is gracious." **Shawn, Shawnah, Shonna, Shonnah.**

SHAWNEQUA American: Contemporary, based on the name Shawn (God is gracious). **Shawneekwa, Shawnekwa.**

SHAWNETTA American: Contemporary, based on the name Shawn (God is gracious).

SHAWN-NEE American: Contemporary, possibly a variation of the Native American Shawnee (southern people) or the Irish Shawn (God is gracious).

SHAWNTELLE American: Contemporary, based on Shawn (God is gracious) and Chantelle (boulder, stone).

SHAYLA American: Feminine form of Shay (seizing by the heel). **Shaela, Sheyla.**

SHAYLE American: Contemporary. **Shaile.**

SHAYLEEN American: Feminine form of Shay (seizing by the heel). **Shaeleen, Shaeline, Shayline, Sheyleen, Sheyline.**

SHAYNA Yiddish: "beautiful." **Shaina.**

SHAYNE American. Irish. Hebrew: "God is gracious."

SHEELA Hindi: "kind."

SHEENA Scottish. Hebrew: "God is gracious." **Sheenah.**

SHEHAN Hebrew: "petition."

SHEILA Irish. Latin: "blind." **Sheela, Sheelah, Sheilah, Shela.**

SHEKEDA Hebrew: "almond tree." **Shekedia.**

SHELAE American: Contemporary. **Shelay.**

SHELAGH American: Contemporary spelling of Sheila (blind). **Sheilah, Shiela, Shielah.**

SHELIA American: Contemporary. Hebrew: "the Lord is mine." **Sheliya.**

SHELITA American: Contemporary.

SHELITHA American: Contemporary.

SHELLENE American: Contemporary. **Shelleen, Shelline.**

SHELONDA American: Contemporary.

SHENDALE American: Contemporary.

SHERA American: Contemporary.

SHERESALLE American: Contemporary.

SHERIAN American: Contemporary. Sherian Grace Cadoria, highest ranking Black woman in the U.S. armed forces, as of 1990.

SHERIDAN Irish: "peaceful."

SHERINA American: Contemporary, possibly influenced by Serena (calm, serene).

SHERRHEA American: Contemporary. **Sherrea, Sherreah.**

SHERRIL American: Contemporary, probably modeled after Cheryl.

SHERRITTA American: Contemporary. **Sherrita, Sheritta, Sherrita.**

SHERRY Spanish: "Spanish wine from Jeres." French: "darling." **Sheree, Sherree, Sherrie.**

SHIANN American: Contemporary, phonetic spelling of Cheyenne (unintelligible speakers). **Shianne, Shyann, Shyanne.**

SHIFRAH Hebrew: "beautiful." **Schifra, Schifrah, Shifra.**

SHIKEISHA American: Contemporary.

SHILANDRA American: Contemporary.

SHIMINEGE Nigeria. Tiv: "to see the future."

SHINELL American: Contemporary, possibly influenced by the French Surname Chanel (canal, channel).

SHIQUINTA American: Contemporary.

SHIRAH Hebrew: "a song." **Shira.**

SHIREE American: Likely a contemporary spelling of Sherry.

SHIRELL American: Variation on the name Cheryl.

SHIRLEENA American: Contemporary, based on Shirley (bright meadow).

SHIRLEY English: "bright meadow." **Shirlee, Shirlie.** Shirley Chisholm, first Black congresswoman. Shirley Graham, biographer. Shirley Bassey, singer. Shirley Verrett, mezzo-soprano.

SHIRLIETTA American: Contemporary, based on Shirley (bright meadow).

SHONA Hindi: "crimson." African: A Bantu language spoken by the Mashona people.

SHONDALETTE American: Contemporary. **Shaundalette, Shawndalette. Shaun, Shaunda, Shawn, Shawnda, Shon, Shonda.**

SHONI American: Contemporary. **Shonee.**

SHO QWA American: Contemporary.

SHOREEN American: Contemporary.

SHRALEEKA American: Contemporary.

SHREEANN American: Contemporary.

SHREELA Hindu: "beautiful, wealthy."

SHREELAE American: Contemporary. **Shreelay.**

SHREELANA American: Contemporary.

SHUALA Hebrew: "fox."

SHUKUMA Swahili: "grateful."

SHUKURA Swahili: "be grateful."

SHULAMMITE American: Contemporary, based on Shulamite, an epithet meaning "princess" that is applied to the maiden in the Song of Solomon.

SHUMANA American: Contemporary.

SHUVANA American: Contemporary.

SHUWANI American: Contemporary.

SHWANNAH American: Contemporary.

SHYLA　Hindi: Another name for the goddess Parvati. American: Contemporary. **Shila, Shilah**.

SHYLONDA　American: Contemporary.

SICILY　American: Borrowed from the name of the Italian island.

SIDNEY　English. French: "follower of Saint Denis; dweller by the wide, wet land." **Sydney**.

SIDRA　American. Latin: "starlike."

SIEDAH　American: Contemporary, perhaps influenced by the Arabic Saida (lucky) or Sayyid (master). Siedah Garrett, singer and songwriter.

SIERRA　Spanish: "mountain." **Siearra**.

SIGELE　Malawi. Ngoni: "left."

SILVIA　Latin: "of the woods." **Sylvia**. Sylvia Rhone, chairman and CEO of Elektra Entertainment Group.

SIMA　Aramaic: "treasure."

SIMONA　Spanish. Hebrew: "heard."

SIMONE　French. Hebrew: "heard."

SINETTA　American: Contemporary.

SINIKKA　American: Contemporary.

SINTEAL　American: Contemporary.

SIONA　Hebrew: "peak, height." **Sione**.

SIRRAH　American: Contemporary variant of Sarah (princess).

SISI　Ghana. Fante: "born on a Sunday."

SIVANA　Hebrew: From Sivan, the ninth month of the Jewish calendar, corresponding to May-June.

SKY　American: "the sky." **Skye**.

SKYLA　American: Elaboration of Sky (the sky).

SMYELLE　American: Contemporary.

SNOWENA　American: Contemporary, perhaps modeled after Rowena (famous friend; joyful fame).

SOLANA　Spanish: A combination of Sol (sun) and Ana (grace, mercy).

SOLANGE　French: "solitary, alone."

SOLEDAD　Spanish: "solitude." **Soledada**.

SOMAYA　Hindu: "gentle, serene."

SOMONA　Spanish. Hebrew: "heard."

SONYA　Russian. Greek: "wisdom, skill." **Sonia, Sonja**. Sonia Sanchez, poet and playwright.

SOPHIA　Greek: "wisdom, skill." **Sofia**.

SOREKA　Hebrew: "vine."

SOWANDE　Nigeria. Yoruba: "the magician sought me out."

SPECINA　American: Contemporary.

STACY　Irish. Russian: "resurrection." **Stacey**. Stacy Dash, actress.

STAR　American: "a star." **Starr**.

STARLENE　American: Contemporary elaboration of Star (a star). **Starleen, Starleene, Starrleen**.

STEPHANIE French. Greek: "a crown, a garland." **Stefanee, Steffanee, Steffanie, Stephanee, Stephany. Steffi, Stevie.**

STEVIE American. Greek: "a crown, a garland." **Steevee, Steevi, Steevie, Stevi.**

SUBIRA Swahili: "patience is rewarded."

SUEANGELA American: A blending of Sue (lily; rose) and Angela (angel).

SUHAYLA Arabic: "Canopus." Canopus is the second-brightest star in the southern skies. **Suhaila, Suhailah, Suhaylah.**

SUMA Tanzania. Nyakyusa: "ask."

SUMONA American: Contemporary.

SUNAYANA Hindi: "beautiful eyes."

SUNNIVA Scandinavian. English: "a gift of the sun."

SUNNY English: "shining; happy, bright personality."

SURAYYA Arabic: "the Pleiades." The Pleiades are stars in the constellation Taurus. The name Surayya is a variant of Thurayya. **Surayyah.**

SUSAN English. Hebrew: "lily; rose." **Suzan. Sue, Susie, Suzie.** Susan L. Taylor, editor-in-chief of *Essence* magazine.

SUSANITA American: "little Susan (lily; rose)." **Sue, Susie.**

SUZETTE French. Hebrew: "lily; rose." **Susette. Sue, Susie, Suzie.**

SWANGEELA American: Contemporary.

SYMONE French. Hebrew: "heard." **Simone.**

SYNDY American: Contemporary form of Cindy (from Kynthos; light).

SYNETTE American: Contemporary.

SYREETA American: Contemporary.

TABIA Swahili: "talents."

TABITHA Aramaic: "gazelle." **Tab, Tabbi, Tabbie, Tabby.**

TABRA American: Contemporary, possibly a blending of Tabitha (gazelle) and Debra (a bee).

TACY English. Latin: "silent."

TADARA American: Contemporary.

TAEA American: Contemporary. **Taeya.**

TAELER American: Variant of Taylor (a tailor). **Tailer, Tayler.**

TAFUI Togo. Mina: "glory to God; honoring God."

TAHANA American: Contemporary.

TAHANI American: Contemporary. Arabic: "congratulations."

TAHIRA Arabic: "chaste, pure." **Tahirah.**

TAHIYYA Arabic: "greetings." **Tahiyyah.**

TAHNDA American: Contemporary.

TAHSIN Arabic: "good deed."

TAISHA American: Contemporary, based on Aisha (life). **Tyaisha, Tyeesha.**

TAIWO Nigeria. Yoruba: "firstborn of twins."

TAKIMRA American: Contemporary.

TAKIYA Arabic: "righteous."

TALEAH   American: Contemporary.

TALEENA   American: Contemporary.

TALIA   Spanish. Latin: "natal day."

TALIBA   Arabic: "seeker of knowledge." **Talibah.**

TALISA   American: Contemporary, based on Lisa (God is my oath). **TaLisa, Taleesa, TeLisa, Telisa.**

TALITHA   Aramaic: "maiden, child." **Taletha.**

TALLACE   American: Contemporary, perhaps influenced by Wallace (a Welshman) or a phonetic spelling of the Spanish Tales (she comes forth in splendor). **Tallase.**

TALLULA   Native American. Choctaw: "leaping water, laughing water." **Talula, Talulah, Talulla, Talullah. Tally.**

TALMA   Aramaic: "hill, mound, furrow."

TALSIA   American: Contemporary.

TALYA   Hebrew: "dew." Aramaic: "lamb."

TALYNN   American: Contemporary, based on Lynn (lake). **Talin, Talinn, Talyn, Talynne.**

TAMANI   American: Contemporary.

TAMANNA   Hindi: "desire."

TAMAR   Hebrew: "date palm, a palm tree."

TAMARA   English. Russian. Hebrew: "date palm, a palm tree." **Tamarah, Tamera, Tammara, Tammarah, Tammera, Tamra, Tamrah, Tami, Tammi, Tammie, Tammy.**

TAMARACK   American. Native American: "the larch tree."

TAMARICK   American: Contemporary, possibly influenced by *tamarack* (a larch tree). **Tamrick. Tami, Tammi, Tammy.**

TAMASA   Hindi: A river name.

TAMASHA   Arabic: "a walking-around."

TAMATHA   Arabic: "a walking-around." **Tamath.**

TAMBALA   African: "rooster." In Malawi, tambala is a monetary unit.

TAMBI   American: Contemporary.

TAMBRA   American: Contemporary, possibly a blending of Tamara (date palm) and Debra (a bee). **Tami, Tammi, Tammy.**

TAMEE   American: Contemporary, based on pet forms of Tamara (date palm, a palm tree) or other names beginning with the element *Tam-*.

TAMELA   American: Contemporary, modeled after Pamela.

TAMIKA   American: Contemporary. **Tamecka, Tameeka, Tameekah, Tammeeka, Tammika. Tami, Tammi, Tammy.**

TAMIKO   Japanese: "people child."

TAMILENE   American: Contemporary.

TAMIMA   American: Contemporary, influenced by Jemima (dove).

TAMISHA   American: Contemporary. **Tameesha, Tameeshah, Tamishah, Tammisha, Tamysha, Tamyshah. Tami, Tammi, Tammy.**

TAMLA   American: Contemporary.

TAMRIKA   American: Contemporary, based on Tamara (a date palm) or Tamarick. **Tammrika, Tamreeka. Tami, Tammi, Tammy.**

TAMYRA American: Variant of Tamara (date palm, a palm tree). **Tami, Tammi, Tammy, Tamy.**

TAMZIE American: Contemporary.

TANA American: "tan." African: After an Ethiopian lake that is the source of the Blue Nile.

TANANA American: Contemporary, possibly after the Tanana River in eastern Alaska.

TANANI American: Contemporary.

TANARIVE American: Possibly after Tananarive, the former name of Antananarivo, the capital of Madagascar. Tanarive Due, author.

T'ANAY American: Contemporary. **Tanae, Tanay, Tanée, Tanee, Tenae, Tenay, Tenée, Tenee.**

TANAYA Hindi: "daughter."

TANDRA American: Contemporary, modeled after Sandra (helper of mankind). Madagascar: "mark of beauty, a mole."

T'ANGELA American: Contemporary, based on Angela (angel). **Tangela.**

TANIKA Hindi: "rope."

TANIQUA American: Contemporary. **Taneekwa, Taneequa, Tanikwa.**

TANIQUE American: Contemporary. **Taneek, Taneeke, Tanik, Tanyke, Tanyque.**

TANISHA American: Contemporary. Nigeria. Hausa: "born on Monday." **Ta-**

neesha, Taneeshah, Teneesha, Tenisha, Tenishah.**

TANNISHTHA Hindi: "dedicated."

TANYA Russian: A pet form of Tatiana, which is of uncertain meaning. **Tania.** Tanya Blount, singer.

TANYIN American: Contemporary.

TAPATHA American: Contemporary.

TAQIYYA Arabic: "pious, God-fearing." **Takiya, Takiyah, Takiyya, Takiyyah, Taqiyyah.**

TAQUANNA American: Contemporary. **Takwanna.**

TARA Irish: "hill." Hindi: "star, destiny."

TARAL Hindi: "flowing."

TARALITA Hindu: "undulating."

TARANA Hindi: "one who uplifts." Nigeria. Hausa: "born during the day."

TARANI Hindi: "a ray of light."

TARAS American: Contemporary.

TAREN American: Contemporary, perhaps based on Tara (hill) or Karen (pure, unsullied). **Taran, Tarin, Taryn.**

TARI American: Variant of Terry.

TARIKA American: Contemporary.

TARINNE American: Contemporary, influenced by Corrine (maiden). **Tarinn, Tarrinn, Tarrynn.**

TARJA American: Contemporary.

TARJANI Hindi: "finger."

TARLA Hindi: "brilliant."

TARNA   American: Contemporary.

TASBIN   American: Contemporary.

TASHA   Russian. Latin: "natal day, Christmas." Originated as a pet form of Natalia.

TASHANEE   American: Contemporary. **Tashani, Tashany, Teshanee, Teshani, Teshany.**

TASHAWNA   American: A contemporary coinage, based on the name Shawn (God is gracious). **Tashauna, Tashaunah, Tashawnah, Tashonna, Tashonnah, Teshauna,   Teshawna,   Teshawnah, Teshonna, Tishauna, Tishawna, Tishawnah, Tishonna, Tishonnah.**

TASHINA   American: Contemporary. **TaSheena, Tasheena, TaShyna, Tesheena.**

TASIA   American: Contemporary variant of Tasha (natal day, Christmas). **Tacia, Tahcia.**

TATIANA   Russian: Unknown meaning. **Tatyana.** Tatyana M. Ali, actress.

TAUNYA   American: Contemporary, most likely based on Tanya and Tawnya. **Taunyah, Tawnya, Tawnyah.**

TAUREA   Latin: "a bull's-hide whip."

TAURINA   Latin: "aficionado of bulls."

TAVANNA   American: Contemporary, most likely based on the name Savanna (a treeless plain). **Tavannah.**

TAWANNA   American: Contemporary.

TAWIAH   Ghana. Ga: "first child born after twins." **Tawia.**

TAWNIA   American: Contemporary, most likely influenced by Tawny (soft brownish yellow) and Tonya (meaning uncertain).

TAWNY   English: "tawny, a soft brownish yellow." **Tauney, Tauny, Tawney.**

TAWSHA   American: Variant of Tasha (natal day, Christmas). **Tawshah.**

TAYAUNA   American: Contemporary.

TAYLAN   English: Contemporary.

TAYLOR   English. French: "a tailor."

TAYNA   American: Contemporary.

TCHIA   American: Contemporary.

TEA   American: Possibly a variant of Tia (aunt; princess). **Teah.**

TEAKA   American: "teak, a hard golden brown wood."

TEAL   English: "blue-green; a duck."

TECHLA   American. Greek: "divine fame." **Tekhla, Tekkla.**

TEEKA   American: Contemporary.

TEESHA   American: Contemporary, possibly based on Ticia, a short form of names such as Leticia. **Teisha, Tiesha, Tiisha, Tysha.**

TEHIA   Hebrew: "birth, resurrection." **Techiya.**

TELEZA   Malawi. Ngoni: "slippery."

TEMANA   Hebrew: "the south, the left side." **Temania.**

TEMECCA   American: Contemporary. **Temeca.**

TEMILYA American: Contemporary.

TEMPEST English: "stormy." **Tempestt**. Tempestt Bledsoe, actress.

TENAYA American: Contemporary. **Tenayah**.

TENÉ American: Contemporary, influenced by René (rebirth). **Tenae, Tenay, Tene, Tennae**.

TENEAL American: Contemporary.

TENESHA American: Contemporary.

TEREA American: Contemporary.

TEREMIAH American: Contemporary, based on Jeremiah (God will uplift). **Teremia, Teremya, Teremyah. Teri**.

TERIAH Hebrew: "new, fresh." **Taria, Tariah, Teria**.

TERRA Latin: "earth."

TERRI English: Originating as a short form of Teresa (harvester). **Teri, Terie, Terree, Terrie**. Teri Lynn Carrington, jazz drummer.

TESSORA American: Contemporary.

TEXANA American: Contemporary, after the southern state of Texas.

THALIA Greek: "joyful."

THANA Arabic: "commendation."

THANDIWE South Africa. Xhosa: "loving one."

THEA English. Greek: "God's gift." Originated as a shortened form of Theodora.

THEBE Greek: Meaning unknown. In Greek mythology, Thebe was a nymph loved by the river god Asopus.

THEKLA Greek: "divine fame." **Tecla, Tekla, Thecla**.

THELIDRIA American: Contemporary.

THELMA English: A nineteenth-century coinage of author Marie Corelli.

THELMARIE American: Blending of the names Thelma and Marie (sea of bitterness).

THEMA Ghana. Akan: "queen."

THEMBA South Africa. Zulu: "trusted."

THEORA American: A contracted form of Theodora (God's gift).

THERETHA American: Contemporary.

THREETHA American: Contemporary.

THURAYYA Arabic: "the Pleiades." The Pleiades are stars in the constellation Taurus. **Thuraia, Thurayyah**.

THYRA Greek: "shield-bearer."

TIA Spanish: "aunt." Greek: "princess."

TIANI American: Contemporary. **Tianee, Tianie, Tiannee, Tiani, Tiannie**.

TIANNA American: Contemporary, modeled after Dianna (divine). **Tiannah**.

TIARA American: "a crown."

TICHERA American: Contemporary.

TICHINA American: Contemporary. **Tisheena, Tishinah, T'Sheena**. Tichina Arnold, actress.

TIERRA American: Contemporary, possibly influenced by Sierra (a saw).

TIFFANY English. French: "Epiphany, manifestation of God." **Tiffaney, Tiffani, Tiffanie, Tiffenii, Tiffini, Tyfani, Tyfanni, Tyfanny.**

TIMAHNA American: Contemporary.

TIMILA Hindi: A musical instrument.

TIMONAE American: Contemporary. **Timonae, Timanee, Timony.**

TIMONAH Greek: "honored."

TINA Greek: "follower of Christ." A short form of Christine. **Teena, Teenah, Tinah.** Tina Turner, actress and singer. Tina McElroy Ansa, novelist. Tina Allen, sculptor.

TIONNE American: Contemporary, possibly modeled after Dionne (divine). Tionne Watkins, singer with the group TLC.

TIPPANY American: Contemporary, possibly influenced by Tiffany (epiphany).

TIRA Hebrew: "camp, encampment." **Tirah.**

TIRANA American: Contemporary. Also, the name of the capital of Albania.

TIRZAH Hebrew: "pleasantness." In the Bible, Tirzah was the youngest of Zelophehad's five daughters. **Thirza, Thirzah, Tirza.**

TISA American: Contemporary, modeled after Lisa. Swahili: "ninth child."

TISHA American: Originally a short form of names such as Latisha. **Ticha.** Tisha Campbell, actress.

TISHARA American: Contemporary.

TISHRA American: Contemporary.

TISHREEA American: Contemporary.

TIVIAN American: Contemporary, probably based on Vivian (alive).

T'NIA American: Contemporary. **T'Nea, T'Neah.**

TOBIANA Spanish. Hebrew: "the goodness of God."

TOIYA Spanish. Greek: "victory."

TOMASINA English. Aramaic: "a twin." **Tomasena, Tomasine. Tommi.**

TOMEKA American: Contemporary.

TOMIKO Japanese: "contented child."

TONDA American: Contemporary.

TONI English: Originating as a short form of Antonia (priceless, of inestimable worth). **Tonee, Tonie.** Toni Braxton, singer. Toni Morrison, Pulitzer Prize–winning author.

TONIA English. Latin: "priceless, of inestimable worth." **Toni, Tonye.**

TONIKA American: Contemporary.

TONNIE American: Contemporary, possibly a variant of Tawny (golden brown) or modeled after Ronnie (judgment power).

TONYA American. Russian: From Tanya, a shortened form of Tatiana, which is of uncertain meaning. **Tonyah.** Tonya Lee Williams, actress.

TORIA Latin: A shortened form of Victoria (victory). **Tori, Torie.**

TORYN American: Contemporary.

TOVA Swedish: "beautiful Thor." **Tove.**

TOWANDA Native American. Delaware: "where we bury the dead."

TOYYA American. Spanish. Greek: "victory."

TRACY English. French: "place of Thracius." Tracy is also a pet form of Teresa (harvester). **Tracee, Tracey.** Tracy Chapman, singer-songwriter.

TRAVISTINE American: Contemporary.

TREASURE American: "hidden riches, wealth."

TREKA American: Contemporary.

TRELACE American: Contemporary, possibly influenced by *trellis* (a support for climbing plants).

TREMAINE English: Celtic: "house of the stones." **Tramaine, Tramayne, Tremain, Tremayn, Tremayne.** Tramaine Hawkins, gospel singer.

TREMIKA American: Contemporary.

TRENA Spanish: "third child." **Trenia.**

TRENELLE American: Contemporary. **Trenell, Trennel, Trennell, Trennelle.**

TRENESSA American: Contemporary. **Trenesa, Trennesa.**

TRENIKAH American: Contemporary. **Trenika, Trenyka, Trenykah.**

TRENISE American: Contemporary, probably influenced by Denise (a follower of the god Dionysus). **Treneese, Trenyse.**

TRENITA Spanish. Latin: "little third child." **Treneta.**

TRESSEA American: Contemporary. **Tressia, Tresea.**

TREVIA Spanish: Borrowed from a type of flowering plant.

TREYLEANNA American: Contemporary, blending of the male name Trey and Leanna. **Treylanna.**

TRICIA English: A short form of Patricia (noble, aristocrat). **Trisha. Trish.**

TRIKELLE American: Contemporary.

TRINADA Latin: "the Trinity; three-in-one."

TRINDI American: Contemporary. **Trindee, Trindie, Trindy.**

TRIOLA American: Contemporary.

TRISTA Latin: "sorrowful."

TROYIA American: Contemporary.

TSIVYA Spanish. Hebrew: "gazelle."

TULANI American: Contemporary.

TULIKA Hindi: "a painter's brush."

TUNISIA African: After the North African country of the same name.

TURKESSA American: Contemporary.

TUULA American: Contemporary.

TVETTE American: Contemporary, influenced by Yvette (little archer).

TWYLA English: "double-threaded." **Twila, Twilah.**

TYANA   American: A blending of the male name Ty and Ana (grace, mercy) or possibly a contemporary name modeled after Dyana (divine). Also, Tyana is an Italian town in the Taurus Mountains. **Tyanna, TyeAnna.**

TYCY   American: Contemporary.

TYEESHA   American: Contemporary. **Tiisha, Tyaisha, Tyiisha.**

TYLEISHA   American: A blending of the male name Ty and Leisha. **Tyleesha, Tylicia, Tylisha.**

TYLYNN   American: Contemporary. **Tylin, Ty Linn, Tylinn, Ty Lyn, Tylyn, Ty Lynne, Tylynne.**

TYNISA   American: Contemporary, perhaps influenced by Tunisia. **Tynisha, Tynisia.**

TYRA   Scandinavian: "of Tyr (the ancient supreme Indo-European god)." Tyra Banks, cover girl.

TYVETTE   American: A blending of the male name Ty and Yvette (little Yves).

TYWANKI   American: Contemporary.

TZEVIYA   Hebrew: "gazelle." **Tzevia.**

UBIRDIA   American: Contemporary.

UCHENNA   Nigeria. Ibo: "will of God."

ULANDRA   American: Contemporary, influenced by Yolanda (violet).

ULIINA   American: Contemporary.

ULIMA   Arabic: "wise."

ULU   Nigeria. Ibo: "second child."

UMA   Arabic: "mother." Hindu: Another name for the goddess Parvati.

UMAYMA   Arabic: "little mother."

UMIKA   Hindi: Another name for the goddess Parvati. **Umeeka, Umeekah.**

UNITH   American: Contemporary.

UNITY   English: "united, harmony."

URANIA   Latin: "the heavenly one." In classical mythology, Urania was the Muse of astronomy. **Uranie.**

URBI   Nigeria. Benin: "princess."

URENNA   Nigeria. Ibo: "father's pride."

USHA   Hindi: "dawn."

USHARA   Hebrew: "fortunate."

UWIMANA   Rwanda. Rwanda: "daughter of God."

VALENCIA   Italian. Latin: "healthy, strong."

VALERIE   French. Latin: "healthy, strong." **Valarie. Val.**

VALETTA   American: "little Val (healthy, strong).

VALICE   American: Contemporary, possibly influenced by *valise* (a small, suitcase).

VALIREE   American: Contemporary spelling of Valerie (healthy, strong). **Valeree, Valeriy, Valery. Val.**

VALKARI   American: Contemporary, possibly influenced by Valkyrie, the maidens from Norse mythology who led the souls of slain heroes to Valhalla.

VALLARI Hindi: Another name for the goddess Parvati.

VALORA English: "valor." **Valoura.**

VANDA Spanish: Variant of Wanda.

VANEDA American: Contemporary.

VANESSA English: An early eighteenth-century coinage of satirist Jonathan Swift. It is said to be a partial anagram of Esther Vanhomrigh, his intimate friend. **Vannessa, Venessa, Vennessa.** Vanessa Williams, actress and first Black woman to be crowned Miss America. Vanessa Bell Calloway, actress.

VANI Hindi: "voice; another name for the goddess Sarasvati."

VANIDA Thai: "girl."

VANIKA Hindi: "little wood."

VANNETT American: Contemporary.

VARDA Hebrew: "a rose."

VARINI Hindi: "a woman."

VARINIA American: Contemporary.

VARNETTE American: Contemporary.

VASHTI Persian: "beautiful."

VEENA Hindi: A musical instrument.

VEGA Arabic: "falling; the great one." Vega is the brightest star in the constellation Lyra.

VELDA American: Contemporary.

VELMA English. German: "resolute protector."

VELNA American: Contemporary.

VELVET English: "velvet; luxurious and soft."

VENDELLA American: A blending of the male name Van and Della.

VENÉ American: Contemporary. **Venae, Venai, Venay.**

VENETIA English: Of debated etymology. Some believe it is a Latin rendering of the Welsh Gwyneth (blessed). Others believe it is borrowed from the name of an ancient Roman province in Italy. **Venecia, Venetta, Venicia.**

VENTRAIA American: Contemporary. **Ventrea.**

VENUS Latin: "love." In Roman mythology, Venus is the goddess of love and beauty. Venus Williams, tennis star.

VENUSIA Latin: "lovely, attractive."

VERA Scandinavian. Russian: "faith." Latin: "truth."

VERALIE American: Coinage based on Vera (faith; truth) or the word *verily* (truly).

VERALYNN American: Blending of Vera (faith, truth) and Lynn (lake). **Veralyn, Veralynne.**

VERBENA Latin: "foliage, branches."

VERLEENA American: Contemporary. **Verleen.**

VERLINDA American: Contemporary, based on Linda (beautiful).

VERLISA American: Contemporary, based on Lisa (God is my oath). **Verleesa.**

VERMEESHA American: Contemporary. **Vermiisha.**

VERNA English: "dweller among the ferns; of Vernon." Verna Aardema, author.

VERNICE American. Greek: "bringer of victory."

VERNISHA American: Contemporary.

VERNSHELLA American: Contemporary.

VERONIKA Greek: "bringer of victory." **Veronica.**

VERONIQUE French. Greek: "bringer of victory."

VERSA Latin: "changing, twisting, whirling."

VERSIE American. Latin: "changing, twisting."

VESHA American: Contemporary.

VESNA Slavic: "spring."

VESTA Latin: "clothed with authority." In Roman mythology, Vesta is the goddess of the hearth.

VIANNA American: Contemporary, possibly influenced by the name Diana. **Viana, Vianah, Viannah.**

VICTORIA Latin: "victory." **Vicki, Vicky, Tori, Toria.**

VIENNA Teutonic: Meaning unknown. From the Austrian city of the same name. **Vienne.**

VIERMA American: Contemporary.

VIETTA American: Contemporary.

VIGNETTE French: "little vine."

VINAYA Hindi: "modesty."

VINETTE American: A feminine form of Vinny (conquering).

VIRENDIA American: Contemporary.

VIRGINIA Latin: "springlike; flourishing." Virginia Hamilton, author.

VITA Latin: "life."

VIVA Spanish: "life."

VIVIAN Latin: "alive." **Viviane, Viviann, Vivianne, Vyvyan. Viv, Vyv.** Dr. Vivian W. Pinn, associate director of research on women's health, National Institute of Health.

VOLANTE French: "violet."

VOLENA American: Contemporary.

VOLETA English. French: "veiled."

VONZELLA American: Contemporary.

WAGAI Ethiopia. Amharic: "the prize is mine."

WAGAYE Ethiopia. Amharic: "my price."

WAHIDA Arabic: "unique." **Waheeda, Waheedah.**

WAJIDA Arabic: "excited."

WALETTA American: Contemporary.

WALIDA Arabic: "an infant, newborn." **Waleeda, Waleedah, Walidah.**

WANETTA English: "little pale one, little wan one."

WANISHA American: Contemporary.

WANYIKA Swahili: "of the bush."

WANZA American: Contemporary, possibly a shortened form of Kwanza (first), the celebration of African culture and heritage.

WASEME Tanzania. Swahili: "let them talk."

WASHINGTONIA American: Contemporary variant of Washington (a surname and place-name). **Washingtonea, Washintonia.**

WAVALEN American: Contemporary.

WAYNINE English: "a wagonmaker."

WEIGELLIA American: Contemporary, after *weigela*, a honeysuckle plant.

WELLICA American: Contemporary.

WENDOLYN Welsh: "fair browed." **Wendolin, Wendoline, Wendolynn. Wendi, Wendy.**

WENISE American: Contemporary, modeled after Denise (of Dionysus).

WESESA Uganda. Musoga: "careless."

WESTINA English: "the western village."

WHITNEY Anglo-Saxon: "Hwita's island." Hwita is an obsolete word and name meaning "white." **Whitnee, Whitni, Whittney, Whittny, Witney, Wittney.**

WILLA English. German: "resolute protector." **Billi, Billie, Willi, Willie.**

WILLADEAN American: Blending of Willa (resolute protector) and Dean (a dean). **Willadeen, Willadine.**

WILLEEN American. German: "resolute protector." **Billi, Billie, Willi, Willie.**

WILLIAMETTE American. German: "resolute protector." **Billi, Billie, Willi, Willie.**

WILMA German: "resolute protector." Wilma Rudolph (1940–1994), Olympic gold medal winner in track.

WINIFRED English. Welsh: "blessed peace." **Winfred, Winnifred. Winni, Winnie, Winny.**

WINONA Native American: "firstborn daughter." **Wenona, Wenonah.**

WYLA American: Contemporary.

WYNELLE American. Welsh: "white, fair, blessed." **Winni, Winnie, Winny.**

WYNETTE American. Welsh: "white, fair, blessed." **Winni, Winnie, Winny.**

WYNNE Welsh: "white, fair, blessed." **Wynn.**

WYVONNE American: Contemporary, based on Yvonne (archer).

XANTHE Greek: "golden, golden yellow."

XAVIERA Spanish: "from the new house." Arabic: "bright."

XENA Greek: "hospitality." **Xenia.**

XENOBIA Greek: "of Zeus." Xenobia Bailey, crafts artist.

XETSA Ghana. Ewe: "one of twins."

YADYRA American: Contemporary. **Yadira.**

YAFA Hebrew: "beautiful."

YAKIRA Hebrew: "valuable, precious."

YAMIKA Hindi: "moonlit night."

YAMINA Arabic: "morally correct." **Yameena, Yameenah, Yaminah.**

YAMINI Hindi: "night."

YANIRA   American: Contemporary.

YASAMIN   Persian: "jasmine."

YASHWINA   Hindi: "successful."

YASMIN   Arabic: "jasmine." **Yasmeen, Yasmeena, Yasmina, Yasminah.**

YEJIDE   Nigeria. Yoruba: "the likeness of her mother."

YEMOJA   Nigeria. Yoruba: In mythology, Yemoja is a wife of Ogun (god of iron) and the goddess of the Ogun River.

YESHARA   Hebrew: "ancient."

YETUNDE   Nigeria. Yoruba: "mother has arrived." Bestowed if the grandmother died shortly before the child's birth.

YOLANDA   English: Meaning uncertain. It might be from the medieval French name Violante (violet). **Yalanda, Ylanda, Yolandah, Yolande, Yolonda.**

YOLANNA   American: Contemporary name, based on Yolanda.

YOLONDRA   American: Contemporary, based on Yolanda.

YONA   Hebrew: "dove."

YONDA   American: A shortened form of Yolanda (violet).

YONKELA   American: Contemporary.

YUMONA   American: Probably modeled after Ramona (wise protector).

YUOVENE   American: Contemporary.

YVELLE   American. French: "little archer."

YVETTE   French: "little Yves." Yves is derived from a word meaning "yew," the type of wood used in making bows and arrows.

YVONNE   French: "archer, yew."

ZADA   Arabic: "lucky, fortunate." **Zaida, Zaidah, Zayda.**

ZAFIRA   Arabic: "to succeed." **Zafirah.**

ZAHARA   Hebrew: "to shine." Swahili: "flower."

ZAHIRA   Arabic: "blossom, flower." **Zahirah.**

ZAHRA   Arabic: "blossom, flower." **Zahara, Zaharah, Zahrah, Zara.**

ZAINABU   Swahili: "beautiful."

ZAKIYA   Swahili: "intelligent." Hebrew: "pure." **Zakia.**

ZAKIYYA   Arabic: "pure, righteous." **Zakiya, Zakiyah, Zakiyyah.**

ZALIKA   Swahili: "well born, noble."

ZAN   Greek: "mankind."

ZANDRA   Greek: "mankind." **Xandra, Xandrah, Zandrah. Xandi, Xandie, Zandi, Zandie, Zandy.**

ZANDRIA   American. Greek: "mankind; defender of mankind." **Zandrea, Zandreah, Zandreeah, Zandriya.**

ZANNA   Polish: "God is gracious." A cognate of Jane. Hebrew: "lily; rose."

ZARA   Hebrew: "princess; east dawn light." Arabic: "blossom, flower." **Zarah.**

ZARIFA   Arabic: "graceful."

ZARINA   Persian: "golden."

ZAUDITU Ethiopia. Amharic: "she is the crown."

ZAWADI Swahili: "gift."

ZAYNAB Arabic: A borrowing of the name of a fragrant plant. The name Zaynab was borne by two of the prophet Muhammad's wives, a daughter, and a granddaughter. **Zainab, Zeinab.**

ZEA Latin: "ripened grain."

ZEBORAH American: Contemporary, based on Deborah (a bee). **Zebora.**

ZEHIRA Hebrew: "protected."

ZELANKA American: Contemporary.

ZELEKA American: Contemporary, probably a variant of Zalika (well born) or Zuleika (beautiful). **Zeleeka.**

ZELFA American: Contemporary.

ZELIE French: "heaven."

ZELPHIA American: Contemporary, probably influenced by Sophia (wisdom).

ZEMBLA American: Contemporary.

ZEMIRA Hebrew: "joyous song." **Zemirah.**

ZENA Persian: "a woman." Greek: "hospitable." **Zenia.**

ZENDA Persian: "womanly; sacred."

ZENIA Greek: "hospitable." **Zeena, Zena.**

ZENITH American: "highest point, peak."

ZEPHIRAH Hebrew: "dawn."

ZERLINDA Hebrew: "beautiful dawn, beautiful as the dawn."

ZERLINE French: From an opera of the same name by nineteenth-century composer Daniel Auber. **Zerlena, Zerlene.**

ZESIRO Uganda. Luganda: "first of twins."

ZHANÉ American: Contemporary, influenced by the French language. **Zhanae, Zhanay, Zhanée.**

ZHANNA American: Contemporary.

ZIA Latin: "a type of grain." Arabic: "light."

ZILPHIA American: Contemporary, possibly modeled after Sylvia (from the forest) or Zilpah (a biblical name).

ZIMIRA Hebrew: "praised." **Zimirah.**

ZIMRIA Hebrew: "praised." **Zimriah.**

ZINAH Hebrew: "abundance." Russian: "the life of Zeus." Spanish: "zinnia." **Zina.** Zina Garrison, tennis pro.

ZINSA Nigeria. Benin: "one of twins."

ZIRAH Hebrew: "arena."

ZIVA Hebrew: "brilliance, splendor."

ZOBEIDA Spanish. Arabic: "rich as cream." **Sabeida, Sobeida, Zabeida.**

ZOE Greek: "life." **Zoë.**

ZOELETH American: Contemporary.

ZOELIE French. Greek: "life." **Zoelle.**

ZOII American. Greek: "life."

ZOILA Spanish. Greek: "life." **Ziola, Zolla, Zoyla.**

ZOLA Italian: "a ball of earth." South Africa. Xhosa: "quietness."

ZOLLIE American: Contemporary, probably based on Zolla (life) or Zola (a ball of earth; quietness).

ZONA Latin and Greek: "girdle, belt."

ZORA Slavic. Latin: "dawn." **Zorah**. Zora Neale Hurston, novelist and folklorist.

ZUBAIDA Arabic: "a marigold; excellent." **Zubaidah, Zubeda, Zubedah**.

ZUELIA Arabic: "peace."

ZULA Africa: A tribal name denoting a pastoral people of South Africa.

ZULEIKA Arabic: "fair one, beautiful." **Zuelekha, Zuleka**.

ZULEMA Arabic: "peace." **Zulemah, Zulima, Zulimah**.

ZULMA American: Contemporary.

ZUNDRA American: Contemporary.

ZURI Swahili: "beautiful."

ZUWENA Swahili: "good." **Zwena**.

MALE NAMES

AARON Hebrew: "exalted; enlightened." **Aron, Arun.** Aaron Douglas (1900–1979), painter known as the father of Black American art. Aaron Neville, singer. Aaron McKie, basketball pro.

ABASI Swahili: "stern."

ABBUD Arabic: "devoted, worshiper of Allah." **Abid, Abood.**

ABD AL JABBAR Arabic: "servant of the Mighty One." **Abdal Jabbar, Abdul Jabbar.**

ABDALLAH Arabic: "servant of Allah." **Abdalla, Abdulla, Abdullah.**

ABDIKARIM Somali. Arabic: "servant of the Generous One."

ABDU Arabic: "servant of." **Abdou.**

ABDU-ALLAH Arabic: "servant of Allah."

ABDUL Arabic: "servant of."

ABDULLAHI Swahili. Arabic: "servant of Allah."

ABEGUNDE Nigeria. Yoruba: "born during the holiday."

ABHIRAHA Hindi: "great king."

ABIADE Nigeria. Yoruba: "born of royalty."

ABIMBOLA Nigeria. Yoruba: "born wealthy."

ABIONA Nigeria. Yoruba: "born during a journey."

ABRAHAM Hebrew: "father of a multitude." **Abe, Bram.**

ABRAM Hebrew: "the father is exalted."

ACANTHUS Greek: Meaning unknown. Acanthus was an ancient city of Greek Macedonia.

ACANYER American: Contemporary.

ACASTUS Latin: Meaning unknown. In Roman mythology, Acastus is the son of Pelias.

ACE American: "expert, excellent, first in quality."

ACESTES Greek: Meaning unknown. In Greek mythology, Acestes is a Trojan king who was host to Aeneas.

ACHERON Greek: "river of woe." In classical mythology, Acheron is the river in Hades across which Charon ferried the dead.

ACHILLES Latin. Greek: Meaning unknown. In Greek mythology, Achilles is the leader and a warrior of the Trojan War.

ACTAEON Latin. Greek: "from Acte." In Greek mythology, Actaeon is transformed into a stag and hunted down by his own hounds. **Acteon.**

ADAM Hebrew: "red earth." Adam Clayton Powell (1908–1972), congressman and civil rights leader.

ADAN Spanish. Hebrew: "red earth." Nigeria. Yoruba: "a large bat."

ADDISON English: "Addy's son." **Addeson.**

ADEAGBO Nigeria. Yoruba: "he brings honor."

ADEBAYO Nigeria. Yoruba: "he came in a joyful time."

ADEL German: "noble." **Adal, Adell.**

ADELAJA Nigeria. Yoruba: "a crown is added to my wealth."

ADELPHO Greek: "brother."

ADEMOLA Nigeria. Yoruba: "a crown is given to me."

ADEYEMI Nigeria. Yoruba: "brown suits me well."

ADIF Hebrew: "choicest." **Adiph.**

ADIKA African: "first child of a second husband."

ADIL Arabic: "judicious."

ADLAI Aramaic: "refuge of the Lord." **Adlay.**

ADMORE American: Contemporary.

ADNAN Arabic: "to settle."

ADOLPHUS Latin. German: "noble wolf."

ADOM Ghana. Akan: "God helps."

ADON Hebrew: "Lord."

ADONAL American. Contemporary, probably based on Donald (world ruler). **Don.**

ADONIJAH Hebrew: "God is my Lord." **Adon.**

ADONIS Greek: Meaning unknown. In classical mythology, Adonis was the handsome foster child of Persephone and Aphrodite. The name implies physical perfection.

ADRIAN English. Latin: "man from Adria."

AEOLUS Greek: "the changeable one." In Greek mythology, the god of the winds. **Aelous.**

AESHAN American: Contemporary, possibly a phonetic spelling of the Nigerian Essien (the child belongs to everyone). **Ayshan.**

AFIBA Nigeria. Yoruba: "by the sea."

AGANJU African: In African mythology, Aganju is the son and husband of Odudua, the Yoruban earth godesss.

AHMAD Arabic: "praiseworthy, more commendable." **Ahmed.** Ahmad Rashad, sportscaster.

AIBRIHM American: Contemporary spelling of Abram (the father is exalted).

AJAMU Nigeria. Yoruba: "he fights for his desires."

AJANI American: Contemporary.

AJAX English. Greek: "alas." In Greek mythology, the name is given to two men renowned for their valor and strength.

AJMAL American: Contemporary.

AKBAR Arabic: "greatest."

AKELLO Uganda. Luganda: "I have brought forth."

AKIBA Hebrew: "supplanted."

AKIL Arabic: "intelligent."

AKIN Nigeria. Yoruba: "hero, brave man, warrior."

AKINLAWON Nigeria. Yoruba: "bravery sustains them."

AKINYELE Nigeria. Yoruba: "valor benefits us."

AKIVA Hebrew: "supplanted, seizing by the heel."

AKONO Nigeria. Yoruba: "my turn."

AKRAM Arabic: "generous."

ALA Arabic: "excellence, supremacy, height." **Alaa**. Alaa Abdelnaby, basketball pro.

ALAN Celtic: "handsome, fair." **Alen, Allan, Allen, Allyn. Al**. Allan Houston, basketball pro.

ALBERT German: "noble and bright." **Al, Bert**. Albert Murray, novelist.

ALBERTO Italian. Spanish. German: "noble and bright." **Al, Berto**.

ALCIDE Spanish: "the governor."

ALDEN English: "old friend; half Dane."

ALDORE American: Possible variant of Aldous (old) or a blending of names.

ALDOUS English: "old." **Aldus**.

ALDWIN English: "old friend." Aldwin Ware, basketball pro.

ALEEM Hindi: "knowledgeable."

ALERON Latin: "eagle."

ALEX Greek: "defender, helper." Alex Haley, author.

ALFONSO Italian. Spanish. German: "noble and ready." **Al**. Alfonso Ribeiro, actor.

ALFREDO Spanish. English: "elf counselor." **Al**.

ALGERNON French: "mustache." **Al**.

ALI Arabic: "exalted, elevated."

ALIKA American: Contemporary.

ALIM Arabic: "scholar." **Aleem**.

ALJAY American: Contemporary.

ALLARD English: "nobly brave."

ALLAWAY English: "noble war; elf war."

ALLAZEAN American: Contemporary.

ALMAR American. Arabic: "golden, coated in gold."

ALMOND American: "an almond, almond-shaped."

ALMOS Nigeria. Hausa: "knife."

ALON Hebrew: "oak tree."

ALONGE Nigeria. Yoruba: "a tall, slim boy."

ALONZO Spanish. German: "noble and ready." **Alonso**. Alonzo Mourning, basketball pro.

ALOYS French. German: "wise." Alois.

ALPHEUS Latin. Greek: "a white or transparent object." Alphie.

ALPHONSE French. German: "noble and ready."

ALPHONSO American. German: "noble and eager." **Alphonzo. Alphie.**

ALSTON English: "from Alston (Al's town); from the old town."

ALTA English: "old."

ALTAIR Arabic: "falcon."

ALTIE American: A pet form of Alta (old) or Alastair (defender or helper of mankind).

ALTON English: "old town." Alton Augustus Adams, composer and band leader.

ALVAR English: "elf army, elf warrior." **Al.**

ALVARO Spanish. German: "guarded, protected." **Álvaro.**

ALVERN English. Latin: "springlike, verdant."

ALVERNON American: Blending of the names Al and Vernon (from the alder grove), or possibly a coinage influenced by Algernon (mustache). **Al.**

ALVIN English: "friend of the elves." **Alvan, Alven. Al, Vinnie, Vinny.** Alvin Davis, baseball pro.

AMAL German: "worker." Hindu: "clean, pure." Arabic: "hopes."

AMBROSE English and French. Latin: "immortal."

AMEDÉE French. Latin: "lover of God."

AMEEL Hindi: "unobtainable."

AMELIO Italian. German: "worker."

AMIKAR Hebrew: "my nation is precious."

AMILAR American: Possibly influenced by the Spanish Amilcar (friend of the god Melkar).

AMIN Arabic: "honest, faithful." **Ameen.**

AMIR Arabic: "king, ruler." **Ameer.**

AMMAN Egyptian: "protected by the god Ammon." Amman is also the name of the capital of Jordan.

AMMAR Arabic: "builder, carpenter."

AMPHION Greek: Meaning unknown. In Greek mythology, Amphion is a son of Zeus and Antiope.

AMOS Hebrew: "a burden, something borne."

ANAN Hebrew: "cloud; fortune-teller." **Anani, Ananya.**

ANAND Hindi: "joy."

ANANSI Ghana. Akan: "the spider." Anansi is the trickster hero of Akan legend.

ANAYA French: "descendant of a friar." Arabic: "to sing, to chant."

ANCHISES Greek: Meaning unknown. In classical mythology, Anchises is the father of Aeneas and Aphrodite.

ANDERSON Scandinavian: "Ander's son."

ANDON American: Variant of Anton (priceless, of inestimable worth).

ANDRAS Welsh. Greek: "manly."

ANDRÉ French. Greek: "manly." **Andrae, Andre.** Andrae Crouch, gospel singer. Andre Rison, football pro. Andre Dawson, baseball pro. André De Shields, actor. André Watts, pianist.

ANDREAS Greek: "manly."

ANDRÉS Spanish. Greek: "manly." **Andres**. Andres Thomas, baseball pro.

ANDREW English. Greek: "manly." **Andy, Drew**. Andrew Brimmer, Ph.D., first Black member of the Federal Reserve Board. Andrew Young, civil rights leader and U.S. ambassador to the United Nations.

ANDRIUS American. Greek: "manly."

ANDROKLES Greek: "man glory." **Androcles**.

ANEESH Hindi: Another name for the god Vishnu.

ANFERNEE American: Contemporary. Anfernee Hardaway, basketball pro.

ANGELO Italian. Spanish. Greek: "angel, messenger of God."

ANGRIS American: Contemporary.

ANJAY Hindi: "unconquerable."

ANKOMA Ghana. Akan: "last-born child."

ANQUELL American: Contemporary.

ANRY American: Contemporary, possibly a phonetic spelling of the French Henri (home ruler).

ANSHU Hindi: "sunbeam."

ANTANAS Lithuanian. Latin: "priceless, of inestimable worth."

ANTARES Greek: "like Mars." Antares is the name of the brightest star in the constellation Scorpio.

ANTAWN American: Contemporary, influenced by Antoine (priceless, of inestimable worth).

ANTHONY English. Latin: "priceless, of inestimable worth." **Tony**. Anthony Braxton, jazz instrumentalist.

ANTJUAN American: Contemporary.

ANTJWON American: Contemporary.

ANTOINE French. Latin: "priceless, of inestimable worth." **Toine**. Antoine "Fats" Domino, jazz great.

ANTON European. Latin: "priceless, of inestimable worth."

ANTONI European. Latin: "priceless, of inestimable worth." **Toni**.

ANTONIO Spanish. Latin: from Antonius (priceless, of inestimable worth). **Tonio**. Antonio Lang, basketball pro. Antonio Lewis Todd, actor.

ANTRIC American: Contemporary.

ANTRON American: Contemporary, possibly based on the Latin name of a town in Thessaly.

ANTULIO Spanish. Greek: "manly."

ANTWON American: Contemporary, a phonetic spelling of Antoine (priceless, of inestimable worth).

ANVAY Hindi: "purpose."

ANWAR Arabic: "brighter, clearer."

APOLLO Greek: Meaning unknown. In Greek mythology, Apollo was the god of medicine, music, poetry, and prophecy. **Apolo**.

AQUILO Latin: "the north wind, the swift-flying thing."

AQURIOUS American: Contemporary, possibly influenced by Aquarius (the water carrier).

ARA Nigeria. Hausa: "borrowed, lent."

ARBERT Teutonic: "eagle bright."

ARCAS Latin: Meaning unknown. In Roman mythology, Arcas is a son of Jupiter and Callisto. He was transformed into the star Arcturus to guard his mother, who had been transformed into the Great Bear constellation.

ARCELL American: Contemporary.

ARCENEAUX French: "keeper of the arsenal."

ARDEAN American: Contemporary.

ARDEN English: "from Arden (dwelling house)." **Ardin**.

ARDON Hebrew: "bronze."

ARDWRIGHT American: Contemporary.

ARES Greek: Meaning unknown. In Greek mythology, Ares is the god of war and a son of Zeus and Hera.

ARGILE American: Contemporary, based on *argyle* (a diamond-shaped pattern).

ARGOLA American. Greek: "of Argolis."

ARGUS Greek: "bright."

ARGUSTUS American: Elaboration of Argus (bright).

ARGUSTER American: Elaboration of Argus (bright).

ARIES Latin: "the Ram." The first sign of the zodiac (March 21–April 20).

ARIF Arabic: "knowledgeable."

ARION Latin and Greek: Meaning unknown. In classical mythology, Arion is a horse endowed with the gifts of speech and prophecy.

ARLINGTON English: "from Arlington (Aelfred's town)."

ARMAND French. German: "soldier, warrior." **Armond**.

ARMANDO Spanish. German: "soldier, warrior."

ARMENOUS American: Possibly based on Arminius (soldier, warrior).

ARMENTRAL American: Contemporary.

ARMIN English. German: "soldier, warrior." Armon Gilliam, basketball pro.

ARMINIUS Latin. German: "soldier, warrior."

ARMON Hebrew: "palace; oak tree." Armon Gilliam, basketball pro.

ARMSTRONG English: "strong in the arm." Armstrong Williams, radio talk show host.

ARNA American: Possibly based on the Scandinavian Arne (eagle). Arna Bontemps, poet and novelist.

ARNAN Arabic: "fruit of the lotus." Hebrew: "roaring stream." **Arnon**.

ARNAV Hindi: "ocean."

ARNOBA American: Contemporary.

ARNOLD German: "powerful as an eagle, eagle ruler." **Arnald**.

ARQUETTE French: "archer."

ARQUILLA Spanish: "operator of a kiln."

ARSENI Russian. Greek: "male, virile." **Arseniy**.

ARSENIO Spanish. Greek: "manly, strong." Arsenio Hall, actor and talk show host.

ART Gaelic: "bear." English: Short form of Arthur (meaning unknown). Art Blakey, jazz drummer.

ARTAN Gaelic: "little bear."

ARTEMIS Greek: Meaning unknown. In Greek mythology, Artemis is the goddess of the moon and hunting. **Artemas, Artemus**.

ARTHUR Celtic: Meaning unknown. **Art**. Arthur A. Schomburg, historian, curator of the Division of Negro Literature, History, and Prints for the New York City Public Library. Arthur Fletcher, member of the U.S. Commission on Civil Rights, known as the Father of Affirmative Action.

ARTIS English. French: "from Arthes." **Artiss. Art**. Artis Gilmore, basketball pro.

ARUN American. Hebrew: "exalted; enlightened." Hindi: "reddish brown."

ASA Nigeria. Hausa: "restlessness." Asa Philip Randolph (1889–1979), national labor leader and civil rights leader.

ASAD Arabic: "happier, luckier." **Assad**.

ASADEL Arabic: "very lucky, greatly successful."

ASBERRY English: "from Ashbury (fort near the ash trees)."

ASEEM Hindi: "infinite."

ASFOUR Arabic: "bird."

ASHAKI African: "beautiful."

ASHANTE American: Contemporary.

ASHBY English: "from Ashby (village near the ash trees)."

ASHLEY English: "dweller near the ash tree forest." **Ashly**.

ASHTON English: "from Ashton (ash tree town)."

ASHUR Arabic: "born during the month of Ashur."

ASIM Arabic: "guardian, protector."

ASTON English: "from Aston (town to the east)."

ATIF Arabic: "understanding."

ATILANO Spanish. Latin: Meaning unknown.

ATISONE American: Contemporary, possibly based on Addison (Addy's son).

ATREUS Greek: Meaning unknown. In Greek mythology, Atreus is a king of Argos and Mycenae.

ATTILA Hungarian. Latin: An old family name of unknown meaning. Attila the Hun (d. 453) was a fierce military leader who fought against the Roman Empire.

ATTILIO Italian. Latin: An old family name of unknown meaning.

AUBIN French. English: "white."

AUBREY   English. Teutonic: "elf ruler."

AUDEN   English: "old friend." **Audin.**

AUDREECE   American: Contemporary.

AUGUST   Latin: "venerable, great." August Wilson, playwright.

AUGUSTUS   Latin: "most venerable, greatest."

AUNDRAY   American. Greek: "manly." **Ahndrae, Ahndray, Ahndrey, Aundrae, Aundrey.** Aundray Bruce, football pro.

AUSTIN   English. Latin: "great, venerable." Austin Carr, basketball pro.

AUTMY   American: Contemporary.

AVERY   English: "elf counselor." Avery Johnson, basketball pro.

AVONDRE   American: Contemporary.

AWOTWE   Ghana. Akan: "eighth child."

AYINDE   Nigeria. Yoruba: "we gave praises and he came to us."

AYMAN   Arabic: "fortunate."

AYUB   Arabic. Hebrew: "supplanting, seizing by the heel."

AYUBU   Swahili. Hebrew: "supplanting, seizing by the heel."

AZANDE   African: Borrowed from the name of a Central African tribe.

AZIBO   Malawi. Ngoni: "earth."

AZIZ   Arabic: "powerful; beloved."

BABATUNDE   Nigeria. Yoruba: "father returns."

BADRAK   Arabic: "merciful."

BADRU   Swahili: "born during a full moon."

BAHIR   Arabic: "dazzling."

BAHJAT   Arabic: "delight."

BAILER   German: "ax-maker." **Bailor, Baylor.**

BAILEY   French: "administrator." English: "worker at the outer court of a castle." Hindu: "savior." **Baily, Baylee.**

BAKARI   Swahili: "of noble promise." **Bacari.**

BALEN   Hindi: "a child."

BALESH   Hindi: "king of children."

BALLARD   English: "bald."

BANDELE   African: "he follows me home."

BARACHEL   Hebrew: "blessed of the Lord." In the Bible, Barachel was one of Job's three friends.

BARAK   Hebrew: "bright, a flash of light."

BARNABAS   Aramaic: "son of exhortation." **Barney.**

BARNABY   English. Hebrew: "son of exhortation."

BARON   English: "a baron, nobleman." **Barone.**

BARRETT   English. French: "commerce, traffic." **Barry.**

BARRY   English. French: "commerce, traffic." Barry Bonds, baseball pro. Barry White, singer.

BARTHOLOMEW   Greek: "son of Talmai." **Bart.**

BARUTI Botswana. Tswana: "teacher, tutor."

BASIL Latin and Greek: "kingly, royal." **Bazil.**

BASIM Arabic: "smiling."

BASIR Turkish: "astute, wise."

BASSAM Arabic: "smiling."

BAXTER English: "baker."

BAYARD French: "auburn, auburn-haired." Bayard Rustin (1910–1987), civil rights and labor union leader.

BEAU French: "handsome."

BEAUCHAMP French: "beautiful plain." **Beau.**

BEAUFORT French: "beautiful stronghold." **Beau.**

BEAUMONT French: "beautiful mountain." **Beau.**

BEAUREGARD French: "beautiful view." **Beau.**

BECK German: "dweller near the brook."

BELLAMY French: "beautiful friend."

BELMA American: Contemporary, possibly a shortened form of Bellamy (beautiful friend).

BEN English. Hebrew: "son of the right hand." **Bennie, Benny.** Ben Vereen, dancer and actor.

BENAJAH American: Contemporary. **Ben, Bennie, Benny.**

BENAYA Hebrew: "God has built." **Benaiah.**

BENDAHAN American: Contemporary. **Ben, Bennie, Benny.**

BENDICK American: Blending of Ben (son of the right hand) and Dick (brave ruler). Also, a contracted form of Benedict (blessed).

BENEDICT English. Latin: "blessed."

BENITO Spanish. Latin: "blessed."

BENJAMIN Hebrew: "son of the right hand." **Benjamen. Ben, Bennie.** Benjamin Banneker (1731–1806), astronomer, inventor, mathematician. Dr. Benjamin F. Chavis Jr., executive director of the NAACP.

BENNIE English: Originated as a pet form of names beginning with *Ben-.* **Benny, Bennye.**

BENO Kenya. Mwera: "member of a band."

BENOIT French. Latin: "blessed." Benoit Benjamin, basketball pro.

BENSON English: "Ben's son." **Ben, Bennie, Benny.**

BENZER American: Contemporary. **Ben, Bennie, Benny.**

BENZION Hebrew: "son of Zion." **Ben, Bennie, Benny.**

BERCHET American: Contemporary, possibly based on the English surname Burchett (dweller by the birch-grove, dweller at the birch-covered headland). **Berchett.**

BERHANU Ethiopia. Amharic: "his light."

BERISH German. Slavic: "bear glory."

BERJES   American. French: "freeman of a borough." **Bergess, Berjess, Berjus, Berjuss.**

BERLIN   German: "from Berlin." **Berlan, Berlyn, Berlyne.**

BERNARD   German: "bold as a bear." **Bernie.**

BERNARDO   Spanish. German: "bold as a bear."

BERNIE   German: "bold as a bear."

BERRY   English: "dweller near the hill or stronghold." American: "a berry." Berry Gordy Jr., founder of Motown Records.

BERTRAM   English: "bright raven." **Bertrem. Bert.**

BERTRAND   English and French: "bright raven." **Bert.**

BERTRESA   American: Contemporary.

BERYLN   American: Variant of Beryl (pale green gemstone).

BEVAN   Welsh. Hebrew: "God is gracious." **Bevin.**

BEVARD   Hebrew: "zoo." English: "dweller near the sign of the beaver."

BEZELL   American: Contemporary.

BHAJAN   Hindi: "adoration."

BIA   Ghana. Akan: In Akan mythology, Bia is a son of Onyame. Deceived by his brother, Tano, Bia received ownership of all undesirable land instead of the most desirable land his father had planned for him.

BILAL   Arabic: "trustworthy." Bilal was the first convert of the Prophet Muhammad.

BILLY   English. German: "resolute protector." **Bill, Billie.** Billy Dee Williams, singer and actor.

BISHOP   English: "a bishop, a high-ranking clergyman."

BLAIN   Scottish: "son of the disciple of Blaan (yellow) or Blane (the lean)." **Blaine.**

BLAIR   Scottish: "dweller on the plain." **Blaire.** Blair Underwood, actor.

BLAISE   French: "the babbler."

BLAKE   English: "black, dark-complexioned; bright, shining."

B'NARD   American: Variant of Bernard (bold as a bear).

BOAZ   Hebrew: "strength in the Lord."

BOBBY   English. German: "bright with fame."

BOLDEN   English: "from Bolden (homestead on the hill)."

BOMANI   Malawi. Ngoni: "fierce fighter."

BOOKER   English: "a writer of books, a scribe." Booker T. Washington (1856–1915), civil rights leader, founder and first president of Tuskegee Institute.

BOULUS   Arabic. Latin: "small." The Arabic form of Paul.

BRADEN   English: "from the broad valley."

BRAM   Irish. Hebrew: "father of a multitude." A shortened form of Abraham.

BRAN   Welsh: "raven."

BRANDON   English: "from the brushwood hill."

BRANDY American: "brandy, a liquor distilled from fermented fruit juice or wine."

BRANFORD English: "dweller near the brushwood by the ford." Branford Marsalis, band leader.

BRAWLEY American: Contemporary.

BRAXTON English: "dweller near Bracca's town." **Braxston**.

BRECK Irish: "freckled."

BRENT English: "the burnt one; from the burned land."

BRENTON English: "from Bryni's (fire, flame; burnt) settlement."

BRETON English: "from Bretton (newly cultivated enclosure)."

BREVIN American: Contemporary.

BRIAN Irish. Celtic: "kingly, strength, valor, high." **Brion, Bryan, Bryon**. Brian Grant, basketball pro.

BRICE English. Celtic: "force, strength, valor." **Bryce**. Bryce Wilson, musician.

BRINSLEY American: Contemporary, based on the English surname Brindley (dweller from the burnt wood clearing).

BRIZELL American: Contemporary.

BRONIUS American: Contemporary, possibly influenced by the Latin Bromius (the noisy one).

BRONZELL American: Contemporary. Bronzell Miller, football pro.

BROOK English: "brook, a small stream; a breaking forth."

BROOKER English: "dweller by the brook."

BROOKLYN American: Borrowed from the name of the New York City borough. **Brooklin, Brooklinn, Brooklynn, Bruklin, Bruklinn, Bruklyn, Bruklynn**.

BROOKS English: "dweller near the brook or water-meadow."

BROOX American. English: "dweller near the brook or water-meadow."

BROUGHTON English: "from Broughton (the village near the brook)."

BRUCE English. French: "from Brieuse."

BRYANT English. Celtic: "kingly; strength, valor; high." Bryant Stith, basketball pro. Bryant Gumbel, television host.

BRYN Welsh: "hill."

BRYNE American: Variant of Bryn (hill) or Brian (kingly; strength).

BRYTON English. Welsh: "from the hill town." Bryton McClure, actor.

BUFORD English: "from Beeford (ford by the bees)." Buford Jordan, football pro.

BUNMI Nigeria. Yoruba: "my gift."

BURGESS English. French: "freeman of a borough."

BURNELL French: "dark-complexioned."

BURNESS Scottish: "from Burness (fair wind point)."

BURRELL English: "from Burrill (hill of the fort)." **Burrel, Burril, Burrill**.

BUTRUS Arabic. Latin and Greek: "a rock, a stone." The Arabic form of Peter.

BWERANI   Malawi. Ngoni: "you are welcomed."

BYRAM   English: "at the cow sheds."

BYRON   English: "at the cow sheds." Byron Houston, basketball pro. Byron Lars, designer.

CABOT   French: "small head."

CADERAL   American: Contemporary.

CADY   Scottish: "descendant of little Cadda (battle)."

CAESAR   Latin: Meaning uncertain, possibly "hairy" or "to cut." Caesar came to be used as the imperial title of the emperor of Rome. **Cesar.**

CAGN   African: In African mythology, Cagn is the supreme god of the Bushmen, the creator of all living things.

CAIN   Hebrew: "smith, craftsman."

CAIRO   American: From the Egyptian city of Cairo (victorious).

CAJERO   American: Possibly a shortened form of the Spanish Cajetaro (from Caieta).

CALBERT   English: "herdsman." **Calbort.** Calbert Cheaney, basketball pro.

CALDWELL   English: "dweller near the cold stream." Caldwell Jones, basketball pro.

CALEB   Hebrew: "dog; faithfulness."

CALVIN   French: "little bald one." **Kalvin. Cal, Kal.**

CALWIN   American: Contemporary, based on Calvin (little bald one). **Calwyn.**

CAMAS   American. Chinook Indian: "sweet; a delicate wild plant with edible bulbs." **Camus.**

CAMERON   Scottish: "crooked nose." **Kameran, Kameron. Cam, Kam.**

CAMP   American: "camp, outdoor settlement."

CANADA   American. Native American: "where the heavens rest upon the earth, horizon." Canada Lee (1907–1951), actor.

CANNOVA   Italian: "worker in a wine cellar." **Canova.**

CAPRICE   American. French: "a whim."

CARDELL   American. Italian: "goldfinch."

CARL   English: "man, freeman." Carl T. Rowan, journalist, first Black to sit on the National Security Council, U.S. Ambassador to Finland. Carl Lewis, Olympic gold medal–winning track star. Carl Weathers, actor.

CARLESTER   American: Combination of Carl (man, freeman) and Lester (a dyer; from Leicester).

CARLOS   Spanish. English and German: "man, freeman."

CARLTON   English: "settlement of freemen." **Carleton. Carl.**

CARMEN   Spanish. Hebrew: "vineyard, orchard."

CARRICK   American. Irish: "rock."

CARRINGTON   English: "from Carrington (Curra's village)."

CARTER English: "a cart driver." Dr. Carter G. Woodson (1875–1950), historian.

CARVELL French: "from Carvell (estate in the marsh)." **Carvel.**

CARVER English: "wood-carver, woodcutter."

CARWELL American: Possible variant of Cardwell (from Chardo's village).

CARWYN Welsh: "fair love, blessed love."

CASCIO Italian. Latin: "vain."

CASEO American: Probable variant of Cascio (vain).

CASIMIRO Italian. Slavic: "proclaimer of peace."

CASSIAN English. Latin: Meaning uncertain, possibly "hollow, empty."

CASTLE American: "a castle."

CAULTON English: "from Caulton (cold town)."

CAYNE American: Contemporary spelling of Cain (smith, craftsman).

CECIL English. Latin: "blind, dimsighted." Cecil Fielder, baseball player.

CEDRIC English: coined by Sir Walter Scott for a character in *Ivanhoe*. Cedric Ceballos, basketball pro. Cedric Jones, football pro.

CELESTER American: Contemporary, possibly influenced by Sylvester (of a wood or forest).

CEOLA American: Possibly a shortened form of Osceola (black drink crier). Osceola was a famous Seminole leader.

CEPHEUS Greek: Meaning unknown. In Greek mythology, Cepheus is an Ethiopian king, husband of Cassiopeia and father of Andromeda.

CHAD English: From the obsolete Ceadda (meaning unknown).

CHADWICK English: "from Chadwick (Ceadda's farm)." **Chad.**

CHAFULUMISA Malawi. Ngoni: "swift."

CHANCELLOR English: "a chancellor, an official secretary."

CHANDA Hindi: "moon."

CHANDAN Hindi: "sandalwood."

CHANDRAN Hindi: "moonlight."

CHANZAN American: Contemporary.

CHAPELLE English: "dweller near the chapel." **Chapell, Chappell, Chappelle.**

CHARLES German: "full-grown, a man." English: "a man, freeman, a peasant." **Charley, Charlie, Chuck.** Charles Barkley, basketball pro. Charles Drew, surgeon, recipient of the Spingarn Medal of the NAACP for his contributions to science. Charles F. Bolden Jr., astronaut.

CHARLESTON English: "from Charlton (the village of free men)." **Charley, Charlie.**

CHARLIE English: "a man, freeman, a peasant." **Charley.** Charley Pride, country singer.

CHARLTON English: "from Charlton (the village of freemen)." **Charley, Charlie.**

CHATHA African: "an ending."

CHAUNCEY English. French: "from Chancey (estate of Cantius)." **Chauncy.**

CHAVEZ Spanish: "descendant of Jaime (supplanter)."

CHAVIS French: "from Chavois (hollow)."

CHAVOUS American: Contemporary, possibly influenced by Chavez (son of Jaime) or Chavis (hollow).

CHAZ American: Contemporary, based on a nickname of Charles (full-grown; a man). **Chas.**

CHAZAIAH Hebrew: "Jehovah sees." **Chazaya. Chaz.**

CHAZIEL Hebrew: "vision of Jehovah." **Chaz.**

CHEIKH Kenya. Kiyuku: "learned."

CHELSEA English: "a port of ships." **Chelsey, Chelsie.**

CHENIER French: "dweller in or near the oak forest."

CHENZIRA Zimbabwe. Shona: "born on the road."

CHESTER English: "camp of the legions." **Chet.** Chester Himes, novelist.

CHET English: "camp of the legions." Chet Lemon, baseball pro.

CHEYNE American: Variant of Shane (God is gracious).

CHEZ French: "dweller at an isolated house."

CHIANTI American. Italian: A dry red wine, originally made in the Chianti Mountains of Italy.

CHIBALE Malawi. Ngoni: "kinship."

CHIGARU Malawi. Ngoni: "hound."

CHIKE Nigeria. Ibo: "power of God."

CHIKOSI Malawi. Ngoni: "neck."

CHILEMBA Kenya. Mwera: "turban."

CHIPITA Malawi. Ngoni: "it has gone away."

CHITOSE American: Contemporary. Chitose is also the name of a Japanese city.

CHRIS European: A short form of Christian (a follower of Christ) and Christopher (bearing Christ).

CHRISTIAN English. Latin: "a Christian, a follower of Christ." **Chris.**

CHRISTOFOR American. Latin: "bearing Christ." **Chris.**

CHRISTOPH German. Latin: "bearing Christ." **Christoff, Kristoph, Kristoff. Chris, Kris.** Kristoff St. John, actor.

CHRISTOPHER English. Latin: "bearing Christ." **Christofer, Cristofer, Cristopher. Chris, Cris, Kit.**

CHUBAKAH American: Contemporary, possibly influenced by the character Chewbacca in the movie *Star Wars*.

CHUMA Zimbabwe. Shona: "beads (wealth)."

CLABERT American: Contemporary.

CLABON American: Contemporary.

CLARDIT American: Contemporary.

CLARELL American: Contemporary. **Clarel.**

CLARENCE English: "from the Clare (shining, bright, illustrious) family." **Clarance, Clarrence.** Clarence Thomas, U.S. Supreme Court Justice. Clarence Weatherspoon, basketball pro. Clarence Gilyard Jr., actor.

CLARK English: "a clerk." Clark Johnson, actor. Clark Terry, jazz trumpeter and big band leader.

CLARKSTON Scottish. English: "from Clarkston (clerk's town)."

CLAUDE English. Latin: "lame."

CLAUDELL American. Latin: "lame." Claudell Washington, baseball pro.

CLAUDIO Italian, Spanish. Latin: "lame."

CLAYBORNE English: "dweller near the clay banks." **Clayborn, Claybourne. Clay.**

CLAYTON English: "from Clayton (the clay town)."

CLEANDRO Spanish. Greek: "man of glory, man of fame."

CLEANT American: Possibly a variant of Cleanthes.

CLEANTHES Latin: Meaning unknown. Cleanthes was a Stoic philosopher. **Cleanthas.**

CLEASTER American: Contemporary.

CLEATHUS American: Contemporary.

CLEAVE English: "dweller near the cliff or slope." **Cleve.**

CLEAVON English: "cliff, slope, bank." **Clevon.** Cleavon Little, actor.

CLEDITH American: Contemporary.

CLELLEN American. Irish: "son of the servant of Fillan (little wolf)."

CLEMEAL American: Contemporary. **Clem.**

CLEMENT English. Latin: "merciful, gentle, mild." **Clem.**

CLEMENTE Spanish and Italian. Latin: "merciful, gentle, mild."

CLEMESHA American: Contemporary. **Clem.**

CLEMIS American: Contemporary. **Clem.**

CLEMON American: Contemporary. **Clem.**

CLENTON American. English: "settlement near the cliff."

CLEOLA American: Contemporary.

CLEON Latin. Greek: "glory."

CLEOPHAS American. Greek: "glory." **Cleophis, Cleophus.**

CLETUS Greek: "called forth, invoked."

CLEVELAND English: "from Cleveland (hilly land)." Cleveland Gary, football pro.

CLEVETT English: "dweller near the small cliff."

CLEVON American: Contemporary. **Cleavon, Kleavon, Klevon.**

CLIDE American. Scottish: River name of unknown meaning.

CLIFF English: "dweller at or near the cliff or slope."

CLIFFORD English: "dweller near the ford by the cliff or steep bank." **Clif, Cliff.** Clifford Alexander Jr., lawyer, deputy special counsel to President Johnson.

CLIFTON English: "from Clifton (town near the cliff)." **Cliffton. Clif, Cliff.**

CLINSTON American: Variant of Clinton (settlement by the cliff).

CLINTON English: "settlement by the cliff." **Clint.**

CLIVE English: "dweller near the cliff or riverbank."

CLOYCE American: Contemporary.

CLYDE Scottish: River name of unknown meaning. Clyde Drexler, basketball pro.

CLYNELL American: Contemporary.

CODELLA American: Contemporary.

COLBORN English: "dweller near the cold stream." **Colborne, Colbourne, Colburn, Colburne.**

COLBY English: "from Colby (Koli's homestead)."

COLE English: "coal; dark-skinned."

COLEMAN English: "a coal man, a seller of coal." Coleman Hawkins, jazz musician. Coleman Young, politician.

COLIN English. Greek: "victory of the people." Colin Powell, first Black National Security Adviser, first Black chairman of Joint Chiefs of Staff.

COLSTON English: "from Colston (Kol's homestead)."

COLT English: "a young male horse."

COLTON English: "from Colton (Cola's homestead)." **Coletan, Coleton, Coletun, Coltan, Colten, Coltun. Colt.**

COLTRIN American: Contemporary. **Coltrun. Colt.**

CONEALUS American: Contemporary, influenced by Cornelius (a horn).

CONNAWAY American. Irish: "hound of the plain."

CONNER English: "examiner, inspector." **Connor.**

CONRAD English. German: "wise counsel."

CONSTANT English. Latin: "constant, steadfast."

COOLIDGE English: "dweller near the pool of cold water."

COOPER English: "maker of casks and barrels."

CORBY Scottish: "from Cor's settlement." **Korby.**

CORDELL French: "maker and seller of rope."

COREY Irish: "from the round hill; spear." **Correy, Korey, Kory.**

CORILLA American: Contemporary.

CORINTHIAN English. Latin: "a Corinthian, from Corinth."

CORNELIOUS American. Latin: "horn." **Cornilius, Cornylyus.**

CORNELIUS Latin: "horn."

CORNELL English. Latin: "horn."

CORNETT English: "player of the cornet."

CORTEZ Spanish: "court, town." Cortez Kennedy, football pro.

CORWIN English: "dweller near the white enclosure or castle." **Korwin.**

COSHAWN American: Contemporary, based on the Irish Shawn (God is gracious). **Coshaun, Coshon, Coshonn.**

COSMO English. Greek: "order, beauty."

COSTELLO Irish: "son of Oisdealbh (fawn, deer)."

COSTIN English. Latin: "constant, steadfast."

COUJOE Ghana. Ewe: "born on Monday."

COURTENAY French: "from Courtenay (estate of Curtius)." **Courtney.** Courtney Vance, actor.

COYE English: "shy, quiet." **Coy, Koy, Koye.**

CRAIG Scottish: "dweller by the crag."

CREIGHTON English: "from Crichton (creek town)."

CREOLA American: "Creole."

CREON Greek: "ruler, prince."

CRIMSON American: "deep red."

CRISPIN English. Latin: "curly-haired."

CRISPUS Latin: "curly, curly-haired." Crispus Attucks (c. 1723–1770), first American to lose his life in the American Revolution.

CRUZ Spanish: "cross."

CRYHTEN American: Probably a variant of Creighton (from Crichton).

CUBA American: Borrowing of the name of an island in the West Indies. Cuba Gooding Jr., actor.

CUDJOE Jamaican. African: "born on Monday." **Cudjo.**

CURTIS English. French: "courteous." **Kurtis.** Curtis Wilkerson, baseball pro. Curtis Mayfield, singer.

CY English: Originated as a short form of Cyrus (lord).

CYLK American: Contemporary, probably based on *silk* (a fine, soft fiber produced by silkworms).

CYRUS English. Greek: "lord." Cyrus Colter, novelist.

DABIR Arabic: "teacher."

DACTRIN American: Contemporary.

DAIQUAN American: Contemporary.

DAJUAN American. Spanish. Hebrew: "God is gracious."

DAKS American: Contemporary.

DALE English: "dweller in the valley."

DALLAS American: From the Texas city of Dallas (place on the plain).

DALLIN English: "from Dalling (the valley meadow)." **Dallen, Dallon.**

DALMAR Somali: "versatile."

DALTON English: "from Dalton (the village in the valley)." Dalton Hilliard, football pro.

DALVIN　American: Contemporary.

DALZELL　American. Scottish: "from Dalziel (the white field)."

DAMAN　Greek: "to tame."

DAMANI　African: "thoughtful."

DAMARIO　Spanish. Greek: "tamer."

DAMEON　American. Greek: "tamer." **Daimmeione, Dameian, Damien, Damion, Damiun, Damon, Daymeon, Daymian, Daymion, Daymiun.**

DAMERON　French: "small man."

DAMETRI　American. Greek: "of Demeter."

DAMIAN　European. Greek: "tamer." **Damien.**

DA'MON　American: Contemporary.

DAMON　Latin. Greek: "tamer." **Daman, Damen.** Damon Stoudamire, basketball pro.

DA'MOND　American: Contemporary.

DAMOND　French: "dweller near the upper waters."

DAMONE　American: Blending of Damian and Ramone (wise protector).

DANA　English: "from Denmark." European. Hebrew: "judged." Dana Barros, basketball pro.

DANAUS　Greek: Meaning unknown.

DANBY　English. Scandinavian: "settlement in the valley." **Dan.**

D'ANDRA　American: Contemporary.

DANDRE　American: Contemporary.

DANIEL　Hebrew: "God is my judge." **Danyel. Dan, Danny.** General Daniel James Jr., first Black four-star general, commander, North American Air Defense Command. Daniel Simmons, artist.

DANJUMA　Nigeria. Hausa: "born on Friday."

DANLADI　Nigeria. Hausa: "born on Sunday."

DANNY　Hebrew: "God is my judge." Danny Glover, actor. Danny Tartabull, baseball pro.

DANSO　Ghana. Ashanti: "reliable."

DANTÉ　French. Italian: "lasting."

DANTE　Italian: "lasting."

DANTON　American: Contemporary.

DANYA　American: Contemporary.

DAPRICE　American: Contemporary, possibly modeled after Caprice (a whim, whimsical).

DARBY　English: "from Derby (deer settlement)."

DARCY　English. French: "from Arcy (in La Manche)."

DARECKO　American: Contemporary.

DARELL　American: Modern variation of Darrell (from the town Airelle). **DaRel, DaRell, Darelle.** Darelle Porter, basketball pro.

DAREN　Nigeria. Hausa: "born at night."

DARIAN European: Variant of Darius. **Darien.**

DARICE American: Contemporary.

DARICK American: Contemporary. **Da-Rick, DaRik, D'Rick, D'Rik.**

DARIO Spanish: The Spanish form of Darius (meaning uncertain). **Dareo.**

DARION American: Variant of Darian. **Darreion, Darrion, Darryon, Derrion, Derriyon, Derryon.** Darion Connor, football pro.

DARIUS Latin and Greek: Meaning uncertain. It is possibly from the name of an ancient Persian king, so it is often defined as "king, kingly." Darius McCrary, actor. Darius Rucker, lead singer of Hootie and the Blowfish.

DARLAND French: "descendant of Arland (looter)."

DARMANDA American: Contemporary.

DARNALL English: "from Darnall (hidden nook)." **Darnell, Darnelle.** Darnell Coles, baseball pro.

DARON American: Contemporary, possibly influenced by the name Darren. **Daron, DarRon, Darron.** Darron Bittman, basketball pro.

DARRELL English. French: "from the town of Airelle." **Darel, Darell, Darill, Darryle, Darryll, Daryl, Daryll.** Daryl Mitchell, actor. Daryl Boston, baseball pro.

DARREN English: Twentieth-century coinage. **Daren, Darin, Darrin, Darryn.**

DARRIS American: Contemporary, possibly based on Harris (home ruler).

DARRNARYL American: Contemporary.

DARSHAN Sanskrit: "to see, to perceive."

DARVIN American: Contemporary, possibly modeled after Marvin (sea hill).

DARWEN English: "from Darwen (clear water, white water)."

DARWIN English: "dear friend." **Darwinn, Darwyn, Darwynn.**

DARWYN American. English: "from Darwen (clear water, white water)."

DASH English: "from Ash (the ash tree)." American: Contemporary, based on *dash* (to rush, to move swiftly).

DASHAWN American: Contemporary, based on Shawn (God is gracious).

DATHAN Hebrew: "fount."

DAULTON American. English: "from Dalton (the village in the valley)."

DAVE Hebrew: "beloved." Dave Stewart, baseball pro.

DAVEAN American: Contemporary.

DAVID Hebrew: "beloved." **Davyd. Dave, Davie, Davy.** David Robinson, basketball pro. Dr. David Satcher, first Black to head the Centers for Disease Control and Prevention. David Bradley, novelist.

DAVIDCHEN American: Contemporary. **David, Dave, Davie, Davy.**

DAVIS English: "son of Davie (beloved)." Davis Levering Lewis, historian.

DAVLIN   English: "little Dave (beloved)." **Dave, Davie, Davy.**

DAWAYNE   American. Celtic: "little dark one."

DAWNEL   American: Contemporary.

DAWUD   Arabic. Hebrew: "beloved."

DAX   American: Contemporary.

DAY   English: "the dairy worker."

DAYLON   American: Contemporary. **Daylen.**

DAYMOND   English: "day protection."

DAYTON   English: "from the settlement in the dale; from the farm by the dike."

DEAN   English: "a dean, an official of a church or university."

DEANCE   American: Contemporary.

DEANDRE   American: Contemporary, based on Andre (manly). **DeAndré, De'Aundray, De'Aundre, De'Aundrey, DeAundray, DeAundre, DeAundrey.** De'Aundre Bonds, actor.

DEANTÉ   American: Contemporary. **Deantae, Deantay, Deiontae, Deiontay, Deionté, Deiontey, Deontae, Deontay, Deonté, Deontey, Diontae, Diontay, Dionté, Diontey.**

DEATRA   American: Contemporary.

DEATRIA   American: Contemporary.

DECARLOS   American: Contemporary, based on Carlos (a man, freeman).

DECIO   Spanish. Latin: "tenth."

DEDRICK   Teutonic: "ruler of the people."

DEE   English: Originated as a pet form of various names beginning with the letter D. Dee Brown, basketball pro.

DEHUNDRA   American: Contemporary.

DEION   American. Greek: "of Dionysus (god of wine and revelry). **Deeon, Deiyon, Deyon.** Deion Sanders, baseball pro.

DEJUAN   American: Contemporary, based on Juan (God is gracious). **DeJuan.**

DEKER   Hebrew: "to pierce."

DEKOVA   American: Contemporary.

DELACROIX   French: "of the cross." **DeLaCroix. Del.**

DELACRUZ   Spanish: "of the cross." **DeLaCruz. Cruz, Del.**

DELACY   French: "from Lassy (Lasciu's estate)."

DELANO   French: "from La Noe (the wet land); of the night."

DELBERT   English: Blending of Del (leader of the people) and Bert (bright).

DELEON   American: Contemporary, based on Leon (lion). **Deleon.**

DELEWIS   American: Contemporary, based on Lewis (famous in war). **DeLouis, D'Lewis, D'Louis.**

DELINO   American: Contemporary. Delino DeShields, baseball pro.

DELL   English: "dell, valley."

DELLBEE   American: Contemporary.

DELMAR   Spanish: "of the sea." **Del Mar. Del.**

DELON American: Contemporary. **Dee-Lon, De'Lon, D'Lon.**

DELOSS American: Contemporary.

DELRIO Spanish: "of the river." **Del.**

DELROY English: Combination of the names Dell (dell, valley) and Roy (king; red). **Dellroi, Dellroy, Delroi.**

DELVIN American: Contemporary, modeled after Melvin (counsel protector). Greek: "dolphin."

DELWIN American. Welsh: "pretty and fair; pretty and blessed." **Dellwin, Dellwinn, Dellwyn, Dellwynn, Dellwynne, Delwinn, Delwyn, Delwynn, Delwynne. Del, Dell.**

DELWYN Welsh: "pretty and fair; pretty and blessed." A female name in Wales, although it's used as a male name in the United States.

DEMARCO American: Contemporary, based on Marco (Mars). **Demarco, De Marko, Demarko.**

DEMARIAE American: Contemporary.

DEMARKUS American: Contemporary, based on Markus (Mars). **De Marcus, Demarcus, Demarkus.**

DEMATTHEW American: Contemporary, based on Matthew (gift of God).

DEMETRI English. Greek: "of Demeter." **Demetry.**

DEMETRIC American. Greek: "of Demeter." **Demetrik.**

DEMETRICE American. Greek: "of Demeter." **Demetris, Demetrise.**

DEMETRIUS Latin. Greek: "of Demeter." Demeter was the mythological Greek goddess of fertility and agriculture.

DEMETRUS American. Greek: "of Demeter."

DEMIAN American. Greek: "tamer."

DEMOND American: Contemporary. Demond Wilson, actor.

DEMONTE French: "dweller near the hill." **DeMontey, DeMonty.**

DEMONTRE American: Contemporary.

DEMOSTHENES Greek: "of the people." Demosthenes (384?–322 B.C.) was an Athenian statesman and orator. **Demosthanes.**

DEMPSEY Irish: "proud."

DENDRIUS American: Contemporary.

DENETRIUS American: Modern variation of Demetrius (of Demeter).

DENIS French. Greek: "of Dionysus." Dionysus was the Greek god of wine and revelry. **Dennis, Denniss, Denys, Dennys. Denny.** Dennis Rodman, basketball pro. Dennis Boyd, baseball pro.

DENTON English: "from the settlement in the valley; from the settlement by the den."

DENZAR American: Contemporary.

DENZELL Cornish: "from Denzell." **Denzel, Denzelle, Denzil.** Denzel Washington, actor.

DEOLA American. Danish: "ancestor."

DEONTAY American: Contemporary. **Deontae, Diontae, Diontay.**

DERALD American: Contemporary, modeled after Gerald (spear ruler).

DEREK German: "ruler of the people."

DERICK American. German: "ruler of the people." **Derik, Derrick, Derrik, Deryck, Deryk.** Derrick Coleman, basketball pro.

DERONN American: Contemporary.

DERRAL American. French: "from the town Airelle."

DERRON American: Contemporary.

DERVIN American: Contemporary.

DESHAD Hindi: "nation."

DESHAL Hindi: "nation."

DESHONE American: Contemporary. **DeShoan, DeShone.**

DESHUN American: Contemporary.

DESMOND Irish: "from South Munster."

DETECTO Italian: "detective."

DETROIT American. French: "strait." Borrowed from the name of the Michigan city.

DEUCE American: "two."

DEVAK Hindi: "divine."

DEVAUGHN Dutch: "carrier of the banner."

DEVEAUX French: "dweller in the valley." **Deveau.**

DEVEREAUX French: "from Evreux." **Devereux.**

DEVERELL Welsh: "from the riverbank." **Deverel, Deveril, Deverill.**

DEVIN American: Contemporary form of Devin (poet). **DeVinn, DeVyn, DeVynn.**

DEVIN Irish: "poet." **Devon.** Devon White, baseball pro.

DEVITT Irish: "son of little David (God is gracious)."

DEVON American: Contemporary. **DeVonn, D'Von, D'Vonn.**

DEVONAIRE American: Contemporary, influenced by the word *debonair* (urbane, cultured).

DEVONE American: Contemporary.

DEVRIES Dutch: "the Frisian, from Friesland."

DEWANN American: Contemporary.

DEWARD American: Contemporary, a possible anagram of Edward (wealthy guardian).

DEWITT Dutch: "light-complexioned, white-haired." **De Wit, Dewitt, De Witte.**

DEXTER English: "dyer of cloth." **Dex.**

DEZARIE American: Contemporary.

DEZELL American: Contemporary, possibly a shortened form of Denzell (from Denzell).

D'HANEY American: Contemporary.

DHAREN Hindi: "supporter."

DIAMAN American: Contemporary, possibly influenced by *diamond* (a diamond, a precious gem).

DIANGELO Italian: "son of Angelo (angel, messenger of God)."

DIATRA American: Contemporary. **Dieatra.**

DIGBY English. Norse: "settlement by the ditch."

DIJI African: "farmer."

DILLAN American. Welsh: Meaning uncertain; some think it's from a Celtic element meaning "sea." **Dilan, Diland, Dilland, Dyllan, Dylland.**

DILLARD English: "the dull one."

DIMPLE American: "one with a dimple."

DION Greek: "of Dionysus (the Greek god of wine and revelry)." **Dionn.** Dion James, baseball pro.

DIONTE American: Contemporary.

DMITRI Russian. Greek: "of Demeter (the Greek goddess of agriculture and fertility)." **Dimitri, Dmitriy.**

DOAK Scottish: "the servant of Saint Cadoc." Doak Walker, football pro.

DOIL American. Irish: "descendant of the dark one."

DOMINIC English. Latin: "belonging to the Lord." **Dominick, Dominik.**

DOMINIQUE French. Latin: "belonging to the Lord." Dominique Wilkins, basketball pro.

DONAL Irish: "world ruler." **Donall. Don, Donny.**

DONALD Gaelic: "world ruler." **Don.** Donald E. McHenry, U.S. ambassador to the United Nations. Donald B. Gibson, writer and professor.

DONDRÉ American: Contemporary. **Dondrae, Dondray, Dondre, Dondrey.** Dondré Whitfield, actor.

DONELL American. Irish: "world ruler." **Donelle, Donnell, Donnelle. Don, Donny.** Donell Nixon, baseball pro.

DONMINIC American: Contemporary variant of Dominic (belonging to the Lord).

DONOVAN Irish: "dark brown."

DONTA American: Contemporary.

DONTAE American: Contemporary, probably based on Danté (lasting).

DONTONIO American: Contemporary, possibly a blending of the names Don (world ruler) and Antonio (of inestimable worth). Dontonio Wingfield, basketball pro.

DONYELL American: Contemporary. Donyell Marshall, basketball pro.

DONZELL American: Contemporary.

DORATHER American: Contemporary.

DORÉ French: "golden."

DORIAN English: An invention of Oscar Wilde (1854–1900) for a character in *The Picture of Dorian Gray.*

DORON Greek: "gift."

DORSEY Irish: "dark man." French: "from Arcy (stronghold)."

DOUGLAS Gaelic: "dark blue, dark gray." **Douglass. Doug.**

DOYLE   Irish: "descendant of the dark one."

DRAFTON   American: Contemporary.

DRAKE   English: "dragon; male duck."

DRESDEN   German: "from Dresden, a city on the Elbe River."

D'SHAWN   American: Contemporary.

DUANE   English. Celtic: "little dark one." **De Wayne, Dewayne, Dwain, Dwaine, Dwane, Dwayne**.

DUFF   Irish: "black, dark-complexioned."

DUGAN   Irish: "little black one." Welsh: "little Dug (a pet form of Richard [stern king])."

DUJUAN   American: Contemporary.

DUKE   English: "a duke, a nobleman whose rank is just below that of a prince."

DULANI   Malawi. Ngoni: "cutting."

DUMITRU   Romanian. Greek: "of Demeter."

DUMONT   French: "of the mount, of the hill." **Du Mont**.

DUNCAN   Scottish: "brown warrior."

DUNEESHI   American: Probably a variant of Dunixi (of Dionysus).

DUNIXI   Spanish. Greek: "of Dionysus (the god of wine and revelry)."

DUNSTAN   English: "dark stone."

DUNYEA   American: Contemporary.

DUPONT   French: "of the bridge."

DUPREE   French: "of the meadow." **Du Pre**.

DURAND   French: "lasting."

DURELL   English: "stern, severe." **Durrell**.

DURIEL   Hebrew: "the Lord is my dwelling."

DUROND   American: Contemporary, possibly modeled after Durand (lasting).

DUSTIN   English: Meaning uncertain, possibly from the Norse name Thorstein (Thor's stone).

DUWARD   American. English: "from the forest of wild animals."

DWALYN   American: Contemporary.

DWAN   Irish: "little black one." American: Contemporary. **D'Wan, D'Wann**.

DWAWNE   American: Contemporary.

DWIGHT   Dutch: "the white one." Dwight Gooden, baseball pro.

DWIVIAS   American: Contemporary.

DYCRONE   American: Contemporary.

DYLAN   Welsh: Meaning uncertain. Some think it's from a Celtic element meaning "sea."

DYSHAWNE   American: Contemporary.

EARL   English: "an earl, a nobleman." **Earle**. Earl Cunningham, baseball pro. Earl Klugh, jazz guitarist.

EARVIN   American: Variant of Ervin (friend of the sea). Earvin "Magic" Johnson, basketball pro.

EARWEN English: A combination name formed from the elements *boar* and *friend*.

EDDIE English: "prosperity, fortune." **Eddy**. Eddie Murray, baseball pro. Eddie Daniels, jazz musician. Eddie "Rochester" Anderson (1906–1977), comedian. Eddie Murphy, actor-comedian.

EDDWYNN American. English: "prosperous friend."

EDET Nigeria. Efik: "born on market day."

EDISON English: "son of Edie."

EDOLPHUS American: Probably a Latinate rendering of Adolph (noble wolf).

EDROY American: Blending of the names Ed and Roy (king; red). **Ed, Eddie**.

EDWARD English: "wealthy guardian." **Ed, Eddie**. Edward Bouchet (1852–1918), first Black to earn a Ph.D. at a U.S. university. Edward Lewis, cofounder of *Essence* magazine.

EDWAYNE American: Blending of Ed and Wayne (a wagoner, one who uses a wagon). **Ed, Eddie**.

EDWIN English: "prosperous friend." **Eddwynn, Edwinn, Edwynn. Ed, Eddie**.

EFRON Hebrew: "a bird." **Ephron**.

ELDON English: "Ella's hill." **Elden, Eldin, Eldyn**. Elden Campbell, basketball pro.

ELDRICK American: Possibly a variant of Eldridge (from Elbridge [the plank bridge]).

ELDRIDGE English: "from Elbridge (the plank bridge)." Eldridge Cleaver, author and civil rights leader.

ELESTER American: Coinage, perhaps a variant of Alistair (defender or helper of mankind).

EL-FATIH Arabic: "the conqueror."

ELI Hebrew: "high, ascend, lifting up." **Ely**.

ELIAS Greek. Hebrew: "Jehovah is God; the Lord is my salvation."

ELIAZ Hebrew: "my God is strong."

ELIJAH Hebrew: "Jehovah is God." **Elija**. Elijah Muhammad (1897–1975), founder of the Black Muslims.

ELIMU Swahili: "knowledge."

ELISHA Hebrew: "God is salvation."

ELKANAH Hebrew: "God created."

ELLAIRD American: Contemporary, based on Ellard (elf guardian).

ELLARD English: "elf guardian."

ELLINGTON English: "from Ellington (Ella's town)."

ELLIOT English. French: "little Elijah."

ELLIOUT American: Variant of Elliot.

ELLIS English. Hebrew: "Jehovah is God; God is salvation." Ellis Burks, baseball pro. Ellis Marsalis, jazz musician. Ellis Wilson, painter.

ELLSWORTH English: "from Elsworth (Elli's homestead)."

ELMO Italian. Greek: "friendly, amiable." Saint Elmo is the patron saint of sailors.

ELMORE English: "from Elmore (the shore where elms grow)." Elmore Spencer, basketball pro.

ELON American: Contemporary, perhaps based on the French élan (spirit, verve).

ELOYCE American: Coinage, perhaps influenced by the French Eloy (worthy of choice).

ELRADER American: Possibly a variant of the Hebrew Elrad (God is the king).

ELTON English: "from Elton (Ella's village; Aethelheah's village)." Elton C. Fax, author and illustrator.

ELVAH American: Contemporary.

ELVARDO Spanish. German: "noble and strong."

ELVESTER American: Coinage, inspired by Sylvester (of a wood or forest).

ELVIN American. English: "friend of the elves; godly friend." **Elvinn, Elvyn, Elvynn.** Elvin Hayes, basketball pro.

ELYSEES American: Variant of Ulysses (hater).

EMERAL American: Contemporary.

EMERSON English: "son of Emery (work ruler)."

EMILE French. German: "industrious." Latin: "rival, trying to equal or excel." Emile Harry, football pro.

EMILTON American: Possibly modeled after Hamilton (from the treeless hill).

EMMANOUIL American. Hebrew: "God with us."

EMMANUEL English. Hebrew: "God with us." **Emanuel.**

EMMET English: "of Emma." **Emmett, Emmit, Emmitt.** Emmitt Smith, football pro.

ENGROM American. English: "from Ingram (grassland enclosure)." Norse: "Ing's raven."

ENNIS Scottish: "dweller on an island or riparian meadow." **Ennes, Enness.**

ENOCH Hebrew: "dedicated."

ENRICHE American: Contemporary, possibly influenced by Enrique (home ruler).

ENRIQUE Spanish. German: "home ruler; ruler of an enclosure." **Anrique, Enrrique, Henrique, Inrique.**

EPHRAIM Hebrew: "very fruitful." **Efram.**

EREL Hebrew: "I will see God."

ERIC Norse: "eternal ruler." **Erich, Erick, Erik, Eryc, Eryk.** Eric Davis, baseball pro.

ERION American: Contemporary variant of Orion (a name from Greek mythology).

ERIQ American. Norse: "eternal ruler." Eriq La Salle, actor. **Erek, Errek, Errick.**

ERMIAS Arabic. Hebrew: "the Lord loosens, God will uplift."

ERNEAST American: Variant of Ernest (earnest). **Ernie.**

ERNEST German: "earnest, resolute." **Earnest. Ernie.** Ernest Riles, baseball pro. Ernest J. Gaines, novelist.

ERNIE German: "earnest, resolute."

ERRICT American. Norse: "eternal ruler."

ERROLL English. Latin: "wanderer." **Errol**. Erroll Garner (1921–1977), jazz musician.

ERRON American. Hebrew: "enlightened."

ERVIN English. German: "sea friend." **Ervinn, Ervyn, Ervynn**.

ERWIN English: "boar; friend." German: "friend of many."

ERYX Greek: Meaning unknown. In Greek mythology, Eryx was a son of Poseidon and Aphrodite.

ESSIEN Nigeria. Ibo: "the child belongs to everyone."

ESTEEN American: Contemporary.

ETHAN Hebrew: "strength, longevity." **Ethen, Ethun**.

EUGENE French. Latin: "well born." Eugene Lee, actor.

EUNIQUE American: "unique."

EURIDEE American: Coinage, perhaps influenced by Euripides. Euripides (479?–406? B.C.) was a Greek writer of tragedies.

EVAN Welsh. Hebrew: "God is gracious." **Evon**.

EVANDER Greek: "manly." Evander Holyfield, heavyweight boxing champion.

EVERETT English. German: "strong as a wild boar." **Everet, Everit, Everitt, Evret, Evrett, Evrit, Evritt**.

EVERT German: "strong as a wild boar."

EVERTEEN American. German: "strong as a wild boar."

EXCELL American: "to excel, to be eminent."

EXREE American: Contemporary.

EZEKIEL English. Hebrew: "God strengthens." **Ezekyel, Zeke**.

EZELL English: "from Isell (Isa's corner)."

EZRA Hebrew: "help."

EZZRETT American: Coinage, possibly influenced by Ezra (help).

FADELL American. Arabic: "generous."

FADIL Arabic: "generous."

FAHD Arabic: "panther, lynx."

FAHIM Arabic: "intelligent."

FANTASIA American: "fantasy; a musical composition with no fixed form." A contemporary name no doubt influenced by the movie *Fantasia*, a Disney classic.

FARAJ Arabic: "remedy."

FARID Arabic: "unique." **Fareed**.

FARIS Arabic: "horseman, rider of horses." **Farees, Fareese**.

FARON French: "maker and seller of candles." **Farron**.

FARRAN Arabic: "baker." **Farren, Ferren**.

FARUQ Arabic: "a distinguisher of right from wrong."

FAWZI Arabic: "achievement."

FAYIZ Arabic: "achiever."

FAYSAL Arabic: "a judge." **Faisal**.

FEDERAL American: "a central authority or government."

FELA Nigerian: "warlike."

FELIPE Spanish. Greek: "lover of horses."

FELTON English: "from the town or farm on the field." Felton Spencer, basketball pro.

FENTON English: "from the homestead by the marsh." Fenton Johnson (1888–1958), poet.

FENTRESS English: "adventurer, risk-taker."

FERDINAND European. German: "prepared for a journey; peaceful journey." **Ferdnand. Ferdi.** Ferdinand La Menthe, jazz musician.

FERRELL Irish: "super valor." Ferrell Edmunds, football pro.

FIELDING English: "dweller near the fields."

FINESSE American: "skill, artfulness, ability."

FITZPATRICK Irish: "son of Patrick (patrician)." **Fitz.**

FITZROY Irish: "son of Roy (red)." **Fitz.**

FLEMMON American: Contemporary.

FLOURNOY French: "dweller at the place of flowers." **Flourney.** Flournoy Miller (1887–1971), actor.

FONTAINE French: "from Fontaine (fountain, bubbling spring)." **Fontain, Fontane.**

FORESTORN American: Contemporary, based on Forest (a forest). **Forrestorn.** Forestorn "Chico" Hamilton, jazz percussionist.

FORREST English: "dweller or worker in a forest." **Forest, Forestt, Forrestt.** Forest Whitaker, actor and director.

FRANCOIS French: "French, a Frenchman."

FRANK German: "a Frank, a member of the Frankish Empire." Frank White, baseball pro.

FRANKLIN English: "a freeman, a landowner of free birth." **Franklinn, Franklyn, Franklynn. Frank, Frankie.** Franklin Stubbs, baseball pro.

FRED English: "elf counselor; peace ruler." Fred McGriff, baseball pro.

FREDERICK English. German: "peace ruler." **Fredrick, Fredrik, Fredryk. Fred, Freddie, Freddy, Rick, Ricky.** Frederick Douglass (1817–1895), author, editor, abolitionist, minister, and consul general to Haiti. Frederick Patterson (1901–1988), founder of the United Negro College Fund. Frederick D. Gregory, astronaut. Frederick O'Neal, actor.

FREEDAIL American: Contemporary.

FREEMAN English: "a freeman, a man who ranks above a serf." Freeman McNeil, football pro.

FUDAIL Arabic: "excellent in character."

FUNSANI Malawi. Ngoni: "request."

GABRIAL American. Hebrew: "God is my strength." **Gabriall, Gabriell, Gabryel, Gabryell. Gabe.**

GABRIEL Hebrew: "God is my strength." **Gabe.**

GAGE English: "measurer, tester."

GALE English. Hebrew: "father of exaltation." Gale Sayers, football pro.

GALEN English. Latin: "calm, serene." **Gaylen.**

GAREN American: Contemporary.

GARETH English: Meaning unknown. First noted in Sir Thomas Malory's collection of Arthurian tales, *Le Morte D'Arthur*, where it is the name of Sir Gawain's brother. **Garreth.**

GARLAND English: "spear land; dweller at the triangular field."

GARMOND English: "spear protector." **Garamond.**

GARNER English: "warrior, protector with a spear."

GARNETT English: "protector with a spear."

GARRET English: "spear rule, spear brave." **Garrett, Garrit. Garry, Gary.** Garrett A. Morgan, inventor of safety devices.

GARRICK English: "from Garrick (Gara's dwelling)." German: "brave with the spear." **Garek, Garrek. Garry, Gary.**

GARRISON English: "son of Gerard (brave with the spear)." **Garry, Gary.**

GARVEN Irish: "little Garbh (rough)." **Garvon.**

GARVIN English. Teutonic: "spear friend."

GARWOOD English: "dweller among the fir trees."

GARY English: "spear of battle." **Garry.** Gary Payton, basketball pro. Gary Sheffield, baseball pro.

GASTON English. French: "from Gascony." Gaston Green, football pro.

GAWAIN Welsh: "battle hawk."

GAYLON American. English. Latin: "calm, serene."

GEDEON Russian. Hebrew: "hewer, one who cuts down."

GEIRROD Norse: "famous with a spear."

GELFON American: Contemporary.

GELMAN German: "a money changer."

GENE English. Latin: "well born." Gene Harris, baseball pro.

GENERAL American: "a high-ranking military officer."

GENNARO Italian. Latin: "January; of Janus, the Roman mythological god of portals and of beginnings and endings."

GENO Italian. Latin: "well born, noble." **Gino.**

GENTRY American: "noble, of high birth."

GEOFFREY French. German: An evolution of several different names whose meanings are "pledge of peace," "traveler of peace," and "land of peace." **Geoffry. Geof, Geoff.** Geoffrey Holder, actor, director, painter.

GEORGE Greek: "farmer, worker of the earth." George Foreman, heavyweight boxer. George Washington Carver (1861–

1943), botanist and chemist whose work helped revitalize the economy of the South. George Benson, jazz guitarist. George Shirley, tenor.

GERALD English. German: "spear ruler." **Gerrald, Gerrold, Jarald, Jarrald, Jarrold, Jerald, Jerrald, Jerrold. Gerry, Jarry Jerry.** Gerald Wilkins, basketball pro. Gerald LeVert, singer.

GERARD French. German: "brave with the spear."

GERMAIN French: "brother." **Germaine.**

GERON French: "little Gero (spear)."

GERONIMO Spanish. Greek: "holy name." **Geromino.** Geronimo Berroa, baseball pro.

GEROY American: Contemporary.

GERRON American: Contemporary.

GERVAIS French: "spear warrior." **Gervaise.**

GESTIN American. French. Latin: "the just." **Gestyn.**

GHEDI Somali: "traveler."

GIANCARLO Italian: Combination of Gian (God is gracious) and Carlo (full-grown; a man).

GIBSON English: "son of Gib (bright pledge)."

GILAM Hebrew: "joy of the people."

GILBERT English. German: "bright pledge." **Gillbert. Gib, Gil.**

GILQUAN American: Contemporary.

GIONET American: Contemporary, probably influenced by the Italian Giannetti (little Gianni).

GI-VONNIE American: Contemporary, likely based on Giovanni (God is gracious).

GLENALLEN American. Celtic: Combination of Glen (a mountain valley) and Allen.

GLENDON English. Celtic: "from the fortress in the glen."

GLENN Gaelic: "a mountain valley, a secluded valley." **Glen.** Glenn Robinson, basketball pro. Glen Braggs, baseball pro.

GLENWORTH American: Contemporary.

GLIDELL American: Contemporary.

GODFREY English: "God's peace."

GODWIN English: "friend of God." **Godwinn, Godwyn, Godwynn.**

GOLDWIN English: "friend of gold." **Goldwyn.**

GORDON Scottish: From a Scottish placename of unknown meaning. Gordon Parks, composer, director, author, and 1972 winner of the Spingarn Award.

GRACEN American: Contemporary, possibly modeled after Grayson (son of Greve).

GRAIG American: Contemporary spelling of Greg (a watchman), modeled after Craig (dweller by the crag).

GRANT English. French: "great, large." Grant Hill, basketball pro.

GRANVILLE English. French: "from the large town." Granville Woods (1856–1910), inventor of railroad telegraphy.

GRASTON English: "from the grassy settlement."

GRAYLIN American: Contemporary variant of Grayland (from the Gray land).

GRAYSON English: "son of Greve (earl)." **Greyson.**

GREG English. Greek: "a watchman, vigilant." Greg Vaughn, baseball pro.

GREGORY English. Greek: "a watchman, vigilant." **Greg, Gregg.** Gregory Hines, actor and dancer.

GROVER English: "dweller at a grove of trees." Grover Washington Jr., jazz musician.

GUILFORD English: "from Guildford (river ford near the marigolds)."

GUILLAUME French. German: "resolute protector."

GUION French: "little Guy (guide, leader)." **Guyon.** Guion Bluford Jr., astronaut, first Black American in space.

GUTHRIE Celtic: "serpent of war, war serpent."

GUYRITHAIN American: Contemporary. **Guyrithian.**

HABIB Arabic: "beloved."

HADDAD Arabic: "blacksmith."

HAFIZ Arabic: "guardian."

HAGEN German: "from the enclosure."

HAHVYER American: Contemporary, modeled after Xavier (the new house).

HAIDAR Arabic: "lion."

HAJI Swahili. Arabic: "born during the month of pilgrimage."

HAKIM Arabic: "judicious." **Ha-Keem, Hakeem.** Hakeem Olajuwan, basketball pro. Hakim Shahid, basketball pro.

HALE English: "dweller in the remote valley."

HALIM Arabic: "patient, mild-mannered."

HAMADI Swahili. Arabic: "praised, commended." **Hamidi.**

HAMAL Arabic: "lamb."

HAMID Arabic: "commendable, praising."

HAMILTON English: "from the blunt hill."

HAMISI Swahili: "born on Thursday."

HAMMOND English: "chief protector."

HAMPTON English: "from Hampton (high town; enclosure in a village)."

HANBAL Arabic: "purity."

HANIF Arabic: "true believer."

HANK English. German: "ruler of an enclosure, home ruler."

HANNA Arabic. Hebrew: "God is gracious." The Arabic form of John.

HAREL Hebrew: "mountain of God."

HARITH Arabic: "earthworker, cultivator."

HARLAN English: "dweller in or near the land of hares." **Harland, Harlen.**

HARLEAN   American: Contemporary, possibly a variant of Harlan (dweller in the land of hares).

HARLEM   American: From the section of New York City in the borough of Manhattan.

HARLEY   English: "from Harley (the hares' woods)."

HARLIN   English: "from Harling (Herela's people)."

HARMONY   American: "order, harmony."

HAROLD   English and German: "ruler of an army." **Harald, Harrald, Harrold. Harry.** Harold R. Perry (1916–1991), first Black clergyman to deliver the opening prayer in the U.S. Congress. Harold Reynolds, baseball pro and sportscaster.

HARRY   English and German: "ruler of an army." Harry Belafonte, singer, actor, and director. Harry Carney, baritone saxophonist.

HARSHAN   Hindi: "joyful."

HARUN   Arabic: "exalted." **Haroon, Haroun.**

HARVEY   English: "battle-worthy."

HASAD   Turkish: "harvesting, reaping."

HASAN   Arabic: "beautiful, handsome." **Hassan.**

HASANI   Swahili. Arabic: "beautiful, handsome."

HASHIM   Arabic: "destroying, crushing." **Hasheem.**

HASIM   Arabic: "decisive." **Haseem, Hassiem.**

HASIN   Hindi: "beautiful."

HASKEL   Hebrew: "wisdom."

HASSANE   American. Arabic: "beautiful, handsome."

HAYDEN   English: "from Heydon (hay hill)." **Haydin, Haydon.**

HAYES   English: "dweller at or near the hedge, dweller at the hedged enclosure."

HAYTHAM   Arabic: "young eagle."

HAYWARD   English: "keeper of the hedged enclosure."

HAYWOOD   English: "from Haywood (hay wood)." **Haywoode.** Haywoode Workman, basketball pro. Haywood Oubre, painter.

HEBERT   German: "bright combat." English: "noble chief; mind bright."

HECTOR   Latin. Greek: "holding fast."

HENDRIK   Scandinavian. German: "ruler of an enclosure, home ruler."

HENLLYS   American: Contemporary.

HENRY   French. German: "ruler of an enclosure, home ruler." **Hal, Hank, Harry.** Henry Blair (nineteenth century), possibly the first Black to obtain patents. Henry O. Flipper (1856–1940), first Black to graduate from West Point. Henry Threadgill, jazz instrumentalist. Henry Louis "Hank" Aaron, baseball great, 1975 winner of the Spingarn Medal.

HENSLEY   English: "dweller in the hen's woods." Hensley Meulens, baseball pro.

HERBERT English: "bright army, famous army." **Bert, Herb, Herbie.** Herbie Hancock, jazz musician.

HERMAN English and German: "army man, soldier." **Hermann, Hermen. Herm, Hermie.**

HERSCHEL German: "dweller at the sign of the stag." **Hershel.** Herschel Walker, football pro.

HERSEY English: "from Hercy; from Herse." Hersey Hawkins, basketball pro.

HERSHEY German: "dweller at the sign of the stag."

HESHIMU Swahili. Arabic: "handsome."

HESSLEY American: Contemporary. **Hessley.** Hessley Hempstead, football pro.

HETONKUS Native American: "bull."

HEZEKIAH Hebrew: "the Lord strengthens."

HIATT English: "dweller at the high gate."

HIAWATHA Native American. Iroquois: "he makes rivers."

HILARION Greek: "cheerful, happy."

HILYARD English: "dweller at the hill enclosure; descendant of Hildegard (battle might)."

HIRAM Hebrew: "exalted brother." Hiram R. Revels (1822–1901), first Black U.S. senator.

HISHAM Arabic: "crushing."

HONDO Zimbabwe. Shona: "war."

HORACE English. Latin: From an old Roman family name of unknown meaning. Horace Grant, basketball pro.

HORATIO English. Latin: From an old Roman family name of unknown meaning. In Roman legend, Horatio was a hero who defended a bridge against the Etruscans.

HOSEA Hebrew: "salvation."

HOUSTON Scotland: "from Houston (Hugh's town)." **Huston.**

HOYCE Dutch: "spirit, mind."

HOYT Dutch: "spirit, mind." **Hoyte.**

HUBERT English. German: "bright heart." **Bert.** Hubert Davis, basketball pro.

HUEDNEY American: Contemporary.

HUNTER English: "a hunter, a huntsman." **Hunt.**

HURVIN American: Contemporary. Hurvin McCormick, football pro.

HUSANI Swahili. Arabic: "handsome."

HUSAYN Arabic: "handsome, beautiful." **Husain, Husane, Hussain, Hussane, Hussein.**

HUSNI Arabic: "excellence, beauty."

IAN Scottish. Hebrew: "God is gracious."

IBRAHIM Arabic. Hebrew: "father of a multitude."

IHSAN Arabic: "charity."

IKE English. Hebrew: "laughter." Originated as a short form of Isaac.

ILLIAM American: Contemporary, probably a shortened form of William (resolute protector). **Illium.**

IMARI American: Contemporary. Also, possibly influenced by the Swahili Imara (solid, firm) or borrowed from the name of a city in Kyushu, Japan.

INGRAM English. Old Norse: "Ing's raven." Ing was another name for the Norse fertility god Frey.

INNES Scottish. Celtic: "from the river island." **Inness, Innis, Inniss.**

INUS American: Coinage, possibly influenced by Innes (dweller on an island).

IRA Hebrew: "watchful; a stallion."

IRLTON American: Contemporary.

IRVING English. Celtic: From a river name of unknown meaning. **Irvin. Irv.** Irving Fryar, football pro.

ISAAK Greek. Hebrew: "laughter." In the Bible, Isaac is the name of one of the three patriarchs. **Isaac.** Isaac Hayes, musician.

ISAIAH Hebrew: "the Lord is salvation." **Isiah.** Isaiah Rider, basketball pro. Isiah Thomas, basketball pro. Isaiah Washington, actor.

ISANDRO Spanish. Greek: "freer of mankind, liberator."

ISHA Hindi: "master, ruler."

ISHAQ Arabic. Hebrew: "laughter."

ISHMAEL Hebrew: "God hears." Ishmael Reed, novelist and poet.

ISHUA Arabic. Hebrew: "God is salvation."

IVORY English: "tusk." Often used in reference to the West African country, Ivory Coast.

IYAN American: Contemporary.

IZELLO American: Contemporary.

JABARI Swahili: "brave; comforter, bringer of consolation."

JACIN American: Contemporary variant of Jason (healer).

JACINTO Spanish: "hyacinth."

JACK English. Hebrew: "God is gracious."

JACKOB American. Hebrew: "supplanting, seizing by the heel." **Jaycob, Jaykob. Jake.**

JACKSON English: "son of Jack (God is gracious)." **Jack, Jackie, Jacky.**

JACOB English. Hebrew: "supplanting, seizing by the heel." **Jacobe, Jakob. Jake.**

JACQUES French. Hebrew: "God is gracious." **Jacque.**

JADRIEN American: Contemporary.

JAFAR Arabic: "stream."

JAFARI Swahili. Arabic: "stream, creek."

JAHA Swahili: "dignity."

JAHAN Hindu: "the world."

JAHI Swahili: "dignity."

JAHIDI Swahili: "dignity."

JAHUE American: Contemporary.

JAI Hindi: "victory."

JAIDEV Hindi: "victory of God."

JAIH American: Contemporary spelling of Jay.

JAIMAN American: Contemporary.

JAKOBI West Africa. Mandinka: "star."

JAKUTA Nigeria. Yoruba: Stone Thrower, another name for Shango (god of the thunderbolt).

JALAL Hindi: "glory." Arabic: "greatness."

JALEN American: Contemporary. Jalen Rose, basketball pro.

JALIL Arabic: "beneficent." **Jaleel**. Jaleel White, actor.

JAMAD American: Contemporary. **Jahmahd, Jamahd, Jammad, Jammahd, Jammod**.

JAMAHL American: Arabic: "beauty." **Jahmahl, Jahmal, Jahmall, Jamall, Jamaul, Jhamahl, Jhamal, Jhamall**.

JAMAL Arabic: "beauty." **Jamaal**. Jamal Mashburn, basketball pro.

JAMALE American. Contemporary, possibly based on Jamal (beauty).

JAMAR American: Contemporary, a blending of Jamal (beauty) and Lamar (famous across the land). **Jahmar, Jamaar, Jamahr, Jamarr, Jammaar, Jammahr, Jammar**.

JAMARC American: Contemporary.

JAMEL American. Arabic: "beautiful, handsome." **Jammel**.

JAMES English. Hebrew: "supplanting, seizing by the heel." **Jaimes, Jaimz, Jaymes. Jim, Jimmy**. James Earl Jones, actor. James Baldwin (1924–1987), author and playwright. James "Eubie" Blake (1883–1983), jazz pianist. James Brown, singer, called the Godfather of Soul.

JA'MICHAEL American: Contemporary, based on Michael (Who is like God?).

JAMIL Arabic: "beautiful, handsome." **Jameel**.

JAMILE American. Arabic: "beautiful, handsome." **Jahmeel, Jahmil, Jahmyl, Jameal, Jamiel, Jamiil, Jamyl**.

JAMILEH Arabic: "beautiful."

JAMISON English: "Jamie's son." **Jamieson, Jamyson. Jami, Jamie, Jamy**.

JAMMAD American: Contemporary.

JAMMAL American. Arabic: "beauty."

JAMSHID American: Contemporary, perhaps a blending of Jamil (beautiful, handsome) and Rashid (rightly guided).

JANNON American: Contemporary.

JAPHET Hebrew: "spacious, beautiful."

JARAAN American: Contemporary.

JARAD Arabic: "locusts."

JARDELL American: Contemporary.

JARED Hebrew: "descendant." **Jarred**.

JARELL American: Contemporary. **JaRel, JaRelle, Jarelle**.

JARMAR American: Contemporary.

JARMICA American: Contemporary.

JARNAIL American: Contemporary.

JAROD American: Contemporary. **Jerod**.

JARON American: Contemporary. **Jahrhon, Jahron, Jahrron, Jarron**.

JARREL American: Contemporary, possibly based on Darrel (from the town of Airelle).

JARRETT English: "brave with a spear." American: based on Jared (descendant). **Jaret, Jarett, Jarret. Jarry**.

JARRY English: Variant of Jerry (brave with a spear).

JARVIS English: "servant of the spear."

JASHON American: Contemporary. **JaShaun, Ja'Shaun, JaShawn, Ja'Shawn, Ja'Shon, JaShonn, Ja'Shonn**.

JASIM Arabic: "strong." **Jaseem, Jassiem**.

JASON English. Latin and Greek: "healer." In Greek mythology, Jason was the leader of the Argonauts.

JASPER English: From Gaspar, a name of uncertain etymology that was assigned to one of the Three Wise Men in the eleventh century. It might be from the Persian *genashber* (treasure master).

JATHAN American: Contemporary, possibly influenced by Nathan (gift).

JAVAN American: Contemporary. **Javon**.

JAVARRON American: Contemporary. **Javvaron**.

JAVED Hindi: "immortal."

JAVIER Spanish: "from the new house." Arabic: "bright."

JAWARA African: "lover of peace."

JAY English: A short form of names beginning with the letter *J*.

JAYDON American: Contemporary. **Jaydan, Jayden, Jaydin**.

JAYFON American: Contemporary.

JAYLON American: Contemporary.

JAYMES American. Hebrew: "supplanting, seizing by the heel." **Jaimes, Jaimz, Jaymz. Jim, Jimmy**.

JAYMIN American: Contemporary.

JAYRON American: Blending of Jay and Ron (judgement power; ruler of decision).

JAYSHON American: Contemporary.

JAYSIO American: Contemporary.

JAYSON American. Latin and Greek: "healer." **Jaeson. Jae, Jay**. Jayson Williams, basketball pro.

JAYTHAN American: Contemporary. **Jaythan**.

JAYTRON American: Contemporary.

JAYZON American: Contemporary form of Jason (healer). **Jazon**.

JEAN French. Hebrew: "God is gracious."

JEANBAPTISTE French: "John the Baptist." In the Bible, John the Baptist was the forerunner of Christ. Jean Baptiste Point de Sable (1750–1818), pioneer trader and first settler of Chicago.

JEANCLAUDE French: Combination of Jean (God is gracious) and Claude (lame).

JEANPAUL French: Combination of Jean (God is gracious) and Paul (small).

JEARWAUN American: Contemporary.

JEDDA American. Arabic: Borrowed from the capital of Saudi Arabia. **Jed.**

JEDIDIAH Hebrew: "beloved by Jehovah." **Jed.**

JEFFERSON English: "son of Jeffrey."

JEFFREY English: "God's peace." **Jeffry. Jeff.** Jeffrey Leonard, baseball pro.

JELANI Swahili: "mighty, strong." **Jehlani.**

JEMEIL American. Arabic: "beautiful, handsome."

JEMISON Scottish: "son of James (supplanting)."

JENNER English: "a military engineer."

JENSEN Scandinavian: "Jens' son."

JENTREE American: Contemporary, probably influenced by Gentry (person of noble birth).

JEOVANI American: Contemporary, influenced by Giovanni (God is gracious).

JERAY American: Contemporary.

JERBAINE American: Contemporary. **Gerbain, Gerbaine, Jerbain.**

JEREMALE American: Contemporary.

JEREMIAH Hebrew: "God will uplift." **Jerry.**

JEREMY English. Hebrew: "God will uplift." **Jaremie, Jaremy, Jaromy, Jeramie, Jereme, Jeromy.**

JEREVON American: Contemporary.

JERMAIN English. French: "brother." **Germayne, Jermaine, Jermayn, Jermayne.** Jermaine Jackson, member of The Jackson Five.

JERMAL American: Contemporary. **Jermel.**

JERMAR American: Contemporary.

JERMONE American: Contemporary.

JERMORE American: Contemporary.

JERMYN Trinidad. English: "from Germany."

JERNELIUS American: Contemporary.

JEROME English. Greek: "holy name." Jerome Kersey, basketball pro. Jerome Walton, baseball pro.

JERON American: Contemporary. **Jerohn, Jeronn.**

JERONE American: Contemporary, based on Jerome (holy name). **Jeronne.**

JERRELL American: Contemporary. **Jerel.**

JERRIK American: Contemporary. **Jarick, Jarrick, Jarrik, Jerick, Jerik, Jerrick.**

JERRIMI American. Hebrew: "holy name."

JERROD American. Hebrew: "descendant." Jerrod Mustaf, basketball pro.

JERROTT American: Contemporary, probably based on Jerrod (descendant).

JERRY English: Originated as a pet form of several names beginning with *Jer-*. **Jarry.** Jerry Browne, baseball pro.

JERVAIN American: Contemporary. **Jervaine, Jervayne.**

JERVAIZ American. French: "spear warrior." **Jervace, Jervaice, Jervaise, Jervase, Jervays, Jervayz.**

JESPER Danish: Danish form of Jasper (treasure master).

JESSE English. Hebrew: "wealth, gift." Reverend Jesse Jackson, civil rights advocate, founder of the Rainbow Coalition, national director of Operation Bread Basket. Jesse Brown, U.S. secretary of Veterans Affairs. Jesse Owens (1914–1980), four-time Olympic gold medal-winning track star.

JESTIN American: Variant of Justin (just).

JEVON American: Contemporary. **Jevin.**

JIMIYU Uganda. Abaluhya: "born during a dry season."

JIMMY English. Hebrew: "supplanted." **Jimmie.**

JIVAN Hindi: "life."

JIVONE American: Contemporary.

JODARI American: Contemporary.

JOE English. Hebrew: "he shall add." Joe Carter, baseball pro.

JOEZON American: Contemporary. **Joe.**

JOHARI Arabic: "jewel." **Johar.**

JOHN English. Hebrew: "God is gracious." **Jack, Jackie, Johnnie, Johnny.** John H. Johnson, publisher. Johnny Mathis, singer. John Coltrane (1926–1967), jazz musician. John Birks "Dizzy" Gillespie (1917–1993), jazz great. Jackie Robinson (1919–1972), first Black major league baseball player.

JOHNALL American: Contemporary.

JOHNIGAN English: "little John (God is gracious)." **Jonigan. John, Johnnie, Johnny.**

JOHNNIE English. Hebrew: "God is gracious." **Johnny.** Johnny Gill, singer.

JOHNTÉ American: Contemporary. **Johntá, Johntae, Johntai, Johntay, Johntey.**

JOLLAND English. French: "jolly, gay." **Jollan.**

JOMARR American: Contemporary.

JONATHAN English. Hebrew: "God has given."

JONES English: "son of John (God is gracious)."

JOPHERY American: Contemporary, a phonetic spelling of the French Geoffroi.

JORDAN English. Hebrew: "to flow down, to descend." **Jorden, Jordon, Jordyn.**

JORECCA American: Contemporary.

JO REES American: Contemporary.

JO'RIN American: Contemporary.

JOSÉ Spanish. Hebrew: "he shall add." **Jose.** Jose Rijo, baseball pro.

JOSEPH Latin. Hebrew: "he shall add." **Joe, Joey.** Joseph H. Rainey (1832–1887), first Black elected to the U.S. House of Representatives. Joseph Seamon Cotter Sr., poet.

JOSHUA English. Hebrew: "the Lord is salvation." **Josh.**

JOURDAIN French. Hebrew: "he shall add."

JOVON American: Contemporary. **Jovaughn, Jovaun.**

JOZAREN American: Contemporary.

JUAN Spanish. Hebrew: "God is gracious."

JUAQUIN American. Spanish. Hebrew: "established by the Lord."

JUAREZ Spanish: "south army." **Juares.**

JUDAH Hebrew: "from Judah (praise)." **Juda.**

JUDGE English: "a judge."

JULES English. Latin: "downy-bearded; youth."

JULIANO Italian. Latin: "downy-bearded; youth."

JULIEN French. Latin: "downy-bearded; youth." **Julian.** Julian Bond, civil rights leader.

JULIO Spanish. Latin: "downy-bearded; youth."

JULIUS Latin: "downy-bearded; youth." Julius (Dr. J) Irving, basketball pro. Julius Lester, novelist.

JUMANA Swahili: "born on Tuesday." **Jumaana, Jumaane.**

JUMOKE Nigeria. Yoruba: "everyone loves the child."

JUNIOR English: "younger." Junior Walker, jazz musician.

JUPITER English. Latin: "Jove is father." In Roman mythology, Jupiter was the supreme God, equated with the Greek Zeus. Jupiter Hammon (c. 1720–1800), poet and first Black American to have his work published.

JURADO Spanish: "an officer of the courts."

JUSTICE English. Latin: "the just." **Justas, Justis, Justus.**

JUSTILIEN American: Contemporary, likely based on Justinien (the just).

JUSTIN French. Latin: "the just."

JUSTINIEN French. Latin: "the just."

JUWAN American: Contemporary. **Jujuan, Juwahn, Juwaun.** Juwan Howard, basketball pro.

KAARIA Kenyan: "he who speaks quietly and wisely."

KADAR Arabic: "powerful."

KADE German: "swamp."

KADEEM American. Arabic: "servant." Kadeem Hardison, actor.

KADIN Arabic: "companion."

KADIR Arabic: "capable." **Kadeer.**

KADISH Turkish: "saint, holy one."

KAHANA Aramaic: "priest."

KAHILL Turkish: "ingenuous."

KAI English. Latin: "rejoiced."

KAISER German: "Caesar, emperor." **Kaizer.**

KAIZ American: Contemporary.

KALIA Hawaiian: A type of tree native to Hawaii.

KALIF   Somali. Arabic: "holy boy."

KALIL   Hebrew: "crown, garland." Greek: "beautiful." **Kailil.**

KALIM   Arabic: "orator, speaker." **Kaleem.**

KAMA   Hawaiian: "child, person." Thai: "gold." Swahili: "like, if."

KAMAL   Hindi: "lotus." Arabic: "perfection."

KAMAR   American: Contemporary. **Kammar.**

KAMAU   Hawaiian: "to persevere, to continue." Kenya. Kikuyu: "quiet warrior."

KAMBUJI   Malawi. Ngoni: "goat."

KAMIL   Hindi: "complete." Arabic: "perfect." **Kameel.**

KAMILI   Hawaiian: "one beloved." Swahili. Arabic: "perfection."

KAMORA   American: Contemporary, perhaps based on the West African name Camara (teacher).

KAMOWA   Malawi. Ngoni: "beer."

KAMRAN   Hindi: "success."

KAMUZU   South Africa. Nguni: "medicinal."

KANAYA   American: Contemporary. **Kenaya.**

KANIEL   Hebrew: "a reed." Arabic: "a spear." **Kaneel, Kaneil.**

KANZAN   American: Contemporary.

KARAM   Arabic: "generosity."

KARIF   Arabic: "born in the autumn." **Kareef.**

KARIM   Arabic: "generous, noble." **Kareem, Kerim.** Kareem Abdul-Jabbar, basketball pro.

KARIO   American: Contemporary, probably modeled after Mario.

KARL   German: "free man." Karl Malone, basketball pro. Karl Kani, designer.

KARLOC   American: Contemporary.

KARLON   American: Contemporary.

KASHAWN   American: Contemporary.

KASHKA   Nigerian: "friendly."

KASIM   Arabic: "distributor of food and goods." **Kaseem.**

KASIYA   Malawi. Ngoni: "separation."

KATARI   American: Contemporary.

KATEB   Arabic: "writer."

KAVOSSY   American: Contemporary.

KAWEAH   American: Contemporary, possibly influenced by the Hawaiian language.

KAYAM   Hebrew: "established."

KAYIN   Nigeria. Yoruba: "long-awaited child."

KAYYAL   Arabic: "measurer."

KEANDRA   American: Contemporary.

KEANJAHO   Kenya. Kikuyu: "mountain of beans."

KEANTA   American: Contemporary. Kenya. Kikuyu: "mountain."

KEANTRA American: Contemporary.

KEANYANDAARWA Kenya. Kikuyu: "mountain of hides."

KEARNEY Irish: "soldier, victorious in battle."

KEATON English: "from Ketton (estate of the Kesteven people)."

KEAZIAH American: Contemporary.

KEDAR Arabic: "powerful."

KEEFE Celtic: "handsome, noble."

KEELAN Irish: "thin, slender." **Kealan, Kelan.**

KEELON American: Contemporary.

KEENAN Irish: "little bold one, little ancient one." Keenan Ivory Wayans, actor.

KEENJAY American: Contemporary.

KEFIR Hebrew: "lion cub."

KEHINDE Nigeria. Yoruba: "second of twins."

KEIF Irish: "gentle, beloved." **Keefe, Keeffe, Keiff.**

KEILER German: "wild boar."

KEILLER Scottish: "dweller by the River Keiller." The river name is of Celtic origin but unknown meaning. **Keillor, Keilor.**

KEIRAN Irish: "little black-haired one." **Kieran, Kieren. Keir, Kier.**

KEITA African: "medicinal."

KEITH Scottish: Uncertain meaning, possibly "the wind" or "the wood." Keith Jar-

rett, jazz keyboardist. Keith Sweat, musician. Keith Hamilton Cobb, actor.

KEKE American: Contemporary.

KELBY English. Scandinavian: "dweller at the farm by the spring; from Kell's (sacrificial cauldron) homestead." **Kelbi.**

KELDRICK American: Contemporary. **Kel.**

KELE American: Variant of Kelly (war, strife). Hawaiian: "navigator." Native American. Hopi: "sparrow hawk."

KELILE Ethiopia. Amharic: "my protector."

KELLAND German: "from the swampy land."

KELLEN German: "from Kellen (swamp)." **Kelen.**

KELLII American. Irish: "war, strife."

KELLY Irish: "war, strife."

KELSEY English: "ship of victory."

KELTHIUM American: Contemporary. **Kel.**

KELTON English: "from Kelton (calf settlement)."

KELVIN Scottish: A Scottish river name of unknown meaning.

KEMAL Turkish: "perfection."

KEMANI Hawaiian: "the smooth one."

KEMBLE English: "bold family." Welsh: "war chief." **Kembal, Kemball.**

KEMPER English: "soldier, warrior."

KEN English: Originated as a short form of any of the names beginning with *Ken-*. Ken Griffey Jr., baseball pro. **Kenn. Kenny.**

KENAN Hebrew: "to acquire, to have."

KENDALL English. Celtic: "belonging to Kendal (the dell of the river Kent)." **Kendal, Kendel, Kendell. Ken, Kenny.**

KENDERICK American. English: "royal ruler." **Ken, Kenny.**

KENDRICK English: "royal ruler." **Ken, Kenny.**

KENIA American: Contemporary, likely a variant spelling of Kenya.

KENIDS American: Contemporary.

KENIKA American: Contemporary, possibly from the Hawaiian *kenika* (tennis).

KENJI American: Contemporary. **Kenjii.**

KENNER German: "connoisseur." **Ken, Kenny.**

KENNETH English. Gaelic: "handsome; born of fire." **Ken, Kenny.** Ken Page, actor. Kenneth I. Chenault, vice chairman of American Express, highest-ranking Black executive of a Fortune 500 company.

KENRICK English: "bold ruler." **Kenric, Kenrik. Ken, Kenny.**

KENSLEY American: Contemporary. **Kensleigh. Ken, Kenny.**

KENTO American: Contemporary. **Ken, Kenny.**

KENYA English: Taken from the name of the African country.

KENYATTA American: An elaboration of Kenya. **Ken, Kenny.**

KENYON English: "from Kenyon." Gaelic: "white head." **Kenian, Kenion, Kenyan.**

KEON American: Contemporary, modeled after Leon (lion). **Keion, Keyon.**

KENSINGTON English: "from the estate of Cynesige (royal victory)." **Ken, Kenny.**

KEPRIN American: Contemporary.

KERMIT Celtic: "free man." Kermit Washington, basketball pro. Kermit Ruffins, singer.

KERVIN American. Contemporary.

KERWIN Irish: "little black one."

KÉSHA American: Contemporary.

KESHAWN American: Contemporary, based on Shawn (God is gracious). **Keeshaan, Keeshaun, Keeshaune, Keeshawn, Keeshon, Keshaan, Keshaun, Keshaune, Keshawn, Keshon, Keyshaan, Keyshaun, Keyshaune, Keyshawn.**

KESHINA Hindi: "lion."

KESSLER German: "kettle maker." **Kesler.**

KEVIN English. Irish: "handsome." **Keven, Kevinn, Kevyn, Kevynn.** Kevin Johnson, basketball pro. Kevin Mitchell, baseball pro.

KEVLIN American: Contemporary.

KEYAN American: Contemporary.

KEYON American: Contemporary. **Keyan.**

KEYWAN American: Contemporary. **Keejuan, Keewahn, Keewan, Keewaun, Kee-**

won, Keyjuan, Keywahn, Keywan, Keywaun.

KEZ American: Contemporary.

KHABBAZ Arabic: "baker."

KHADEEM Arabic: "servant."

KHAJANA American: Contemporary.

KHALDUN Arabic: "eternal."

KHALFANI Swahili: "born to lead."

KHALID Arabic: "eternal." **Khaled, Khaleed**. Khalid Reeves, basketball pro.

KHALIL Arabic: "best friend, companion." **Kahlil**.

KHAMADI African. Arabic: "born on Thursday."

KHAMIS Arabic: "Thursday."

KHAMISI Swahili. Arabic: "born on Thursday."

KHAN Turkish: "lord, prince." **Khanh**.

KHARI African. Arabic: "charitable."

KHAROUF Arabic: "lamb."

KHARY American: Contemporary, possibly influenced by the Arabic Khayri (charitable) or the Irish Kerry (black-haired one). **Khayra**.

KHAYRI Arabic: "charitable."

KHAYYAT Arabic: "tailor."

KIE-AIRE American: Contemporary.

KIHLON American: Contemporary.

KIJANA Swahili: "youth." **Keejana, Ki-Jana, Ki-jana**. Ki-jana Carter, football pro.

KIMANE Kenya. Kikuyu: "large bean."

KIMATHI Kenya. Kikuyu: "earnest provider." **Kim**.

KIMBLE English: "from Kimble (royal hill)." **Kimball, Kimbel. Kim**.

KIMOTHY American: Contemporary, based on Timothy (honoring God). **Kim**.

KIN American: "blood relative, a relation."

KINDRED English: "related; bold counsel." **Kin**.

KING English: "king, sovereign." King Oliver, band leader.

KINGSLEY English: "dweller near the king's meadow or the king's wood." **Kinsley. Kin**.

KINNARD Gaelic: "from the high mountain." **Kin, Kinn**.

KINSLEIGH American: Contemporary, possibly a modern variant of Kingsley (dweller near the king's meadow) or a combination of the names Kin (blood relative) and Leigh (wood, clearing, meadow). **Kin**.

KINTU Uganda: The name of the legendary first king of Uganda. Kintu was supposedly descended from the gods.

KIRBY English: "from Kirby (the church settlement)." Kirby Puckett, baseball pro.

KIRK English. Norse: "church." Kirk Franklin, gospel singer.

KITO Swahili: "precious."

KITRI American: Contemporary.

KITWANA Swahili: "pledged to live."

KIVI Finnish: "dweller by the stone."

KIWANE American: Contemporary.

KNIGHTY American. English: "a knight."

KNOX Scottish: "from Knock, from Knock hill."

KOBINA American: Contemporary.

KOFI Ghana. Akan: "born on Friday."

KOICE American: Contemporary, possibly influenced by Roice (Roy's son). **Koyce.**

KOII American. English: "shy, quiet."

KOJO Ghana. Ashanti: "born on Monday."

KONATA African: "noble."

KONNER American. English: "examiner, inspector." **Kennor.**

KORLEONE Italian: "lion heart." **Corleone.**

KORONDE American: Contemporary.

KORVESH American. Hebrew: "farmer, digger in the earth."

KOVEY American: Contemporary.

KRACY American: Contemporary.

KREG American: Variant of Craig (crag, rock).

KUBWEZA Malawi. Ngoni: "give it back." This type of name is used to disguise the child's true worth from the spirit world.

KUMI Ghana. Akan: "forceful."

KURTIS German. French: "courteous."

KURVÉ American: Contemporary.

KWAME Ghana. Akan: "born on Saturday."

KWANTIKA American: Contemporary.

KWENDE Malawi. Ngoni: "let's go."

KWESI African: "born on Sunday." **Kwasi, Kweisi.**

KYAN American: Contemporary, probably influenced by Ryan (little king). **Kian, Kyen.**

KYLER American. German: "wild boar."

KYNDALL American. English: "the dell of the river Kent."

KYWAN American: Contemporary. **Ky-Juan, Kyjuan.**

LACEY English. French: "belonging to Lacy or Lassy (the estate of Latius)."

LACROIX French: "the cross."

LACROSSE French: "the crutch, the hockey stick." Lacrosse is the name the French gave to a Native American ball game. **LaCrosse.**

LADON American: Contemporary.

LADRELL American: Contemporary.

LAEL Hebrew: "belonging to God."

LAFAID American: Contemporary.

LAFAYETTE French: "dweller near the small beech grove." **Lafayette.**

LAFFITTE French: "dweller at the boundary marker." **Laffite, Lafitte.**

LAFOLLETTE American: Contemporary, based on Follette (little foolish one). **Lafollett, Lafollette.**

LAFORGE French: "worker at the forge." **LaForge, L'Forge.**

LAFRANC French: "the freeman." **La Frank.**

LAHMARD American: Contemporary.

LAIZAR American. Hebrew: "whom God helps."

LAKEITH American: Contemporary, based on Keith (meaning uncertain).

LAMAR Teutonic: "famous land, famous across the land."

LAMARCUS American: Contemporary, based on Marcus (warlike).

LAMARR French: "dweller near the pool." **La Mar, Lamar.**

LAMEACH American: Contemporary.

LAMOINE French: "the monk."

LAMOND Scottish. Scandinavian: "the lawyer." **Lamont.** Lamond Murray, basketball pro.

LAMONTE American: Contemporary, based on Monte (mountain).

LAMOUNT American. Scottish: "the lawyer."

LAMSON English: "son of Lam (bright land)."

LANCE French. German: "land." Lance Johnson, baseball pro.

LANCELOT English: Meaning unknown. In Arthurian legend Lancelot was King Arthur's best and most trusted knight. **Lance.**

LANDIS French: "from Landes (swampy place)."

LANDO German: "country, land."

LANDON English. French: "from Langdon (long hill)."

LANDRON American: Contemporary.

LANDRY French: "powerful country; country ruler."

LANGSTON English: "from Langstone (long stone)." Langston Hughes (1902–1967), poet, author, and lyricist.

LAPHONSO American: Variant of Alphonso (noble and ready). **LaFonso, Lafonso, Laphonso.** Laphonso Ellis, basketball pro.

LARELL American: Contemporary.

LARENZ American. German. Latin: "man from Laurentum." Larenz Tate, actor.

LARHAN American. French. Latin: "man from Laurentum." **Larhaun.**

LARI American: Variant of Larry (man from Laurentum).

LARKIN English: "little Laurence (man from Laurentum)."

LARMON American: Contemporary.

LARNELL American: Contemporary, influenced by Darnell (hidden nook). Larnell Harris, gospel singer.

LARNEY American: Contemporary.

LAROM American: Contemporary.

LARONCE American: Contemporary variant of Laurence (man from Laurentum). **LaRance, LaRaunce.**

LAROY American. English: "red-haired; king."

LARRANCE American: Variant of Laurence (man from Laurentum). **Larry.**

LARRON American: Contemporary. **LaRon, Laron, LarRon.**

LARRY English. Latin: "man from Laurentum (laurel)."

LARVELLE American: Contemporary.

LASALLE French: "from La Salle (the large room)." LaSalle Thompson, basketball pro.

LASEAN American. Irish: "God is gracious." **LaShaun, Lashaun, LaShawn, Lashawn, LaShawne, Lashawne, LaShon, Lashon.**

LASERO Spanish. Hebrew: "whom God helps." **Lasario, Lasaro, Laserio.**

LASHAN American: Contemporary.

LASZIO Spanish. Hebrew: "whom God helps."

LASZLO Hungarian: "glorious lord."

LATHAN American: Contemporary, based on Nathan (gift).

LATICH American: Contemporary.

LATIF Arabic: "gentle, kind." **Lateef.**

LATISHAR American: Contemporary.

LATRELL American: Contemporary. **Latrell, Latrelle.** Latrell Sprewell, basketball pro.

LATRON American: Contemporary.

LATROY American. French: "from Troyes in Aube, Normandy." **Latroy.**

LAURENCE English. Latin: "man from Laurentum (town of laurel)." **Lawrence. Larry.** Laurence Fishburne, actor.

LAURENT French. Latin: "man from Laurentum (town of laurel)."

LAURINDO American: Variant of Laurence (man from Laurentum), influenced by the Spanish language.

LAURITZ Danish. Latin: "man from Laurentum (town of laurel)."

LAURSCOTT American: Contemporary, blending the names Laurence (man from Laurentum) and Scott (an Irishman, a Scotsman).

LAVALLE French: "dweller in the valley." **LaVal, Laval, Lavalle.**

LAVANCE American: Contemporary.

LAVAR American: Contemporary, possibly influenced by the French *laver* (to wash). **LaVar, LaVarr, Lavarr, LeVar, Levar, Levarr.** LeVar Burton, actor and director.

LAVAUGHN American. Celtic: "the small one." **La Vaun, LaVaun, La Von, Lavon, La Vonn, Lavonn.**

LAVELLE French: "dweller in the town." **La Vell, Lavell.**

LAVIK Hindi: "small particle."

LAVINE Irish: "little ruler."

LAVOUN American: Contemporary.

LAVOYAL American: Contemporary.

LAWAYNE American: Contemporary, based on Wayne (a wagoner). **Lawaine, Lawane, La Wayne.**

LAWON American: Contemporary, **La-Wan, Lawan, LaWaun, Lawaun, Lawon.**

LAWSON English: "son of Law (Lawrence)."

LAWYER English: "a lawyer."

LAYNE English: "dweller in an open tract of land."

LAYSON American: Contemporary.

LAYTAUN American: Contemporary.

LAZARO Spanish and Italian. Hebrew: "whom God helps." **Lazarro, Lazzaro.**

LAZARUS Hebrew: "whom God helps." **Lazaris.**

LEANDER Latin. Greek: "lion man."

LEANDO American. Greek: "lion man."

LEANDRON American. Greek: "lion man."

LEAROH American: Contemporary.

LEARON American: Contemporary.

LEATHE English: "from Leath (the hillside), dweller on the hillside." **Leatha.**

LEATHEL American: Contemporary.

LEATRICE American: Contemporary.

LEBARON French: "the baron."

LEBRON Spanish: "rabbit farmer, one who raises large rabbits."

LEDARION American: Contemporary.

LEDELL American: Contemporary. Ledell Eackles, basketball pro. **LeDell, Leedell.**

LEE English: "meadow, clearing, forest." Lee Smith, baseball pro. Lee Elder, golf pro, first Black to play in a Masters golf tournament.

LEEDO American: Contemporary.

LEERON American: Blending of Lee (meadow, forest) and Ron (ruler of decision).

LEEVAI American: Contemporary form of Levi (joining, adhesion).

LEJORRIE American: Contemporary.

LELIOUS American: Contemporary. **Lee.**

LEMARD American: Contemporary. **LaMard, Lamard, LeMard.**

LEMOINE French: "the monk." **LeMoine.**

LEMONT American. Scottish: "the lawyer." **Lemontt.**

LEMORN American: Contemporary. **LaMorn, Lamorn.**

LEMUEL English. Hebrew: "dedicated to God." **Lemual, Lemuell.**

LENDAL English: "from Lendal (the river near the alder tree)." **Lendall.**

LENDON American: Contemporary.

LENIOUS American: Contemporary.

LENIS American: Contemporary. **Lennie, Lenny.**

LENNARR American: Contemporary.

LENNIER American: Contemporary. **Lennie, Lenny.**

LENNOX   Scottish: "from Lennox (place of elms)." **Lennie, Lenny.**

LENNY   English. German: "lion-hearted." **Lennie.** Lenny Harris, baseball pro.

LENSLEY   American: Contemporary.

LEO   Latin: "lion."

LEOLA   American. Latin: "lion."

LEOLEN   American. Latin: "lion."

LEOMER   American: Contemporary.

LEOMIE   American: Contemporary.

LEON   European. Latin: "lion."

LEONARD   English. German: "lion-hearted." **Leanard, Lenard, Lennard. Lennie, Lenny, Leo.** Dr. Leonard E. Lawrence, president of the National Medical Association.

LÉONCE   French. Greek: "lionlike."

LEONCIO   Italian. Greek: "lionlike." **Leonso.**

LEONID   Russian. Greek: "lionlike."

LEONIDAS   Greek: "lionlike."

LEONIS   English: "the house of Leon (lionlike)." **Leonus.**

LEONZIO   Italian. Latin: "lion." **Leonzo.**

LEPORT   American: Contemporary.

LERAY   American: Contemporary. **LaRay, Laray, LeRay.**

LERON   Hebrew: "the song is mine." **Lerone, Liron, Lirone.** Lerone Bennett Jr., author.

LEROY   English. French: "the king." **Le Roi, Leroi, Leroy.** Leroy "Satchel" Paige (1906–1982), legendary baseball pitcher. Leroy Kelly, football pro.

LEROYAL   American: "the royal one."

LESLIN   American. Scottish: "garden of hollies; the gray fort." **Leslinn, Leslyn, Lesslin, Lesslinn, Lesslyn.**

LESONN   American: Contemporary.

LESTER   English: "dyer of cloth."

LETHANEL   American: Contemporary, influenced by Nathaniel (gift of God).

LETHON   American: Contemporary.

LEVAY   American: Contemporary. **Levae.**

LEVELDRO   American: Contemporary.

LEVELL   English: "beloved power, beloved ruler."

LEVI   Hebrew: "joining, adhesion."

LEWIS   English. German: "famous in war." Lewis Latimer (1848–1928), associate of Thomas Edison, supervised the installation of the first electric street lighting in New York City.

LEX   German. Greek: "defender." Originated as a short form of Alexius.

LE-ZHAN   American: Contemporary.

LIAM   Hebrew: "my people." Irish. German: "resolute protector."

LIBERTY   American: "freedom."

LIDDELL   English. Scottish: "from Liddel (river valley)."

LIEUTENANT American: "military officer."

LIGONGO Malawi. Yao: "Who is this?"

LIMOUS American: Contemporary, possibly influenced by the French region of Limousin.

LINC English: "lake colony." Originated as a short form of Lincoln.

LINCOLN English: "from Lincoln (the lake colony)." **Linc.**

LINDELL English. Scandinavian: "from the lime tree valley; from the valley of the linden trees."

LINDEN Swedish: "dweller near the linden trees."

LINDSEY English: "from Lindsey (the linden tree wetland)."

LINDSLEY American: Elaboration of Lindsey (from Lindsey).

LINER English: "flax dresser, a maker or seller of flax." **Lyner.**

LINNELL English: "little Leon (lion)."

LINWOOD English: "from Linwood (lime tree wood)." **Linnwood, Lynnwood, Lynwood. Lin, Linn, Lyn, Lynn.**

LIONEL English: "little lion." **Lionell, Lyonel, Lyonell.** Lionel Richie, singer-songwriter. Lionel Hampton, jazz great.

LIRON Hebrew: "my song."

LISIMBA Malawi. Yao: "lion."

LITASHE American: Contemporary.

LIU Malawi. Ngoni: "voice."

LLOYD Welsh: "gray." Lloyd McClendon, baseball pro.

LOGAN Celtic: "dweller at the little hollow." **Login.**

LONDO Spanish. German: "fame of the land." Originated as a short form of Rolando.

LONNIE English: Meaning uncertain. Lonnie R. Bristow, M.D., first Black president of the American Medical Association. Lonnie Smith, baseball pro.

LONZELL American: Contemporary. **Lonzel, LonZell. Lonzie.** Lonzell Hill, football pro.

LONZIE American: Contemporary.

LONZO Italian: Short form of Alonzo (noble and ready).

LOREN English: "laurel." **Lorien, Lorin, Lorren.**

LORENZ German. Latin: "man from Laurentum (laurel town)."

LORENZEN German: "from Lorenzen (man from Laurentum)."

LORENZI Italian. Latin: "man from Laurentum (laurel town)." **Lorenzy.**

LORENZO Italian and Spanish. Latin: "man from Laurentum (laurel town)." Lorenzo White, football pro.

LORRANCE American: Variant of Laurence (man from Laurentum). **Lorence. Lorri.**

LOTHAR German: "famous warrior."

LOTRY American: Contemporary.

LOU English. German: "famous in war." Lou Rawls, rhythm and blues singer. Lou Whitaker, baseball pro.

LOUAY American: Contemporary, based on the phonetics of the French Louis (famous in war).

LOUDEAM American: Contemporary.

LOUIS French. German: "famous in war." **Lewis.** Louis Gossett Jr., actor. Louis Farrakhan, minister, national representative of the Honorable Elijah Muhammad, Nation of Islam. Louis Armstrong (1900–1971), jazz great.

LOY American: Contemporary, possibly modeled after Roy (king; red). Loy Vaught, basketball pro.

LOYMON American: Contemporary.

LUC American. Latin: "light."

LUCAN Italian. Latin: "man from Luciania."

LUCAS Latin: "light." **Lukas. Luke.**

LUCIOUS American: Contemporary, possibly a variant of Lucius (light). Lucious Harris, basketball pro.

LUCIUS Latin: "light."

LUMAN American: Contemporary.

LUTALO Uganda. Luganda: "warrior."

LUTHER German: "famous in war." Luther Vandross, singer.

LUZIGE Malawi. Ngoni: "locust."

LYMAN American. English: "from the homestead by the wood."

LYMONT American: Variant of Lamont (lawyer).

LYNARD American: Variant of Leonard (lion-hearted).

LYNDASHA American: Contemporary. **Lyn.**

LYNNEIER American: Contemporary. **Linneier. Linn, Lynn.**

LYNX American: "a lynx, a wildcat."

MACALE American: Contemporary, probably based on the surname MacHale (son of Cathal).

MACEOLA American. Contemporary, possibly influenced by Osceola (black drink crier).

MACIO American. Spanish: Short form of Tomacio (twin). **Maceo, Mascio, Masio.**

MACKAY Scottish: "son of Aodh (fire)."

MAC KEAN Scottish: "son of Eáin (John)." **Mackean, Mac Keen, Mackeen. Mac, Mack.**

MADRONE American. Spanish: "mature." Borrowed from the madroña tree, which has smooth red bark and leathery leaves. **Madrona.**

MAHER Arabic: "clever."

MAHMOUD Arabic: "fulfillment." **Mahmud.**

MAIMUN Arabic: "fortunate."

MAISON French: "house."

MAJID Arabic: "glorious." **Majeed.**

MAKALANI Kenya. Mwera: "a clerk."

MAKARI Russian. Greek: "blessed."

MAKEBA African: Used in honor of Miriam Makeba, a South African singer.

MALCOLM Celtic: "servant of Saint Columba (dove)." **Malcom**. Malcolm X (1925–1965), Black Muslim leader and leader of the Black Pride movement. Malcolm-Jamal Warner, actor.

MALCOMB American: Celtic: "servant of Saint Columba (dove)."

MALIK Arabic: "prince, king." Hindu: "king." **Maleek, Malek**. Malik Yoba, actor. Malik Sealy, basketball pro.

MALLALIEU American. French: "a place for trunks."

MALONE Irish: "servant of Saint Eòin (John)."

MALVIN Celtic: "chief, high."

MAMBASA African: Borrowed from a city in the Democratic Republic of Congo (Zaire).

MANAL Arabic: "achievement."

MANAR Arabic: "beacon."

MANFORD English: "a small crossing over a brook." **Manny**.

MANFRED English: "man of peace." **Manny**.

MANNY English: Originated as a pet form of names such as Manfred (man of peace) and Emmanuel (God with us).

MANU Ghana. Akan: "second born." Hawaiian: "a bird."

MANVILLE French: "from Mannville (the great estate)." **Manvill**.

MANYA American: Contemporary. Russian. Hebrew: "sea of bitterness." A pet form of the feminine Mariya.

MARC French: "of Mars (the Roman mythological god of war); warlike; manly."

MARCELLUS Latin: Meaning uncertain, perhaps "manly" or "soft, tender."

MARCHE French: "market; bargain."

MARCUS Latin: "warlike; manly." **Markus. Marc, Mark**. Marcus Allen, football pro. Marcus Garvey (1887–1940), founder of the Universal Negro Improvement Association (UNIA).

MAREO American. Latin: "of Marius (Mars; warlike)."

MARIANO Italian. Latin: "of Marius (Mars; warlike; manly)." Mariano Duncan, baseball pro.

MARINO Spanish and Italian. Latin: "of the sea."

MARIO Italian. Latin: "of Marius (Mars; warlike; manly)." Mario Van Peebles, actor-director.

MARION French: "little Marie (sea of bitterness)." Marion Butts, football pro. Marion Brown, jazz alto saxophonist.

MARISTONE American: Contemporary.

MARIUS Latin: "of Mars, the mythological god of war; warlike; manly."

MARK English: Latin: "warlike; manly." Mark Curry, actor. Mark Jackson, basketball pro.

MARKEE American. French: "a marquis, a nobleman ranking above an earl."

MARKEL   American: Contemporary.

MARLEN   English. Celtic: "sea hill." **Marlon**. Marlon Riggs, filmmaker.

MARLIN   American: Possibly a variant of Marlen (sea hill) or a borrowing of the name of the fish.

MARQUEESE   American. French: "a nobleman ranking above an earl." **Markquece, Markweece, Markweese, Marquece, Marqueece**.

MARQUES   French: "a nobleman ranking above an earl."

MARQUIS   American. French: "a nobleman ranking above an earl." **Marqui**. Marquis Grissom, baseball pro.

MARRON   English: "dweller near the River Marron (pool)." French: "a large European chestnut." American: Contemporary.

MARS   Latin: "warlike." In Roman mythology, Mars was the god of war.

MARSALLUS   American: Contemporary, based on Marcellus (meaning uncertain).

MARSDEN   English: "dweller in the marsh valley." **Marsdon**.

MARSERVETTE   American: Contemporary.

MARSHALL   English. French: "horse servant, groom, farrier; high officer of the state." **Marshal, Marshel, Marshell**.

MARSHAUND   American: Contemporary.

MARSTON   English: "settlement near the marsh." **Marsten**.

MARTIN   European. Latin: "of Mars, warlike." **Martyn. Marty**. Reverend Dr. Martin Luther King Jr. (1929–1968), civil rights leader and recipient of the Nobel Peace Prize (1964).

MARTINEZ   Spanish: "son of Martin."

MARVELL   English: "from Marvell (pleasant, open country)." **Marvel, Marvele**. Marvell Wynne, baseball pro.

MARVELT   American. French: "wonderful, marvel."

MARVIN   English. Welsh: "sea hill." **Marvyn**. Marvin Allen, football pro. Marvin Hagler, boxer. Marvin Gaye (1939–1984), singer.

MARZELL   American: Contemporary.

MASCIO   Italian: "manly, vigorous."

MASKINI   Tanzania. Swahili: "poor."

MASOMAKALI   Tanzania. Nyakyusa: "sharp eyes."

MASON   English: "a bricklayer, a stonemason."

MASUD   Arabic: "happy, fortunate." **Masoud**.

MATEEN   American: Contemporary, possibly influenced by the Hebrew Matan (gift).

MATEO   Spanish. Hebrew: "gift of God." **Matt**.

MATHANI   Kenya. Kikuyu: "commandments."

MATHESON   Scottish: "son of Matthew (gift of God)." **Mathison. Matt**.

MATTHEW   English. Hebrew: "gift of God." **Matt**. Matthew A. Henson (1866–

1955), member of the 1909 Peary expedition to the North Pole.

MATTHIAS Greek. Hebrew: "gift of God." **Matt.**

MATTIEL American: Contemporary. **Matt.**

MAULIDI Swahili: "born during the Islamic month of Maulidi."

MAURICE French. Latin: "Moorish, a Moor, dark-skinned." Maurice Hurst, football pro. Maurice Hines, dancer and actor.

MAURIECE American. French. Latin: "Moorish, a Moor, dark-skinned." **Mahreece, Mahreese, Maureece, Maureese, Moreece, Moreese, Morreese.**

MAX German. Latin: "greatest."

MAXWELL English: "dweller near the pool of Macceus." **Max.**

MAZI Nigeria. Ibo: "sir."

MCALLISTER Scottish: "son of Allister (Alexander)." **Macalister, Macallister, McAlister. Mac.**

MCCLENNON Scottish: "son of the servant of Finnan (little fair one)." **McClennan, McClennen. Mac.**

MCCLUSTER American: Contemporary. **Mac.**

MCDADE Irish: "son of Daibhéid (David)." **MacDaid.**

MCKINLEY Irish: "son of Cinfaoladh (learned leader, skilled leader)." **MacKinlay, MacKinley, McKinlay. Mac, Mack.**

MCLAREN Irish: "son of Labhran (man from Laurentum)."

MELAKU Ethiopia. Amharic: "the angel."

MELBOURNE English: "from Melbourne (the mill brook)." **Melburn, Melburne. Mel.**

MELTON English: "from Melton (mill stead; middle farm)." **Mel.**

MELVIN English: "council protector." **Melvyn. Mel.** Melvin Franklin, member of the Temptations.

MELVON American: Contemporary.

MELVONE American: Contemporary.

MENDEZ Spanish: "descendant of Mendel (wisdom, knowledge)."

MENSAH Ghana. Ewe: "third born." **Mensa.**

MERCER English: "storekeeper, trader." Mercer Ellington, jazz musician and bandleader.

MERLIN English. Welsh: "sea hill, sea fortress." **Merlyn. Merl.**

MERLINO Italian. Celtic: "sea hill."

MERRILL English. Celtic: "sea bright." **Merrell.** Merril Hoge, football pro.

MERRITT French: "a tenant farmer."

MERVYN Celtic: "sea hill." **Mervin, Myrven, Myrvin.** Mervyn Dymally, U.S. representative, chairman of Congressional Black Caucus.

MESHACH Hebrew: "agile." Meshach Taylor, actor.

MHARQUES American. French: "a nobleman ranking below an earl."

MIAZEL American: Contemporary.

MICAH Hebrew: "Who is like God?"

MICHA German. Hebrew: "Who is like God?"

MICHAEL Latin and Greek. Hebrew: "Who is like God?" **Mick, Micky, Mike.** Michael Jordan, basketball pro. Michael Espy, first Black Secretary of Agriculture.

MICKY English. Hebrew: "Who is like God?" Originated as a pet form of Michael. **Mick.** Micky Leland (1944–1989), U.S. representative and chairman of the Congressional Black Caucus and House Select Committee on Hunger.

MICUE American: Contemporary.

MIGUEL Spanish. Hebrew: "Who is like God?" **Migael, Migel, Miguil, Miquel.**

MIKE English. Hebrew: "Who is like God?" **Mikey.**

MILES Welsh. Latin: "soldier; the crusher." Miles Davis, jazz trumpeter.

MILO Latin and Greek: "the crusher."

MILROY Irish: "descendant of Maolruadh (red chief)."

MILTON English: "from Milton (the mill farm, the middle farm)." **Milt.** Milton Olive III, first Black soldier awarded the Congressional Medal of Honor during the Vietnam War.

MINGO African: Possibly of Bobangi origin and meaning "they" or "to transgress." Mingo was a common slave name.

MINKAH Ghana. Akan: "justice."

MINOR English: "junior, youngster."

MIQUAIL American: Contemporary, influenced by Miguel (Who is like God?).

MITCHELL English. Hebrew: "Who is like God?" **Mitch.**

MIVEN American: Contemporary.

MIZA Hebrew: "empty." **Mizah.**

MODIBO African: "one who helps."

MOHAN Hindi: Another name for Lord Krishna.

MOISES Portuguese. Hebrew: "drawn out of the water." Moises Alou, baseball pro.

MONET French: "little Mon (protection)."

MONETA American. French: "little Mon (protection)."

MONGO Nigeria. Yoruba: "famous."

MONQUENCIO American: Contemporary.

MONROE Scottish: "dweller at the red morass (marsh)." **Monro.**

MONTAGUE Latin: "from the peaked mountain."

MONTE Spanish: "mountain." **Montey, Monti, Monty.**

MONTELL American: Contemporary. **Montel.** Montell Jordan, singer. Montell Williams, actor and talk show host.

MON'TER American: Contemporary.

MONTERREY Spanish: "sun mountain." **Monte, Monty, Rey.**

MONTGOMERY English: "from the prosperous mountain." **Monty.**

MONTICELLO Italian: "little mountain." **Monti.**

MONTROSE Scottish: "mountain of roses."

MONTSHO Botswana. Tswana: "black."

MONTSERRAT Spanish. Latin: "sawtooth mountains." **Montesserat, Montsserat. Monte, Monty.**

MONYALE American: Contemporary.

MORDECAI Hebrew: "worshiper of Marduk; warlike." **Mordechai. Mordy.**

MORDEHEY American: Variant of Mordecai (warlike). **Mordy.**

MORDELL American: Contemporary. **Mordel.**

MORENIKE Nigerian: "good luck."

MORGAN Welsh: "sea dweller." Morgan Freeman, actor.

MORI Hebrew: "my teacher."

MORISCO American. Spanish: "a Moor, Moorish, dark-skinned."

MORITZ French. Latin: "a Moor, Moorish, dark-skinned."

MORLON American: Contemporary. Morlon Wiley, basketball pro.

MORRIS English. Latin: "a Moor, Moorish, dark-skinned."

MOSEGI Botswana. Tswana: "tailor."

MOSELLE American. French: From a river in northeastern France and western Germany. Also the name of a type of wine from the river valley. **Mosel, Mosell, Mozell, Mozelle.**

MOSES English. Hebrew: "drawn out (of the water); son." **Mozes.** Moses Malone, basketball pro.

MOSEZELL American: Contemporary, probably based on Moselle (the Moselle River).

MOSI African: "firstborn child."

MOSWEN Botswana. Tswana: "white, light-colored."

MOTHUDI Botswana. Tswana: "smith."

MOYENDA Malawi. Ngoni: "on a journey."

MOZOLIVER American: Probable blending of Moses (drawn out; son) and Oliver (olive tree). **Mosoliver.**

MSAMAKI Tanzania. Swahili: "like a fish."

MUDADA Zimbabwe. Shona: "the provider."

MUENA KULU Zaire. Luba: "The One from Above." Another name for the supreme deity, Nzambi.

MUHAMMAD Arabic: "praiseworthy." Muhammad, borne by the Prophet and founder of Islam, is the most popular name in the Muslim world. **Mohamad, Mohammad, Mohammed.** Muhammad Ali, heavyweight boxing champion.

MUNIM Arabic: "benefactor."

MUNIR Arabic: "luminous."

MUNTRELLE American: Contemporary. **Muntrel, Muntrell.**

MURRAY Scottish: "sailor, seaman."

MUSA   Arabic. Hebrew: "drawn out of the water." **Mousa.**

MUSAD   Arabic: "lucky, fortunate." **Musahd.**

MYKEAL   American: Variant of Michael (Who is like God?). **Mikell, Mykel, Mykell.**

MYLAR   American: Contemporary, possibly influenced by the name of a type of polyester made into very thin sheets.

MYREE   American: Contemporary.

MYRON   Greek: "myrrh, a fragrant resin." **Miron.**

NAAMAN   Hebrew: "pleasant." Nigeria. Hausa: "sweet herbs." **Nahman, Nahmon, Namon.**

NAARAI   Aramaic: "boy."

NADIER   American: Contemporary, possibly a variant of Nadir (rare, precious).

NADIF   Somali: "born between two seasons."

NADIM   Arabic: "drinking companion." **Nadeem.**

NADIR   Arabic: "rare, precious." Hebrew: "oath." **Nadeer.**

NAEEM   Arabic: "benevolent."

NAHAAS   Arabic: "metalworker."

NAJIB   Arabic: "noble, distinguished." **Najeeb.**

NAKARI   American: Contemporary.

NALIN   Hindi: "lotus."

NAMARION   American: Contemporary.

NAMIR   Hebrew: "a swift cat."

NAMMAR   Arabic: "carpenter."

NANGILA   Uganda. Abaluhya: "born while parents are on a journey."

NAPOLEON   French. Greek: "from the new city." **Napolean, Napoleone.**

NAREN   Hindi: "king."

NARVA   American: Contemporary.

NASEEM   Arabic: "breeze."

NASIR   Arabic: "supporter, helper in victory." **Nasser.**

NASR   Arabic: "victory." **Nazr.**

NASSOR   Swahili. Arabic: "victorious."

NAT   English. Hebrew: "gift; gift of God." Nat King Cole (1919–1965), singer.

NATHAN   Hebrew: "gift." **Nat, Nate.** Nathan Morris, singer with Boyz II Men.

NATHANAEL   Hebrew: "gift of God." **Nathaniel. Nat, Nate.**

NATHEN   American. Hebrew: "gift." **Nathin, Nathon. Nat, Nate.**

NATHION   American: Contemporary.

NATRON   American: Contemporary, possibly borrowed from *natron* (hydrated sodium carbonate) or from Lake Natron in Tanzania.

NATRONE   American: Contemporary, possibly influenced by Natron. Natrone Means, football player.

NAVARRO   Spanish: "from Navarre (plain among the hills)." **Novarro.**

NAVIN Hindi: "young."

NAZIM Arabic: "wonderful." **Nazeem.**

NAZREE American: Contemporary.

NDUKE African: "life is supreme."

NEAL English. Celtic: "chief."

NEDAVIAH Hebrew: "generosity of the Lord." **Nedavia, Nedavya, Nedavyah. Ned.**

NEHEMIAH English. Hebrew: "comforted by the Lord."

NELSON English: "Nel's son; Neil's son." **Nels.**

NEMIAH American: Probably a shortened form of Nehemiah (comforted by the Lord). **Nemiyah.**

NEMROY American: Contemporary.

NEOSHA American: Contemporary.

NESHAUN American: Contemporary. **Neshaune, Neshawn, Neshawne, Neshon.**

NESHELL American: Contemporary.

NESTOR Greek: "one who is departing."

NEVAL American. Latin: "new town."

NEVILLE English. Latin: "new town." **Nevil, Nevill.**

NEVIN English. Celtic: "servant of the little saint."

NICHOLAS English. Greek: "victory of the people." **Nickolas. Nick, Nicky.**

NICO Greek: "victory."

NIECHAE American: Contemporary.

NILE American: From the river in northeastern Africa.

NILTON American: Contemporary.

NINJE Malawi. Yao: "try it."

NIRAM Hebrew: "cultivated fields."

NISAN Hebrew: "miracle."

NIZAM American. Arabic: "to order, to govern."

NJAU Kenya. Kikuyu: "young bull."

NKOLE Zaire. Luba: "The Strong One." Another name for the Central African supreme deity, Nzambi.

NKOZI African: "ruler."

NOAH Hebrew: "rest, comfort."

NOASKA American: Contemporary.

NOLAN Irish: "little noble one." **Noland, Nolen.**

NORMAN English. German: "north man, man from the north." **Norm.** Norman Brown, jazz musician.

NORTON English: "from the northern town."

NORVILLE English. French: "from the northern town." **Norval, Norvel, Norvell, Norvil, Norvill.**

NOUR Arabic: "light."

NOY Hebrew: "beauty."

NUMAIR Arabic: "panther."

NURIEL Hebrew: "fire of the Lord."

NURUL American: Possibly a variant of Nuriel (fire of the Lord).

NZAMBI   Central Africa: The supreme deity of the Bantu.

OBADELE   Nigeria. Ibo: "the king comes home."

OBA-ORUN   Nigeria. Yoruba: "King of the Sky." Native name for the god of creation, also known as Olorun.

OBASI   Nigeria. Ibo: "in honor of the supreme god." **Obassi**.

OBDULIA   Swahili: "servant."

OBI   Nigeria. Ibo: "heart."

OBINNA   African: "he is dear to the father."

O'BRIAN   Irish: "descendant of Brian (kingly, strength, valor)."

OBTALA   Nigeria. Yoruba: "King of the White Cloth." In Yoruban mythology, Obtalla is the creator of land over the water, the shaper of human beings, Olorun's second son and representative, and founder of Ife, the first Yoruban city.

OCTAVIUS   Latin: "eighth."

ODE   Nigeria. Benin: "born along the roadside."

ODELL   Teutonic: "wealth."

ODERO   Kenya. Luo: "granary."

ODESSA   American: Borrowing of the name of a Texas city. Greek: "the Odyssey." Odessa Turner, football pro.

ODION   Nigeria. Benin: "first of twins."

ODIS   American: Contemporary, possibly influenced by Otis (keen-eared). **Odies, Odus**.

ODUDUWA   Nigeria. Yoruba: In Yoruban mythology, Oduduwa is the first ruler of Ife, the first city. Many equate him with Obtala. **Odu**.

ODYSSEUS   Greek: "hater." Odysseus was a leader of the Trojan War and the hero of the Odyssey.

OGUN   Nigeria. Yoruba: In Yoruban mythology, Ogun is the god of iron and the patron of hunters, warriors, and smiths.

OJO   Nigeria. Yoruba: "a difficult birth."

OKELLO   Uganda. Ateso: "born after twins."

OKORIE   Nigeria. Ibo: "born on Oryo market day."

OLA   Nigeria. Yoruba: "wealth."

OLANIYAN   Nigeria. Yoruba: "honor surrounds me."

OLDEN   English: "half Dane." German: "old." Olden Polynice, basketball pro.

OLEAN   American: Contemporary, possibly influenced by Olin (ancestor).

OLERON   American: Contemporary, possibly a variant of Olorun (the god of creation).

OLIN   Swedish: "ancestor." **Olen**.

OLIVIER   French. Latin: "olive."

OLORUN   Nigeria. Yoruba: "Owner of the Sky." A native name for the god of creation.

OLUFON   Nigeria. Yoruba: "King of the White Cloth." Another name for Obtala.

OLU-IGBO Nigeria. Yoruba: "Owner of the Bush." In Yoruban mythology, Olu-Igbo is the god of the bush and the jungle.

OLUJIMI Nigeria. Yoruba: "the lord awakens."

OLUWA Nigeria. Yoruba: "our lord." Another name for the god of creation.

O'MAR American: Contemporary, influenced by Omar (thriving, prosperous). **O'Mahr, O'Marr.** O'Mar Ellison, football pro.

OMAR Arabic: "thriving, prosperous." Hebrew: "eloquent." **Omer.**

OMARI Swahili. Arabic: "thriving, prosperous."

OMEGA Greek: "great."

OMOREDE Nigeria. Benin: "prince."

ONANI Malawi. Ngoni: "look."

ONYAME Ghana. Akan: The supreme deity. In mythology, Onyame is creator and representative of the natural universe. **Nyame.**

ORAN Aramaic: "light." Yoruba: A short form of Oranmiyan.

ORANMIYAN Nigeria. Yoruba: In Yoruban mythology, Oranmiyan is a son of Oduduwa (the first ruler of Ife). **Oran.**

ORANYAN Nigeria. Yoruba: Another name for Oranmiyan. **Oran.**

OREAN American: Contemporary, possibly a variant of Oren (fir tree; eagle).

OREN Hebrew: "fir tree." Swedish: "eagle." **Orin, Orren, Orrin.**

ORIEN American: Variant of Orion.

ORION Greek: Meaning unknown. In classical mythology, Orion, a hunter, was the beloved of the goddess Diana. He was placed in the heavens after being accidentally killed. The name takes the traditional definition of "hunter."

ORISHA-OKE Nigeria. Yoruba: "Sky God." Another name for the god of creation. **Oke, Orisha.**

ORISHA-OKO Nigeria. Yoruba: In Yoruban mythology, Orisha-Oko is the orisha (god) of agriculture and the patron of farmers. **Oko, Orisha.**

ORLANDO Italian and Spanish: "fame of the land."

ORON Hebrew: "light."

ORTEGA Spanish: "dweller at or near the sign of the grouse." **Ortege, Ortego.**

ORUNMILA Nigeria. Yoruba: "the Sky knows who will prosper." In Yoruban mythology, Orunmila is the god of divination and oldest son of Olorun. **Orun.**

ORVIN English: "spear-friend." **Orvon.**

OSAIAS Greek. Hebrew: "helped by God."

OSANYIN Nigeria. Yoruba: In Yoruban mythology, Osanyin is the orisha (god) of medicine and divining.

OSCAR English: "god-spear." Oscar Micheaux, author and filmmaker. Oscar Robertson, basketball pro. Oscar Peterson, jazz pianist.

OSEI Ghana. Fante: "noble."

O'SHEA Irish: "son of Séaghdha (hawk-like, stately)." **O'Shay.**

OSHEA Hebrew: "helped by God."

OSIAS Spanish. Hebrew: "God is my strength." **Osías.**

OSMUND English: "protected by God." **Osman, Osmand, Osmun.**

OSREAL American: Contemporary, probably influenced by Israel (contender with God).

OSWALD English: "divine ruler, god ruler."

OTHELLO Italian: "rich." **Othella.**

OTHIENO Kenya. Luo: "born at night."

OTHNIEL Hebrew: "God is my strength."

OTIS Greek: "keen-eared." **Ottis.** Otis Williams, member of the Temptations. Otis Thorpe, basketball pro. Ottis Anderson, football pro. Otis Redding (1941–1967).

OTONIEL American: Variant of Othniel (God is my strength).

OTTONE Italian. Teutonic: "happy."

OVERTON English: "from Overton (homestead or town on the ridge or riverbank)."

OWEEN American: Variant of Owen (lamb; young warrior).

OWEN English. Celtic: "lamb; young warrior."

OZNI Hebrew: "my hearing."

PAKI South Africa. Xhosa: "witness."

PARIS American. French: "the land of the Parisii." **Parris.**

PARISH English: "from the parish (a church district)." **Parrish.**

PARLIN English: "little Peter (rock)."

PARNELL English: "little Peter (rock)."

PASCAL English and French. Latin: "of Easter."

PATRICK Irish. Latin: "patrician." **Pat.** Patrick Ewing, basketball pro.

PAUL European. Latin and Greek: "a rock, a stone." Paul Williams, member of the Temptations. Paul Laurence Dunbar (1872–1906), poet and novelist. Paul Robeson, actor.

PAYDEN American: Perhaps influenced by Payton (from Peyton).

PERCIL American: Perhaps a variant of Percival (pierce the valley) or of Purcell (little pig).

PERCIVAL French: "pierce the valley." **Perceval, Percivall. Percie, Percy.**

PERCY French: "belonging to Percy (estate of Persius)." **Percey, Persey.** Percy Rodriguez, actor.

PERRIN French: "little Peter (rock)."

PERRY English: "pear tree."

PERTHA Celtic: "thorny thicket."

PERVIS French. Latin: "dweller at a portico or passageway." Pervis Ellison, basketball pro.

PERVIUS Latin: "thoroughfare, passageway."

PETER English. Latin and Greek: "a rock, a stone." **Pete.**

PETRICK English: "little Peter (rock)."

PHELONISE American: Contemporary, possibly influenced by Peloponnesus (a Greek peninsula).

PHELPH English. Greek: "lover of horses."

PHILIP English. Greek: "lover of horses." **Phillip. Phil, Phill.** Philip Butcher, essayist and scholar.

PHILIPPE French. Greek: "lover of horses."

PILI Swahili: "second born."

POLONIUS English: After the father of Ophelia in Shakespeare's *Hamlet.*

PONCE Spanish. Latin: "fifth."

PORTER English: "a porter, a carrier."

PRENTICE English. Latin: "apprentice." **Prentis, Prentise, Prentiss.**

PRESCOTT English: "from the priest's cottage."

PRESIDENT American: "president, leader."

PRICE English. Welsh: "son of Rhys (ardor)."

PRIMEAU French: "superior, first." **Primeaux.**

PRINCE English: "a prince, a ruler just below a king or queen."

PRINCEOLA American: Contemporary.

PRINCETON American: After the New Jersey city, which was named for the English Prince of Orange.

PURCELL English. French: "little pig."

QADIR Arabic: "capable." **Kadir.**

QASIM Arabic: "distributor of food and goods."

QUADRE American. Latin: "four, fourth child."

QUADREES American. Latin: "four, fourth child."

QUAID Irish: "son of Uad (master)." **Quade.**

QUANTRELL French: "little singer." **Quentrell.**

QUENTON English: "from the queen's town."

QUINCY English: "from Quincay (estate of Quintus)." **Quinci, Quinsey.** Quincy Jones, composer.

QUINN Irish: "counsel, advice."

QUINNELL English: "war woman." **Quennell, Quinel, Quinnel.**

QUINTIN French. Latin: "five, fifth child." **Quentin.** Quintin Dailey, basketball pro.

QUITMAN German: "grower and seller of quinces." **Quitmon.**

QUSAY Arabic: "distant." **Qussay.**

RAAMAH Hebrew: "thunder."

RAANAN Hebrew: "luxuriant, fresh."

RABI Arabic: "calming breeze." **Rabbi.**

RACHIM Aramaic: "compassion."

RADI Arabic: "content." **Radee.**

RAEF American. English: "counsel wolf; wolf adviser."

RAFA Hebrew: "to heal."

RAFAEL Spanish. Hebrew: "the Lord heals." **Rafal, Rafala, Raefael, Refael**.

RAFFERTY Irish: "bringer of riches." **Rafferty, Raffarty. Rafe, Rafer, Raffer**.

RAFI Arabic: "praising, exalted."

RAFIK Arabic: "friend." **Rafeek, Rafeeq, Rafiq**.

RAFIKI Swahili. Arabic: "friend."

RAGHIB Arabic: "willing."

RAHIM Arabic: "compassionate." **Raheem**.

RAHMAN Arabic: "merciful, forgiving."

RAHSAAN American: Contemporary.

RAH-SHUN American: Contemporary.

RAIHEAM American. Arabic: "compassionate."

RAIMEY American: Possibly influenced by the French Rémy (oarsman).

RAIMONDS American: Variant of Raimond (wise protector).

RAIMUNDO Spanish. German: "wise protector." **Raimondo, Ramondo, Ramundo, Raymondo, Raymundo**.

RAJ Hindi: "kingdom."

RAJA Hindi: "king."

RAJAB Arabic: "to glorify." Rajab is the seventh month of the Islamic calendar.

RAJAN Hindi: "king."

RAJESH Hindi: "king of kings."

RAJIH Arabic: "excellent."

RAJIV Hindi: "a blue lotus." **Rajeev**.

RAKIN Arabic: "writer."

RALPH English. Teutonic: "wolf counsel; wolf adviser." **Ralphe, Ralf**. Dr. Ralph Bunche (1904–1971), first Black to win the Nobel Peace Prize (1950), undersecretary of the United Nations. Reverend Dr. Ralph Albernathy (1926–1990), organizer and president of the Southern Christian Leadership Conference.

RAMEL American: Contemporary.

RAMI Arabic: "love."

RAMIREZ Spanish: "son of Ramon (wise protector)."

RAMIRO Spanish: "great judge."

RAMÓN Spanish. German: "wise protector." **Ramon**. Ramon Martinez, baseball pro.

RAMSEY English: "Hram's (raven) island; ram's island." Norse: "Ramm's (strong) island." **Ramsay**. Ramsey Lewis, singer.

RANDALL English. German: "shield-wolf." **Randal, Randell, Randle. Rand, Randy**. Randall Cunningham, football pro.

RANDELLE American: Contemporary, based on Randall (shield wolf). **Rand, Randy**.

RANDY English. German: "shield wolf." **Rand**. Randy Milligan, baseball pro. Randy Brooks, actor.

RANKLAN American: Contemporary, possibly influenced by Ranken (little Rand) or Franklin (a freeholder).

RANSOM English: "Rand's (shield wolf) son." **Ransen, Ransome, Ranson**.

RAPHAEL Greek. Hebrew: "God has healed."

RAPHELD American: Contemporary, based on Raphael (God has healed).

RASAUN American: Contemporary. **Rassaun.**

RASHAAM American: Contemporary. Rashaam Salaam, football pro.

RASHAD Arabic: "good judgment."

RASHAMEL American: Contemporary. **Rashamael.**

RASHARD American: Contemporary, probably a phonetic spelling of the French Richard (brave ruler). Rashard Griffith, basketball pro.

RASHAUN American: Contemporary. **Rashaune, Rashawn, Rashawne, Rashon, Reshaun, Reshaune, Reshawn, Reshawne, Reshon.**

RASHID Arabic: "trustworthy adviser, rightly guided." **Rasheed.** Rasheed Wallace, basketball pro.

RASHIDI Swahili. Arabic: "rightly guided."

RAUF Arabic: "compassionate."

RAUL French and Spanish. German: "wolf counsel; wolf adviser." **Raoul.**

RAVEL French: "from Ravel (the rebellious house)."

RAVIV Hebrew: "rain, dewdrops."

RAY German: "wise protection." Ray Charles, music great. Ray Bryant, pianist-composer.

RAYMEE American: Contemporary, probably a phonetic spelling of the French Rémy (oarsman).

RAYMOND English. German: "wise protection." **Raimond. Ray.** Raymond Andrews, novelist.

RAYSHARD American: Contemporary. **Ray.**

RAYVON American: Contemporary. **Rayvonn. Ray.**

RAZELLE American: Contemporary, possibly a variant of Roselle (little rose) or Raziel (secret of the Lord). **Razell.**

RAZIEL Aramaic: "secret of the Lord." **Raz, Razi.**

RAZIN Arabic: "dignified."

RAZIQ Arabic: "provider."

REDA SIRAJ Arabic: "light of contentment."

REDDELL English: "dweller at or near the red hill; dweller near the reeds." **Reddel, Redell.**

REGGIE English. German: "ruler of judgment." Reggie Williams, basketball pro. Reggie Jackson, baseball pro.

REGINALD English. German: "ruler of judgment." **Rejinald. Reggie, Rejjie.**

REHAHN Arabic: "choice of God." **Rehaan, Reyham, Reyhan.**

REINARD German: "brave counsel."

REJÉAN American: Contemporary.

REJINALDO Spanish. German: "ruler of judgment."

REMELL   American: Contemporary.

REMSHARD   German: "marsh   forest."
Remi, Remmie.

REMUS   Latin: "protector." **Remous**.

RENNICK   English: "from   Renwick."
Renni, Rennie, Renny.

RENNY   English: "strong   advice;   strong
counsel." **Renney, Renni, Rennie**.

RENZO   Italian. Latin: "laurel." A short
form of Lorenzo. **Renzi**.

RESHAWN   American: Contemporary,
based on Shawn (God is gracious). **Reshaun, Reshawne, ReShon, Reshon**.

RESHE   Nigeria. Hausa: "branch." **Reshey**.

RESHELET   American: Contemporary, possibly based on Reshe (branch).

REUBEN   Hebrew: "behold, a son!" **Reu-
bin, Reuvan, Reuven, Ruben, Rubin.
Rube**. Ruben Sierra, baseball pro.

REX   Latin: "king."

REYMELLE   American: Contemporary.

RHAMELLE   American: Contemporary.

RHEESE   English.   Welsh: "warrior."
Rheece, Reece, Rees, Reese.

RHODNEY   American: Variant of Rodney
(Hróda's island).

RHUBIN   American. Hebrew: "behold, a
son!" **Rube**.

RHYS   Welsh: "warrior."

RICHARD   European.   German: "brave
ruler." **Rich, Richie, Rick, Ricky**. Richard
Wright (1908–1960), novelist. Richard

Cummings, actor. Richard Pryor, comedian
and actor.

RICHARE   American: Contemporary, possibly a phonetic spelling of the French
Richard (brave ruler).

RICHLAND   American. English: "land of
riches."

RICHMOND   German: "mighty protector."
Richmon.

RICO   Spanish: Originated as a short form
of names ending in -rico. Also from rico
(rich).

RIDDICK   English. Celtic: "from Reddoch
(smooth field)." Riddick Bowe, boxer.

RIGEL   Arabic: "foot." Rigel is the name of
a star in the constellation Orion.

RIKKY   American: German: "brave ruler."

RIO   Spanish: "river."

RIOCKY   American: Contemporary.

RIVER   English: "river." **Rivers**.

RIVERA   Spanish: "bank, shore; river."

RIX   American: Contemporary.

RIYAD   Arabic: "gardens." Riyadh is the
capital of Saudi Arabia. **Riyadh**.

ROAMY   American: Contemporary.

ROBAIR   American: Contemporary, a phonetic spelling of the French Robert (famous
and bright).

ROBERT   French. German: "famous and
bright." **Bob, Bobby, Rob, Robby**. Dr.
Robert C. Weaver, first Black member of
the U.S. cabinet, secretary of the Depart-

ment of Housing and Urban Development. Robert Guillaume, actor. Robert Cray, jazz guitarist.

ROBERTO Spanish. German: "famous and bright." Roberto Clemente (1934–1972), baseball pro.

ROBLEY American: Contemporary. **Robely, Robly.**

ROCCO Italian. German: "rest."

ROCH French. Italian. German: "rest."

ROCHAN Hindi: "red lotus."

ROCKLIFFE English: "from Rockcliff (the rocky cliff)." **Rocklif, Rockliff, Rocliffe. Rocky.**

RODERICK English and French. German: "famous ruler." **Roddrick, Rodrick. Rick, Ricky, Rod, Roddy.**

RODGELY American: Contemporary.

RODGERICK American: Contemporary, a blending of Roger (famous spear) and Roderick (famous ruler).

RODNEY English: "Hróda's (fame) island." **Rodny. Rod.** Rodney Dent, basketball pro.

ROEHL German: "shield-wolf."

ROELL American. German: "shield wolf." **Roel.**

ROFICK American: Contemporary.

ROGAN Gaelic: "red-haired, reddish."

ROGER English. German: "spear fame." **Rodger. Rodg.** Roger Lawson, actor. Roger Robinson, actor.

ROHAN Irish: "little Ruadh (red, red-haired)." **Rohain.**

ROLAND German: "fame of the land."

ROLANDO Portuguese. German: "fame of the land." **Rolondo. Lando, Londo.** Rolando Roomes, baseball pro. Rolando Blackman, basketball pro.

ROLDAN Spanish. German: "fame of the land."

ROMAIN French. Latin: "a Roman." **Romaine.**

ROMAN European. Latin: "a Roman."

ROMANE American. French: "a Roman."

ROMELYN American: Contemporary.

ROMEO English: "from Rome."

RONALD Scottish. Norse: "judgment power." **Ron, Ronnie, Ronny.** Ronald McNair (1950–1986), physicist, astronaut, killed in the Challenger explosion.

RONDEL French: "little round one, little plump one." **Rondell.**

RONEL Hebrew: "song of the Lord." **Ronayl.**

RONELL American: Contemporary. **Ronnell, Ronnelle.**

RONEY English. Celtic: "red, reddish."

RONGIE American: Contemporary.

RONTREK American: Contemporary. **Rontrec, Rontreck, Rontric, Rontrik. Ron, Ronny.**

ROOSEVELT Dutch: "dweller at or near the rose field." **Rosie.** Roosevelt Grier, actor.

ROSAMOND English. Teutonic: "horse protection." **Rosamund. Rosie.**

ROSCOE English. Scandinavian: "from Roscoe (the roe wood)." **Rosco, Roscow.** Roscoe Lee Browne, actor.

ROSHAN Hindi: "illumination." Persian: "light, dawn; splendid."

ROSHAY American: Contemporary.

ROSHON American: Contemporary. **Rochon, Roshaun, Roshawn.**

ROVON American: Contemporary.

ROWAN English. Gaelic: "little red-haired one." Scandinavian: "dweller at or near the rowan tree." **Rowand, Rowen.**

ROXICE American: Contemporary.

ROY English. French: "king." **Roye.** Roy Campanella, baseball pro.

ROYAL English: "from Ryal (a hill where rye grew); wolf ruler." American: "noble, kingly."

ROYCE English: "son of Roy (red-haired one; king)." **Roice, Royse.**

ROYER French: "wheel maker."

ROYLAND American. English: "from the king's land." **Roy.**

ROYNAL American: Contemporary.

ROZELL English: "little rose." **Rosell, Roselle, Rozelle. Rosie, Rozie.**

RUDDICK English: "robin red-breast."

RUDO Zimbabwe. Shona: "love."

RUDOLPH German: "famous wolf." **Rudolf. Rudi, Rudy.** Rudolph Fisher, novelist.

RUDY German: "famous wolf." **Rudi.**

RUEBONAY American. French: "good street."

RUFUS Latin: "red, red-haired." Rufus Porter, football pro.

RUMEAL American: Contemporary. Rumeal Robinson, basketball pro.

RUNAKO Zimbabwe. Shona: "handsome."

RUSHAN American: Probable variant of the Persian Roshan (light, dawn; splendid).

RUSHAUN American: Contemporary. **Rushawn, Rushawne, Rushon.**

RUSHIL Hindi: "charming."

RUTELEIOUS American: Probably influenced by the Latin Rutilius (the red one).

RYLAND English: "dweller at or near the rye land." **Rylan.**

SABER Arabic: "patient."

SADAKA Swahili: "a religious offering."

SADIK Arabic: "truthful, faithful." **Sadiq.**

SADIKI Swahili. Arabic: "truthful, faithful."

SAFFOURI Arabic: "whistler."

SAFI Arabic: "exalted."

SAGHIR Arabic: "short."

SAID Arabic: "lucky, fortunate." **Saeed, Saiyd.**

SAJAN Hindi: "beloved." **Sajen.**

SALAM Arabic: "peace."

SALEH Arabic: "able, skilled."

SALIM Arabic: "safe, secure." **Saleem, Selim.**

SALOMON French. Hebrew: "peaceful." **Saloman. Sal.**

SAMAL Aramaic: "symbol."

SAMARA Hindi: Meaning uncertain. A king of the Bharata dynasty.

SAMEH Arabic: "forgiver."

SAMI Aramaic: "exalted."

SAMIR Hindi: "wind, breeze." Arabic: "companion in evening conversations."

SAMMAN Arabic: "grocer."

SAMPSON Greek. Hebrew: "sun." **Samson. Sam, Sammy.**

SAMUEL Latin. Hebrew: "name of God." **Samual. Sam, Sammy.** Vice Admiral Samuel L. Gravely Jr., first Black admiral, commander, Third Fleet. Samuel L. Jackson, actor. Sammy Davis Jr., (1925–1990), performer. Samuel R. Delany, science-fiction writer.

SANDERS Scottish and English. Greek: "defender of mankind."

SANDFORD English: "from Sandford (the sandy ford)." **Sanford. Sandy.**

SANFORD Teutonic: "peaceful counsel."

SANJIV Hindi: "love."

SANTANA Spanish: "Saint Ana (grace, mercy)."

SANTIAGO Spanish: "Saint James (supplanting)."

SANTOS Spanish: "saints."

SAQR Arabic: "falcon."

SARAZAR American: Possible variant of Salazar (corral; manor house).

SAUL Latin. Hebrew: "asked of God."

SAULIUS Latin. Hebrew: "asked of God." **Saul.**

SAVILLE French: "from Saville (the willow town)." **Savill.**

SAWYER English: "a cutter of timber."

SAXBY English. Scandinavian: "from Saxby (the Saxon's estate)."

SAYYAD Arabic: "hunter."

SCHAPPEL American: Contemporary, possibly modeled after Chappelle (dweller near a chapel) or Shappell (the corner where sheep were raised).

SCHEA American. Irish: "learned."

SCOTT English: "an Irishman, a Scotsman."

SEABERN Teutonic: "sea warrior." **Sebie.**

SEABERT Teutonic: "sea bright." **Sebie.**

SEALER English: "a maker of seals." **Sealar.**

SEAN Irish. Hebrew: "God is gracious." Sean Nelson, actor.

SEARCY English. French: "from Cerisy or Cercy (estate of Cercious)."

SEBASTIAN English. Latin: "man from Sebastia."

SÉBASTIEN French. Latin: "man from Sebastia."

SEBERT   English: "bright hero; bright victory." **Sebie.**

SEDALE   American: Contemporary. Sedale Threatt, basketball pro.

SEKAI   Malawi. Ngoni: "laugh."

SEKANI   Malawi. Ngoni: "laughter."

SEKOU   Guinea: "learned; fighter."

SELASSIE   Ethiopia. Amharic and Tigrinya: "trinity."

SELVIN   American: Contemporary, based on Melvin (council protector). **Selvinn, Selvyn, Selvynn.**

SELWYN   English: "hall-friend, friend of the hall."

SEMAJ   American: Contemporary.

SENECA   American. Dutch. Native American. Mohegan: "people of the standing rock." **Senyca.**

SENEGAL   American: Borrowed from the West African country of the same name.

SENNETT   French: "old age, elderly." **Sennet.**

SENTELL   American: Contemporary.

SENUR   American: Possibly based on *senior* (elder).

SERGIO   Spanish and Italian. Latin: "protector." **Serjio.**

SESSION   English. French: "from Soissons."

SEVERIN   French. Latin: "severe."

SEVILLE   French: "from Saville (the willow estate)."

SEYMOUR   English. French: "from Saint Maur (a Moor)." **Seymore, Seymoure.**

SHAANAN   Hebrew: "peaceful." **Shanan.**

SHAARON   American: Contemporary.

SHACHAR   Hebrew: "dawn, sunrise."

SHACHOR   Hebrew: "black."

SHA'DEON   American: Contemporary.

SHADI   Arabic: "singer."

SHAFAN   Hebrew: "a rabbit."

SHAFER   Aramaic: "handsome."

SHAFIQ   Arabic: "sympathetic, compassionate."

SHAH   Persian: "king."

SHAHEEN   Arabic: "desired."

SHAI   Aramaic: "gift."

SHAILENDRA   Hindi: "king of the mountains."

SHAKEEL   Hindi. Arabic: "handsome."

SHAKIL   Arabic: "handsome."

SHAKIR   Arabic: "thankful."

SHAKRA   Hindu: Another name for Indra, the chief god of the early Hindu religion.

SHAKTI   Hindi: "energy."

SHALAWN   American: Contemporary. **Shalahn.**

SHALID   American: Contemporary. **Shaleed.**

SHALIN   Hindi: "noble."

SHAM American: Possible variant of Shem (name; famous).

SHAMAL Hindi: "dark-complexioned."

SHAMAR American: Contemporary, possibly a variant of Shamir (diamond; flint).

SHAMEEM American. Arabic: "fragrant." **Shaameem, Shahmeem, Shahmiim.**

SHAMIM Arabic: "fragrant."

SHAMIN Arabic: "scent."

SHAMIR Aramaic and Hebrew: "sharp thorn; piece of flint." Arabic: "diamond."

SHAMMAI Aramaic: "name." **Shamai.**

SHAMMGOD American: Contemporary.

SHAMMOND American: Contemporary. **Shamond, Shamonde.**

SHAMON American: Contemporary.

SHAMREAL American: Contemporary.

SHANDAR Hindu: "proud."

SHANDERIC American: Contemporary.

SHANDON American: Contemporary.

SHANDUE American: Contemporary.

SHANE Irish. Hebrew: "God is gracious."

SHANGO Nigeria. Yoruba: In mythology, Shango is the orisha (god) of the thunderbolt.

SHANNON Irish: from the river Shannon (old river). **Shannan, Shannen.**

SHANTA American: Contemporary. Swahili: "knapsack."

SHANTE American: Contemporary. **Shantae, Shantay, Shanté, Shauntae, Shauntay, Shaunte, Shaunté, Shauntey, Shawntae, Shawntay, Shawnte, Shawnté, Shawntey.**

SHANTEL American: Contemporary.

SHANTREY American: Contemporary.

SHANTRON American: Contemporary.

SHAPIR Aramaic: "beautiful."

SHAPIRO Hebrew. Aramaic: "beautiful."

SHARIF Arabic: "noble, honorable." **Shareef.**

SHARMAN English: "cutter of woolen cloth; shearer of wool."

SHARONE American: Contemporary. Sharone Wright, basketball pro.

SHARREEF American. Arabic: "noble, honorable." **Shariff, Shariffe, Sharyf, Sharyfe.**

SHARRELL American: Contemporary.

SHAUN Irish. Hebrew: "God is gracious." **Shaune.**

SHAW English: "dweller at or near a wood or grove of trees." **Shawe.**

SHAWKI Arabic: "striving for right conduct."

SHAWN Irish. Hebrew: "God is gracious." **Shawne.** Shawn Kemp, basketball pro. Shawn Stockman, singer with Boyz II Men.

SHAWNASEY American. Irish: "descendant of Seachnasach (elusive). **Shaunasey, Shaunassey, Shaunnassey, Shawnassey, Shawnnassey.**

SHAWNEL American: Contemporary, based on Shawn (God is gracious). **Shawnell.**

SHAWNTA American: Contemporary. **Shaunta, Shonta.**

SHAWON American: Contemporary. Shawon Dunstan, baseball pro.

SHAY Irish. Hebrew: "supplanting; seizing by the heel." Shay originated as a pet form of Shamus.

SHAYQUAN American: Contemporary.

SHEA Irish: "descendant of Seaghdha (learned; majestic)." **Shay, Shaye.**

SHEDRICK American: Possibly a variant of Sheldrick (a type of duck) or of the Hebrew Shadrach (of uncertain meaning).

SHEIKH Arabic: "old man." In Arabic countries, a sheikh is the chief of a family, tribe, or village as well as an official of the Muslim religion.

SHELBY English. Scandinavian: "from Selby (the farm at the hall)."

SHELDON English: "from Sheldon (the ledge on the hill)."

SHELLAY American: Contemporary.

SHELLON American: Contemporary.

SHELTON English: "from Shelton (the farm by the ledge)."

SHEM Hebrew: "name; famous."

SHEMAR American: Contemporary. **Shemarr, Shemmar.** Shemar Moore, actor.

SHENOAH American: Contemporary, probably based on Noah (rest, comfort).

SHEPHARD English: "shepherd." **Shepard, Shepherd, Sheppard, Shepperd, Sheppherd. Shep.**

SHERAGA Aramaic: "light."

SHERARD English: "splendidly brave."

SHERELL American: Contemporary. **Sherrell.**

SHERIDAN Irish: "peaceful; seeker." **Sherridan.**

SHERMAN English: "one who shears or cuts." **Shermann.** Sherman Douglas, basketball pro. Sherman Hemsley, actor.

SHERMARKE African: "he brings good fortune."

SHERRED American: Contemporary.

SHERROD English: "bright and hard."

SHERWIN English: "to shear the wind; a fleet-footed runner." **Sherwen, Sherwinn, Sherwyn, Sherwynn.**

SHERWOOD English: "from Sherwood (the bright woods)."

SHEVI Hebrew: "return."

SHEVON American: Contemporary, possibly a phonetic spelling of the Irish Siobhán (God is gracious).

SHIMKA American: Contemporary.

SHIMRI Hebrew: "my guardian."

SHLOMO Hebrew: "sun." **Shelomo.**

SHOHARI American: Contemporary, possibly influenced by Johar (jewel). **Shohara.**

SHOMARI Swahili: "forceful."

SHON American: Contemporary, a phonetic spelling of the Irish Sean (God is gracious).

SHONE American. German: "beautiful."

SHONNARD American: Contemporary.

SHONTRE American: Contemporary. **Shontrae, Shontray, Shontrea, Shontreah, Shontrey.**

SHOUNTEZ American: Contemporary. **Shauntez, Shawntez, Shontez.**

SHUN American: Contemporary.

SHUNAN American: Contemporary.

SHUNNAR Arabic: "pheasant."

SHWAN American: Contemporary.

SIDNELL American: Contemporary.

SIDNEY English. French: "follower of Saint Denis; dweller by the wide, wet land. Sidney Bechet (1897–1959), jazz soloist. Sidney Poitier, actor.

SIEVEN American: Contemporary.

SIGMUND German: "victorious protection." **Siggy.**

SILAS Latin. Aramaic: "asked for."

SILESTER American: Variant of Silvester (dweller in the forest).

SILVANUS Latin: "of the forest." In Roman mythology, Silvanus was the god of the forests.

SILVESTER Latin: "dweller in the forest." **Sylvester. Sil, Sly.**

SIM English. Hebrew: "heard." **Simmie.**

SIMEON European. Hebrew: "heard." **Simion. Sim, Simmie.**

SIMIYA African: "drought." **Sim, Simi.**

SIMON English. Hebrew: "heard." Simon Esters, bass-baritone.

SION Welsh. Hebrew: "God is gracious." **Sione.**

SIRQUENCE American: Contemporary.

SIR RELL American: Contemporary. **Sirrell.**

SIVAN Hebrew: The ninth month of the Jewish calendar. It corresponds to May-June.

SLOANE Irish: "warrior, soldier." **Sloan.**

SOCRATES Greek: Meaning unknown. Socrates (c. 470–399 B.C.) was a famous teacher and philosopher.

SOLIMON American. Hebrew: "peaceful." **Sol.**

SOLOMON Latin. Hebrew: "peaceful." **Sol.**

SONTRELL American: Contemporary.

SORRELL English. French: "reddish brown." **Sorrel.**

SPENCER English. French: "dispenser of provisions, larder keeper." **Spenser. Spence, Spense.**

SPENGER American: Contemporary, possibly influenced by the German Spengler (tinsmith).

SREDRICK American: Contemporary, modeled after Frederick (peaceful ruler).

STACEY English. Russian: "resurrection." Stacey Augmon, basketball pro.

STAFFORD   English: "a pole used to ford a river."

STAGALEE   American: Contemporary.

STALEY   English: "from Staveley (the meadow enclosed by staves or slats)."

STANFIELD   English: "dweller at or near the stony field." **Stansfield. Stan.**

STANFORD   English: "dweller near the stony ford." **Stan.**

STANLEY   English: "dweller near the stony meadow." **Stanly.** Stanley Burrell (a.k.a. Hammer), rap musician. Stanley Clarke, jazz guitarist.

STANTON   English: "from Stanton (the stone dwellings); dweller at or near the stone settlement."

STEADMAN   English: "man from the stead (farmhouse, plot of land)." **Stedman.**

STEAVEN   American. Greek: "crown, garland." **Steave.**

STEDHAM   English: "from Stedham (the stallion enclosure)." **Stidem, Stidham.**

STEDRICK   American: Contemporary.

STEFAN   European. Greek: "crown, garland."

STEFFAINE   American: Contemporary.

STEFFAIRE   American: Contemporary.

STEPHEN   English. Greek: "crown, garland." **Steven. Steve.**

STEPHON   American. Greek: "crown, garland."

STEPHONE   American. Greek: "crown, garland." Stephone Paige, football pro.

STERLING   Scottish: "from Stirling (the dwelling of Velyn)." English: "one with the characteristics of a starling." American: "sterling silver; high-quality, excellent." **Stirling.** Sterling A. Brown (1901–1989), poet and professor of literature.

STEVERSON   English: "son of Steven (crown, garland)."

STEVELAND   American: Contemporary. **Steve, Stevie.** Steveland "Stevie" Wonder, musician.

STREITER   German: "battle, strife."

SUDI   Swahili: "success, luck."

SULAIMAN   Arabic. Hebrew: "peaceful."

SUNDAI   Zimbabwe. Shona: "to push."

SUNDAV   Hindi: "handsome."

SURGEL   American: Contemporary.

SYDELL   American: Contemporary, possibly a blending of names such as Sydney (follower of Saint Denis) and Della (a small valley).

SYED   American. Arabic: "lucky, fortunate."

TAB   English: "drummer." **Tabb.**

TABIB   Turkish: "healer, physician."

TACIO   Spanish. Greek: "active, diligent."

TACY   American: Contemporary.

TAD   English: Short form of Theodore (God's gift) and Tadley (Tada's woods).

TADARA   American: Contemporary.

TADLEY English: "from Tadley (Tada's [father's] woods or clearing)." **Tadly. Tad, Tadd.** Tadley "Tadd" Dameron (1917–1965), jazz pianist-arranger.

TAHIR Arabic: "stainless, pure." **Taher.**

TAIMESHIE American: Contemporary.

TAISHIA American: Contemporary.

TAJ Hindi: "crown."

TAJI Hindi: "crown."

TALAUS Greek: Meaning unknown. In classical mythology, Talaus was one of the Argonauts.

TALBOT French: "looter."

TALIB Arabic: "seeker."

TALMADGE English. French: "wallet, knapsack." **Talmage.**

TALMAI Aramaic: "hill, mound."

TALON American: Contemporary.

TAMARICK American: Contemporary, probably based on *tamarack* (the American larch tree).

TAMBALA African: "rooster." The tambala is a monetary unit of Malawian.

TAMBI American: Contemporary.

TAMER American: Contemporary.

TAMIR Arabic: "owner of many dates." Hebrew: "a sacred vessel; a palm tree."

TAMLIN Scottish: "little Tom (twin)." **Tamlinn, Tamlyn. Tam.**

TANAY Hindi: "son."

TANDY Scottish. Greek: "manly." **Tandie.**

TANIS Lithuanian. Latin: "immortal." American: Contemporary, based on Janis (God is gracious) or borrowed from the name of a city of ancient Egypt.

TANNER English and German: "one who tans hides."

TANNOCH Celtic: "dweller at or near a meadow." **Tannock.**

TANO Ghana. Akan: In Akan mythology, Tano is a son of Onyame and the owner, by means of deception, of all the desirable land.

TANYIN American: Contemporary.

TANZAY American: Contemporary, possibly influenced by the African country of Tanzania.

TAPP English: "peg."

TARAGEE American. Arabic: "hope."

TARIK Hindi: "one who crosses the river of life."

TARIL Hindi: "one who crosses the river of life."

TARIQ Arabic: "one who knocks at the door." **Tarik.**

TARIUS American: Contemporary.

TARLEAK American: Contemporary.

TARLETON English: "dweller at Thor's village."

TARON American: Contemporary. **TaRon, TaRonn, Taronn, TarRon, Tarron, T'Ron.**

TARQUIN Spanish. Latin: "from Tarquinium." **Tarquino.**

TARRY American: Variant of Terry. **Tarrie.**

TARRYL American: Contemporary, modeled after Darryl (from Airelle). **Tarrel, Tarril, Taryl, Terral, Teryl.**

TARUN Hindi: "young man, youth."

TARUS American: Contemporary.

TASKER English: "one who threshes grain with a flail."

TATIUS Latin: Meaning unknown. Titus Tatius was an ancient king of the Sabines.

TAUREAN American: Contemporary, probably influenced by Taurus (a bull), the second astrological sign of the zodiac. Alternatively, it might be influenced by the sound of Dorian (a native of Doris, Greece). Taurean Blacque, actor.

TAVARES American: Likely modeled after the Spanish Alvarez (son of Alvaro).

TAVAS Hebrew: "peacock."

TAVI Aramaic: "good."

TAVIS Scottish. Gaelic: "son of David (beloved)." **Taviss.**

TAVISH Irish: "twin."

TAWEEL Arabic: "tall."

TAWFIQ Arabic: "good fortune."

TAY American: Contemporary, possibly a shortened form of Taylor (a tailor).

TAYLEEJO American: Contemporary.

TAYLOR English. French: "a tailor." **Tay.**

TAYMON American: Contemporary.

TAYSHAWN American: Contemporary. **Tayshaun, Tayshaune, Tayshawne, Tayshon, Tayshonn.**

T'BOO American: Contemporary.

TCHEKY American: Contemporary.

TEAGUE Irish: "poet."

TECUMSEH Native American: After the Shawnee chief who attempted to unite the western tribes.

TEDWARD American: Blending of the names Ted (God's gift) and Edward (wealthy protector). **Ted.**

TEEGAN Irish: "poet." **Tagan, Teagan, Tegan.**

TEFERI Ethiopia. Amharic and Tigrinya: "he who is feared, ferocious."

TEGENE Ethiopia. Amharic: "my protector."

TELAMON Greek: Meaning unknown. In Greek mythology, Telamon was one of the Argonauts.

TEMAN Hebrew: "the right side; the south."

TEMANI Hebrew: "man from the south, man from Teman."

TENNEKH American: Contemporary.

TENZIN American: Contemporary.

TERACH Hebrew: "wild goat."

TERALD American: Contemporary, modeled after Gerald (spear rule). **Terrald.**

TEREMIAH American: Variant of Jeremiah (the Lord will uplift). **Teremiyah. Terry.**

TEREMUN American: Contemporary.

TERENCE English. Latin: "from Terentum; soft, tender." **Terance, Terrance, Terrence. Terry.** Terrence Rencher, basketball pro.

TERONN American: Contemporary. **Te-Ron, Teron, TeRonn, Terran, Terren, Terron.**

TERREVIA American: Contemporary. **Terry.**

TERRILL English. French: "stubborn, obstinate." **Terrel, Terrell, Tirelle, Tirrel, Tirrell, Tirrelle.** Terrell Brandon, basketball pro.

TERRY English: Originated as a short form of Terence (from Terentum; soft, tender). **Tery.**

TESHER Hebrew: "gift."

TESSEMA Ethiopia. Amharic: "he is listened to."

TEVIN American: Contemporary, modeled after Kevin (handsome, comely). Tevin Campbell, singer.

TEZ American: Contemporary.

THADDEUS Latin. Greek: Meaning uncertain. **Thaddius. Tad, Tadd, Thad, Thadd.**

THADDIS English. Aramaic: "praise."

THALAMUS Latin: "inner chamber."

THANDIWE South Africa. Zulu: "beloved."

THAYER English: "army of the people."

THAYMON American: Contemporary.

THAYNE English: "freeborn man." **Thain, Thaine, Thane, Thayn.**

THEARL American: Contemporary, possibly based on Earl (an earl). **Thirl.**

THEARON American: Variant of Theron (the hunter).

THEDO Greek: "divine gift."

THELONIOUS English: Latinized form of Saint Tillo (lord). **Thelonius.** Thelonious Monk (1920–1982), jazz pianist. Thelonious Monk Jr., singer.

THEMBA South Africa. Xhosa: "hope."

THEODORE English. Greek: "God's gift." **Ted, Theo.** Theodore Ward, playwright.

THEODUS Latin. Greek: "divine gift." **Theodis.**

THEOLA Greek: "divinely loved."

THERLO American: Contemporary.

THERMEN American: Variant of Thurmand (Thor's protection). **Therm.**

THERON Greek: "the hunter."

THETIS Latin: "the sea." In Roman mythology, Thetis was a sea nymph, the mother of Achilles.

THIERRY French. German: "ruler of the people."

THIRENCE American: Contemporary.

THOM English. Aramaic: "a twin." **Tom.**

THOMAS Latin. Aramaic: "a twin." **Thom, Tom.** Tommy Flanagan, jazz pianist.

THURGOOD English. Old Norse: "Thor-Gaut (a Germanic tribe)." Thurgood Marshall (1908–1993), first Black U.S. Supreme Court justice.

THURLOW English: "from Thurlow (the assembly hill)." **Thurl.** Thurl Bailey, basketball pro.

THURMAN English and Scandinavian: "Thor's protection." **Thurmand, Thurmon, Thurmond, Thurmun, Thurmund.** Thurmand Thomas, football pro.

THURSTON English: "Thor's settlement." Scandinavian: "Thor's stone."

THYEIS Latin and Greek: "a citrus tree." **Thyias.**

THYREA Latin: "of Thyrea (a town in Argolis)." **Thyria.**

TIGER American: "a tiger; fierce." Tiger Woods, golf pro.

TIJUAN American: Contemporary, based on the Mexican city of Tijuana. **Tijwana.**

TIKO South Africa. Xhosa: In Xhosan mythology, Tiko is the supreme being.

TILDON English: "from Tilden (Tila's valley)."

TILLMON English: "tiller of the soil, a plowman." **Tillman, Tillmann, Tilmon.**

TILON Hebrew: "small mound."

TIMATHY American. Greek: "honored of God, honoring God." **Tim, Timmy.**

TIMOTHY English. Greek: "honored of God, honoring God." **Tim, Timmy.** Timothy Thomas Fortune (1856–1928), journalist, editor, and advocate of the term "Afro-American."

TITUS Latin: "giant."

TJADER American: Contemporary.

TOBIAS Greek. Hebrew: "Jehovah is good." **Toby.**

TOBY English. Hebrew: "Jehovah is good."

TODD Scottish: "a fox." **Tod.** Todd Day, basketball pro.

TOI American: Contemporary.

TOMASA European. Aramaic: "a twin." **Tom.**

TONE American: Contemporary, probably based on Tony (priceless, of inestimable worth).

TONY English. Latin: "priceless, of inestimable worth." Originated as a short form of Anthony. Tony Gwynn, baseball pro.

TORAL Hindi: "mood."

TORIAN American: Contemporary, modeled after Dorian.

TORNELL American: Contemporary. **Tornel, Tornelle.**

TORNERRO American: Contemporary.

TORRANCE Scottish: "from Torrance (little hills)." **Torrence. Torrey, Torry, Tory.**

TORRAYE American: Contemporary. **Torreye.**

TORRELL American: Contemporary. **Torell, Torrel.**

TORREY English: "gift of God." Originated as a pet form of Theodoric. Scottish: "from Torrie (hill)." **Torey, Torry.**

TORYN Irish: "chief." **Toren, Torin.**

TOWNSEND English: "dweller at the end of a village."

TRAIAN American: Contemporary. **Trayan.**

TRAJAN American: Contemporary.

TRAMMEL American: Contemporary.

TRANEL American: Contemporary. **Tranell, Tranelle, Trannel, Trannell, Trannelle.**

TRAVEIL American: Contemporary, perhaps influenced by *travail* (toil, hard work).

TRAVERS English. French: "dweller at the crossroads." **Traverse. Trav.**

TRAVON American: Contemporary.

TRAYA American: Contemporary.

TRAYVICK American: Contemporary.

TRELAWN English. Celtic: "dweller at the church town."

TREMAINE English. Celtic: "from Tremaine (town of stones; house of stones)." **Tremain, Tremane, Tremayn, Tremayne.**

TRENELLE American: Contemporary.

TRENT English: "from the river Trent (stream, current)."

TRENTON American: "from Trenton (Trent's town)." **Trent.**

TREVAHN American: Contemporary. **Trevaughn, Trevaun, Trevon, Trevonn.**

TREVAY American: Contemporary. **Travay. Trev.**

TREVONNE American: Contemporary. **Trev.**

TREVOR English. Celtic: "prudent, discreet." **Trevar, Trever. Trev.**

TREY American: "third." **Trae, Tre, Tré.**

TREYMAINE American. Celtic: "from Tremaine (town of stones; house of stones)." **Treymain, Treymane, Treymayn, Treymayne. Tre, Trey.**

TREZELLE American: Contemporary. **Trezell.** Trezelle Jenkins, football pro.

TRIENE Latin: "third."

TRIFON American: Contemporary.

TRINIDAD Spanish. Latin: "three in one." Central doctrine of the Christian religion. **Trinedad.**

TROIX American: Contemporary variant of Troy (from Troyes).

TRON American. Greek: "instrument." Popular use of this name might be attributed to the futurist motion picture *Tron.*

TRONDEAN American: Blending of the names Tron (instrument) and Dean (a dean).

TRONDEAUX American: Contemporary.

TROY English. French: "from Troyes." The name is also borrowed from the ancient Phrygian city, which was the sight of the Trojan War. In this case, the name is from the Greek personal name Tros (meaning unknown). **Troye.**

TROYLAND American: Contemporary.

TUCKER   English. French: "a fuller of cloth."

TUCSON   American: Borrowed from the Arizona city. **Tuscon, Tuson.**

TYAS   English. Teutonic: "a Teuton, a German." **Tyus.** Tyus Edney, basketball pro.

TYDEUS   Greek: Meaning unknown. In Greek legend, Tydeus was one of the Seven against Thebes, an expedition of seven heroes formed to regain the throne of Thebes.

TYE   English: "dweller at or near a common area or enclosure."

TYEASE   American: Contemporary, possibly modeled after Tyeis (a Teuton, a German). **Tyeas, Tyas.**

TYEIS   French. Teutonic: "a Teuton, a German."

TYLER   English: "a tile or brick maker or worker."

TYNDALL   English. Celtic: "from Tindale (the river valley)."

TYREE   Scottish: "from Tyrie (land)." **Tyrey.**

TYRELL   English. Teutonic: "Thor's might, powerful Thor." **Tirrell, Tyrelle.**

TYRONE   Greek: "sovereign, lord." Tyrone Hill, basketball pro. **Tyronne.**

TYRONN   American. Greek: "sovereign, lord." **Tyron, Tirone, Tironn.**

TYRUS   Latin: "purple." Tyrus was the name of a Phoenician city famous for its purple cloth.

TYSHAUN   American: Contemporary.

TYSON   English: "son of Tyas (a Teuton); son of Dye (of Dionysus)."

TZEVI   Hebrew: "a deer."

TZIPPY   American: Contemporary.

UDALE   English: "from Udale (the yew valley)." **Udael, Udall, Udell.**

UDAY   Hindi: "prosperity."

UDO   African: "peace."

UJU   African: "abundance."

ULYES   American: Probable variant of Ulysses (hater). **Ules.**

ULYSSES   Latin. Greek: "hater." Ulysses Kay, composer.

UQUHARDT   American: Probably based on Urquhart (a division of land).

URI   Hebrew: "my flame."

URIAH   Hebrew: "God is my light."

URQUHART   Scottish: "from Urquhart (a division of land)."

USENI   Malawi. Yao: "tell me."

USHONE   American: Contemporary.

UTE   Native American: Denotes a member of any of the Shoshonean tribes.

UTHER   English: Origin and meaning uncertain. In legend, Uther is the father of King Arthur.

UTHMAN   Arabic: "a baby bustard (bird)."

UWALDO   American: Variant of Waldo (ruler).

UZIAH Hebrew: "God is my strength." **Uziya.**

VADEN Swedish: "dweller at or near a ford."

VALDES Spanish: "from Valdes (the table-land); the son of Baldo (prince of fame)." **Valdez.**

VALLONE Italian: "from the wide valley."

VANARD American: Contemporary.

VANCE English. French: "dweller near or at the winnowing fan; dweller near a small hill."

VANDARELL American: Contemporary. **Van.**

VANDELL American. Dutch: "from the valley."

VANLEE American: Contemporary.

VANOY American: Contemporary. **Van-oye.**

VANRON American: Contemporary. **Van-Ron. Ron, Van.**

VANSHON American: Contemporary.

VANTRON American: Contemporary. **Tron, Van.**

VARDAAN Hindi: "giver of prosperity."

VAREN Hindi: "best." **Varin.**

VAUDOIS French: from Vaud (a canton in Switzerland); the French dialect spoken in Vaud.

VAUGHN English. Celtic: "small, little." **Vaughan.**

VAUGHNCEAL American: Contemporary, based on Vaughn (small).

VELDER Dutch: "from the field."

VELMER American: Contemporary.

VELTRAY American: Contemporary.

VELTRON American: Contemporary.

VENNARD French: "firm hope."

VENNELL Scottish: "dweller at or near the alley." **Venall, Vennel.**

VENSON French: "from Vence (estate of Vencius)."

VENTRON American: Contemporary.

VERDIS Latin: "verdant, green."

VERNARD American: Variant of Bernard (bold as a bear).

VERNEAL American: Contemporary. **Vern.**

VERNETT American: "little Vern."

VERNON French: "from Vernon." **Vern.** Vernon E. Jordan, executive director, National Urban League.

VEROAN American: Contemporary.

VERSHEL American: Contemporary.

VERSIL American. Latin: "changing."

VERSILIS Latin: "changing."

VERUS Latin: "true."

VEURGIES American: Contemporary.

VICENTE Spanish. Latin: "conquering."

VIMAL Hindi: "pure."

VINCENT European. Latin: "conquering." **Vince**. Vince Coleman, baseball pro.

VINTON English: "from Feniton (town by the boundary stream)." Venton.

VIRGIL English. Latin: "flourishing, abundant." **Virgel. Virg**.

VIRTUSH American: Contemporary.

VOIGT German. Latin: "overseer, warden." **Voight**.

VONDALE Dutch: "from the valley."

VONTÉ American: Contemporary. **Vontae, Vontay, Vonte**. Vonte Sweet, actor.

VONTEEGO American: Contemporary.

VYASA Hindi: "separation into pieces."

VYRON American: Contemporary.

WAFIYY Arabic: "loyal."

WAHIB Arabic: "donor."

WALDEMAR German: "famous ruler."

WALI American: Possibly a variant of Wally. Arabic: "chief, all-governing." African: "moon."

WALID Arabic: "newborn." **Waleed**.

WALLACE Scottish. French: "a Welshman." **Wallas. Wally**. Wallace Johnson, baseball pro.

WALLACESTENE American: Coinage, based on Wallace (a Welshman). **Wally**.

WALLIS English. French: "a Welshman." **Wally**.

WALTER English. German: "mighty army." **Wally, Walt**. Walter Fauntroy, preacher and civil rights activist. Walter Payton, football pro. Walter Raines, actor.

WALTERT American: Contemporary variant of Walter (mighty army). **Wally**.

WANYA American: Contemporary. Wanya Morris, singer with Boyz II Men.

WARD English: "watchman, guard."

WARDELL English: "dweller at or near the watch hill." **Wardel, Whardell. Ward**.

WAREZ American: Phonetic spelling of the Spanish Juarez (south army).

WARREN English. French: "dweller at or near the game preserve; keeper of the game preserve." Warren Moon, football pro.

WARRICK English: "fortress; builder of scaffolds." **Rick**.

WASHINGTON English: "from the estate of the Hwaes's (sharp, keen) family."

WASIFU Swahili. Arabic: "one who describes."

WASIM Arabic: "handsome." **Waseem**.

WASSIF Arabic: "one who describes."

WATKIN English: "little Walter (mighty army)."

WAUKEEN American: Phonetic spelling of the Spanish Joaquin (God gives strength).

WAVER English: "flickering, wavering; aspen trees."

WAYDE American. English: "to go; ford, wading place."

WAYLAND English: "from Wayland (the land by the path or way)." **Waylan, Waylon, Weylan, Weyland.**

WAYMAN English: "man of the way or path." **Weyman.** Wayman Tisdale, basketball pro.

WAYNE English: "wagon maker."

WEBSTER English: "weaver."

WELBERE American: Possible variant of Wilbur (bright will).

WELDON English: "dweller at or near the hill with the spring."

WELTON English: "from Welton (the town by the spring)."

WENDELL Teutonic: "a wanderer."

WENDEN American: Contemporary.

WESTIN English: "the western village." **Weston.**

WHALEN Irish: "little wolf." **Whalin, Whalon, Whaylon.**

WILBERT English: "bright will." **Will, Willie, Willy.**

WILEY English. German: "resolute protector."

WILFERT American: Variant of Wilford (ford near the willows) or Wilfred (much peace). **Will, Willie, Willy.**

WILFORD English: "dweller at or near the ford by the willows." **Will, Willie, Willy.**

WILFRED English: "desire for peace." **Will, Willie, Willy.**

WILLARD English: "resolutely brave." **Will, Willie, Willy.**

WILLIAM French. German: "resolute protector." **Bill, Billie, Billy, Will, Willie, Willy.** William Wells Brown (1815–1884), novelist and dramatist, first Black to publish a novel. William "Count" Basie (1904–1984), legendary jazz musician and bandleader. Dr. William (Bill) Cosby, comedian, actor, philanthropist. William Marshall, actor.

WILLIE English. German: "resolute protector." **Will.** Willie Dixon, blues musician. Willie Mays, baseball great.

WILLIS English: "son of Will (resolute protector)." **Will, Willie, Willy.** Willis Richardson, playwright.

WILMER English. German: "resolute one; resolute and famous." **Wilmar.**

WILSAR American: Contemporary.

WILSON English: "son of Will (resolute protector)." **Will, Willie, Willy.** Wilson Pickett, blues musician.

WILTON English: "from Wilton (the town by the willows)." **Wilt.** Wilt Chamberlain, basketball pro.

WILTZ German: "son or descendant of Willihard (resolute and brave)."

WINFIELD English: "from Winfield (Wigga's field)."

WINSTON English: "from Winston (the friend's town)." Winston Garland, basketball pro.

WOODROW　English: "dweller at the hedgerow near the woods." **Woodie, Woody.**

WOODWARD　English: "forester, warden of a wood." **Woodey, Woodie, Woody.**

WOODY　English: "a wood, a forest." **Woodey, Woodie.** Woodie Kind, actor.

WRENFORD　English: "from Wrenford (the ford near the wrens)."

WYCLEF　American. English: "dweller at the white cliff." **Wycleff, Wycleft, Wyklef, Wykleff.**

WYCLIFFE　English: "dweller at the white cliff." **Wycliff.**

WYLIE　English: "dweller near the River Wiley (tricky river)."

WYNDHAM　English: "from Wyndham (the enclosure with a winding path)." **Windham.**

WYNDOM　American: Variant of Wyndham (the enclosure with a winding path).

WYNN　Welsh: "fair, beautiful." **Wynne.**

WYNTON　English: "from Winton (the friendly settlement)." **Winton, Wynnton.** Wynton Marsalis, Grammy Award–winning jazz musician.

XANDER　European. Greek: "defender of mankind."

XAVIER　Spanish: "from the new house." Arabic: "bright." Xavier McDaniel, basketball pro.

XDAMIEN　American: Contemporary, based on Damian (tamer).

XENO　Greek: "strange, stranger."

XERIC　American: Contemporary, possibly based on *xeric* (dry, desertlike) or a variant of Eric (eternal ruler).

XERXES　Persian: Meaning uncertain, perhaps "prince." Xerxes (519?–465? B.C.) was a king of Persia and a son of Darius I.

XHAVAR　American: Contemporary, possibly based on Xavier (from the new house).

YACOUB　Arabic. Hebrew: "supplanting; seizing by the heel."

YAKAR　Hebrew: "cherished."

YALE　Teutonic: "one who yields, one who pays."

YALMAN　Turkish: "peak of a mountain."

YAMAL　Hindi: "a pair."

YAMIN　Hindi: "night."

YARNELL　English: Variant of Arnold (eagle ruler). **Yarnall.**

YASIN　Arabic: From the Arabic letters y and s, the opening letters of the thirty-sixth sura of the Koran.

YASIR　Arabic: "wealthy."

YAUVAN　Hindi: "youth."

YAZID　Arabic: "ever-increasing."

YENNY　American. German: "fair lady."

YERED　Hebrew: "to descend, to flow down."

YETEL　American: Contemporary.

YONEL American: Contemporary. Yonel Jourdain, football pro.

YOSEF Hebrew: "he shall add."

YOSHA Hebrew: "wisdom."

YUSUF Arabic. Hebrew: "he shall add." **Yusef, Yussef.**

ZAAN American: Contemporary.

ZACHARIAH Latin. Hebrew: "God remembers."

ZACHARY English. Hebrew: "God remembers." **Zack, Zak.**

ZAFAR Arabic: "victory."

ZAFIR Arabic: "victory." Hebrew: "bright."

ZAHAVI Hebrew: "gold."

ZAHIR Arabic: "flourishing."

ZAID Arabic: "increasing."

ZAKARIYYA Arabic. Hebrew: "God remembers." **Zakaria. Zack, Zak.**

ZAKI Arabic: "pure, virtuous." **Zakee.**

ZAKKAI Hebrew: "pure, innocent." **Zakai.**

ZAKUR Hebrew: "masculine."

ZAMBEZI African: "big river." Borrowed from the African river of the same name.

ZAMIR Hebrew: "a nightingale; singing."

ZAN Hebrew: "nourished."

ZANDALL American: Contemporary. **Zandell. Zan.**

ZANDER German. Greek: "defender of mankind." **Zan.**

ZANTE American: Contemporary. Alternatively, the name might be borrowed from that of a Greek island, also known as Zákinthos.

ZARED Hebrew: "ambushed."

ZARION American: Contemporary.

ZAYAS Spanish: "from Zayas."

ZAYD Arabic: "to increase." **Zaid.**

ZEBEDEE Hebrew: "gift of God."

ZEBULON Hebrew: "dwelling place." **Zeb.**

ZEDEKIAH Hebrew: "God is righteousness." **Zed.**

ZEMARIAH Hebrew: "a song." **Zem.**

ZEPHENIAH Hebrew: "the Lord has hidden." **Zeffy.**

ZEPHYR American. Greek: "the west wind."

ZEPHYRUS Greek: "the god of the west wind."

ZESIRO Uganda. Luganda: "first of twins."

ZETAN Hebrew: "olive tree."

ZEVADIAH English. Hebrew: "gift of the Lord." **Zevadia. Zev.**

ZEVIEL Hebrew: "gazelle of the Lord." **Zev.**

ZHAHQUEZ American: Contemporary, possibly a phonetic spelling of Jacques (God is gracious), the name of a character in Shakespeare's play *As You Like It*.

ZHAWN American: Contemporary, based on Shawn (God is gracious) and influenced by the phonetics of the French Jean (God is gracious). **Zhon**.

ZIKOMO　Malawi. Ngoni: "thank you (for this child)."

ZIMRI　Hebrew: "mountain goat; my branch."

ZINJ　American. Arabic: "East Africa."

ZINJAN　American. Arabic: "East Africa." Zinjan is possibly based on Zinjanthropus, a type of primitive man whose fossil remains were found in Tanganyika.

ZIVI　Hebrew: "brilliance." **Ziv**.

ZIYA　Arabic: "splendor, light."

ZIYAD　Arabic: "an increase."

ZOAN　American: Contemporary. Alternatively, the name might be based on the biblical name of Tanis, a city in ancient Egypt.

ZOHAR　Hebrew: "brightness."

ZOSHANGANA　African: In Shangaanan legend Zoshangana was a Zulu general who conquered the Tsonga. **Zosha**.

ZOUAVE　American. French. Arabic: The name of a tribe living in the mountains of Algeria.

ZUBERI　Swahili: "strong."

ZUHAYR　Arabic: "little flowers."

ZURI　Swahili: "good."